FEMINIST PERSPECTIVES ON
SUSTAINABLE DEVELOPMENT

FEMINIST PERSPECTIVES ON SUSTAINABLE DEVELOPMENT

EDITED BY

Wendy Harcourt

ZED BOOKS LTD

London & New Jersey

in association with the

SOCIETY FOR
INTERNATIONAL DEVELOPMENT
Rome

Feminist Perspectives on Sustainable Development was first
published by Zed Books Ltd, 7 Cynthia Street, London N1 9JF, UK,
and 165 First Avenue, Atlantic Highlands, New Jersey 07716, USA,
in association with the Society for International Development,
Palazzo della Civiltà del Lavoro, 00144 Rome, Italy,
in 1994.

Cover designed by Andrew Corbett.
Cover photograph © Margaret Murray/Christian Aid, 1994.
Typeset by Ray Davies.
Printed and bound in the United Kingdom
by Biddles Ltd, Guildford and King's Lynn.

A catalogue record for this book is
available from the British Library

US CIP data is available from the Library of Congress.

ISBN Hb 1 85649 243 5
ISBN Pb 1 85649 244 3

Contents

Contributors

Janet N. Abramovitz received her MSc in Plant Ecology and Biostatistics from the University of Maryland and has completed postgraduate course work in economics and law. As an Associate with the World Resource Institute for five years until January 1993, she undertook research on biodiversity and conservation. She has published several articles on gender and biodiversity in both popular and scientific journals.

Franck Amalric, a graduate from the Ecole Polytechnique and ENSAé in Paris, is currently completing his PhD in Economics at Harvard University. He has spent two years as a research fellow at the World Conservation Union in Islamabad, Pakistan, and, with Tariq Banuri, Executive Director of the Sustainable Development Policy Institute, Islamabad, Pakistan, has co-edited several research articles on governance and responsibility.

Frédérique Apffel-Marglin is Associate Professor of Anthropology at Smith College, Massachusetts, USA. She has co-edited several books on alternative development in the WIDER series *Studies in Development Economics* and has written widely in the fields of cultural anthropology and the epistemology of development.

Lourdes Arizpe is Professor at the National University of Mexico and President of the International Union of Anthropological and Ethnological Sciences. In addition to six books on rural development, indigenous communities and women in development, she has written extensively on sustainable development issues. She is Programme Chairperson of the Society for International Development 21st World Conference in Mexico.

Mette Bryld is Associate Professor and Director of the Department of Slavonic Studies, Odense University, Denmark. She has published books and articles on Russian culture and feminist studies. Her current research focuses on the theme 'Gender, Cosmos and New World Views'.

Raff Carmen has worked for 15 years in Africa, mainly with grassroots organizations. Now a lecturer at the Centre for Adult and Higher Education (CAHE) at the University of Manchester, he is involved in programmes and research concerned with social development, adult education, management, adult literacy and the popular media.

Frances Connelly is Administrator of the Foundation for International Environmental Law and Development. She contributed to *My Country is the Whole World: An Anthology of Women's Work on Peace and War*, 1984 (Pandora Press, London) and *Pacific Paradise, Nuclear Nightmare*, 1987 (CND Publications, London). She is actively involved in the women's peace movement.

Willy Douma, Heleen van den Hombergh and **Ange Wieberdink** are all members of the women's studies team at InDRA, the Institute for Development Research Amsterdam, the Netherlands, which is working on youth, poverty and emancipation, gender from a South-North perspective and environment, development and countervailing power.

Corinne Kumar D'Souza is a writer and a peace and human rights activist working with the Collective for International Education and Development (CIED) in Bangalore, India.

'Atu Emberson-Bain, a former lecturer in sociology at the University of the South Pacific in Fiji, is now a freelance researcher, writer and radio/video producer on mining, development and gender issues in the Pacific and contemporary politics in Fiji. A graduate of Oxford University and the University of London, she completed her PhD at the Australian National University, Canberra.

Wendy Harcourt joined the Society for International Development (SID) in Rome, Italy, in 1988, as editor of *Development: Journal of SID* and co-ordinator of SID's international Women in Development programme. She received her PhD from the Australian National University, Canberra, in 1987, and has written widely on gender and development issues. Her current research focuses on alternative economics from a gender perspective.

Sabine Häusler worked in Nepal from 1985 to 1989, advising that country's largest international NGO. She has since received her MA at the Institute of Social Studies, The Hague. She is a contributor to and an editor of *Women, the Environment and Sustainable Development: Towards a Theoretical Synthesis* (Braidotti et al, eds. Zed Books, 1994). Since 1992 she has been working on an interdisciplinary research project at the Institute of Social Studies and the University of Utrecht.

Hazel Henderson is an international development policy analyst and author of *Creating Alternative Futures*, 1978 (G.P. Putnam, New York); *The Politics of the Solar Age*, 1981 (Doubleday, New York); and *Paradigms of Progress*, 1991 (Knowledge Systems, Indianapolis). She served on the original Advisory Council of the US Office of Technology and Assessment and is currently a member of the SID Sustainable Task Force.

Nina Lykke is Associate Professor and Head of Department of Feminist Studies, Odense University, Denmark. The author of a number of books and articles, a main line of her research as been the philosophy of gender and the relationship between feminism and psychoanalysis. Her dissertation on this subject has recently been published in German. In common with her co-contributor, Mette Bryld, her current research focuses on the theme 'Gender, Cosmos and New World Views'.

Julia Martin teaches English at the University of the Western Cape, South Africa. She is a member of the interdisciplinary research team working on women and environment with Professor Rosi Braidotti at the University of Utrecht. She is actively engaged in the women's and political ecology movement in South Africa.

Helga Moss, a sociologist and environmentalist, is active in the Norwegian and international women's movement. She is currently working with the city of Oslo to put into place an urban sustainable and participatory development programme.

Gita Sen is a Professor at the Indian Institute of Management in Bangalore, India, and has been Visiting Professor at the Harvard Centre for Population and Development Studies. Her research focuses on gender and development, recently centring on the gender dimensions of population policies and the linkages between population, livelihoods, and the environment. She is co-author with Caren Grown of *Development, Crises and Alternative Visions: Third World Women's Perspectives* (Earthscan, London, 1987), and a founding member of DAWN (Development Alternatives with Women for a New Era), where she is currently research co-ordinator on alternative economic frameworks.

Suzanne L. Simon is a post-graduate student in Anthropology at Smith College, Massachusetts, USA.

Marja-Lisa Swantz is an anthropologist and Africanist who has pioneered participatory and grassroots action approaches to development research in Africa, mainly in Tanzania. Author of several monographs and numerous articles on culture and development with special reference to women, she has recently retired as the Director of Research at the Institute of Development Studies in the University of Helsinki, and is a member of the SID governing council.

Corinne Wacker is a Lecturer in Anthropology at the Institute of Ethnology, University of Zurich, where she is completing her PhD on women's groups in Kenya. She has worked extensively in Southern Africa as a consultant on women, the environment and development for the Swiss Development Corporation. Her extensive research and development assistance work is combined with an active role in the national and international WED contribution to the sustainable development debate.

Roundtables and Magic Circles

Corinne Kumar D'Souza

Circles are symbols in all cultures; circles are images in all civilizations.

Whether we look at a Mayan sun mask or a Nepalese Vishnu mandala or a Navajo sand painting or a sun disc from New Guinea or a Tingari ceremonial bark painting – they are all in circles.[1]

Circles are the most primordial images:
A wise one once said: 'When the eagle builds a nest, the nest is in a circle. When we look at the horizon, the horizon is in a circle.'

Circles speak of a wholeness; whether in time or in space.

Circles have no beginnings; any point can be a beginning;
Circles have no end.
The moon cycle, the day and night cycle, the cycle of time;
Cyclical time so different from linear time, digital time.
We are losing our sense of the circle in relation to time.

The circle as 'mandala' (Sanskrit for circle).
A 'mandala' that holds the meaning of a cosmic order.
Personal circles; connected with the universal circle.[2]

Among the Navajo Indians, healing ceremonies are conducted through sand paintings which are mostly 'mandala' paintings on the ground. The idea of a sand painting with 'mandala', and their use for meditation purposes appears also in Tibet.

We are all connected, we say.

It was the midnight until the dawn of the day that the Earth Summit opened in Rio in 1992. There was an all-night vigil on Leme Beach called by the *Planeta Femea* (The Women's Planet) to protest the state of the world but also 'to reaffirm this strange and obstinate belief in life'. It invited people to dance and sing and tell stories 'until the sun rises in Rio'.

Then with pieces of glass, with mirrors, we tried to hold a piece of the sun, walking to the water's edge, decorated with floating flowers; we symbolically lay the light of our hopes there, so that Yemanje, the Goddess of the Sea and Iansa, the Goddess of the Wind, would carry our hopes to the shores of different lands.

There were flowers everywhere.
There were women everywhere.

People sang and danced with the spirit and grace typical of Cariocas. Bahian women, dressed in traditional white, danced while they sang 'Listen to the women'.
A silver trumpet sounded the alvorado, announcing the dawn.

In a circle, we danced
Everything is connected, we say

'Look how the water flows from this place and returns as rainfall, everything returns, we say.
We are all part of this, we say
And the way of the waters is sacred
and the grove of trees is sacred, and
we ourselves, we tell you, are sacred'[3]

Look at this circle

'See us come from every direction
from the different spheres of the Earth

See the lines that stretch to the horizon
the procession, the gifts borne
see us fuel the fire

Feel the earth's life renewed ...

And the circle is complete again
and the medicine wheel is formed anew
and the knowledge within each one of us
made whole ...

And we dance
the dance of the circling stars'[4]
to the music of the spheres
to the song of the wind.

Notes

1. J. Campbell, *Power of Myth*.
2. Ibid.
3. Susan Griffin, *Made from this Earth*.
4. Starhawk, *Power, Authority and Mystery*, in *Re-weaving the World*.

Preface

In the 1960s, the contradictions in models of economic growth that ignored social and political development became visible; in the 1970s, they were denounced and analysed mainly within ideological frameworks; in the 1980s, research delved deeper into particular issues: women, the environment, population, employment, poverty, debt, food scarcities; the 1990s now seem to be the decade of discussion of sustainable alternatives to such economic growth.

This book offers such a broadening of the discussion and a bringing forward of the debate on feminist and cultural alternatives to redirect development. The advances being made in such debates can be seen in this book. It is no longer only a question of stating that women are important in giving life to sustainable lifestyles and livelihoods: the authors show that a feminist perspective that looks at women not as victims but as agents of change has strong commonalities with other movements seeking a more sustainable future for humanity.

In fact, a common thread throughout the book is the proposal to strengthen alliances: between feminists and progressive economists and policy makers; between scientists and environmental and social movements; between those working on a cultural critique of modernization; and those involved in the debate on power and knowledge in the new global context.

Interestingly, the *goals* of an environmentally sound human development become clearer every day, but proposals to achieve them are so varied and culturally distinct that they seem elusive. There is a consensus in this book that development should mean gender equity, secure livelihoods, ecological sustainability and political participation. Yet we must understand that the diversity itself which is being proposed as a principle for development will, necessarily, produce a multi-coloured pattern of proposals for the future. We can no longer believe that all these distinct, valuable alternatives must converge; in following our own critique of abstract, mechanistic, patriarchal thinking we must go forward into a world that *articulates diversity yet builds a global commonality that will hold us together*.

This book is one more step into this new world. In the fact that it brings together authors from all continents – women and men – of diverse disciplines, it is already creating such a new plurality. At the same time, it points towards the intellectual and policy hot-spots that need to be developed for the future: in a world threatened by entropy, we need to think of regeneration; in a world increasingly fragmented by ethnicity and special interests, we need alliances; in a world fraught by lethal indifference to the natural world, we need to rethink our place in this planet.

The Society for International Development has created a social space to allow for free discussions of such urgent topics and in so doing has developed the Women's Programme that sponsored this book. I would like to congratulate Wendy Harcourt for her work on the SID-WID Programme, and especially for having brought together the authors of this most interesting book.

Lourdes Arizpe

Introduction

Wendy Harcourt[1]

What are the feminist perspectives on sustainable development? How does one explain or understand the dilemmas facing women from the Laikipa, Kenya who in pre-colonial times were the region's farmers and cultivators of 16 different crops but who, in independent Kenya, are squatters with no usufructory rights? How successful is their strategy of sharing the risks and insecurities of their situation with members of their women's group in a network of over 300 such groups? How does one find ways to change the situation at the Vatukoula mine in Fiji where the 24-hour shift system and poor pay for men has led to the women working long and arduous hours to supplement their husbands' income? How can these women bear the burden of growing food, fishing, gathering firewood, selling mats and working the gardens, as well as cooking, washing, ironing, cleaning and child-care in order for the household to survive? Does one call it development or sustainable if the congested and culturally alienating mining settlements have broken down traditional social mores to the extent that night-time male drinking has encouraged violence and assaults against women? How do students growing up amongst the conflict and struggles of South African apartheid seek to understand the meaning of waste, development, consumption, mental apartheid, interdependence and the need for engagement within their own environment? In Oslo, Norway, how do socially and environmentally conscious women make meaningful choices about which products to buy when they have little time, poor information and are continually bombarded by entreaties to consume more?

Beginning from the dilemmas facing these women, and in response to the international interest in the links between environment and development, these are the types of questions which feminist perspectives on sustainable development seek to draw out and understand.

Central to these enquiries is just how will the policies and plans for sustainable development, as first popularized by Norwegian Prime Minister Gro Harlem Brundtland in 1987 and discussed in such detail by the world's governments and non-governmental (NGO) community at the United Nations Conference on Environment and Development (UNCED), help to solve the dilemmas facing these women in their very different environments and with their very different needs? The official goal of sustainable development – to establish equity between generations and to balance economic, social and environmental needs in order to conserve non-renewable resources and to lessen the economic and social costs of the wastes and pollution produced by industrialization – does not appear designed to reach the realities of these women's lives.

There is an uncomfortable fit between the mainstream concerns with sustainable development and those women existing on the margins of development. Feminists, in seeking to understand their own position and that of women of the two-thirds world,[2] who bear the brunt of the current ecological and environmental crises, are raising quite different issues and questions about environment and development. Working on the margins of development policy and institutions, feminists have found themselves entering into the sustainable development debate in order to bring these 'other' concerns to the debate now thriving among the newly emerging 'ecocracy' of the international development community. Feminists involved in the ecological and women's movements are concerned that the complex social, cultural, economic and political relations, which inform women's lives and gender inequities, are not being addressed by the mainstream debate. In this, they welcome the current interest in sustainable development as an opportunity to further feminist methodology, thinking and practice, and also as a political space where women can negotiate for better conditions which respect their choices and meet their different cultural and economic needs.

This book, based on the papers given at a four-day Roundtable on 'women, environment and alternatives to development' held at the Institute of Social Studies, The Hague in May 1993, takes up the questions raised by the realities of different women's interaction with their environment. As researchers and activists affected by the global environment and economic development crisis, they pose and analyse their questions, concerns and proposals for solutions.

The book is divided into four parts. Part One sets out the parameters of the debate by examining how the feminist position in sustainable development is currently situated and how it differs from other alternative and mainstream positions as both a methodology and a political stance. Part Two explores the gendered alternatives to the explanations of dominating knowledge systems of environment and development. The chapters challenge the assumption that the Western model of economic development is universally applicable to all cultures and argue for a recognition of the importance of women's role in cultural and social production. They discuss alternatives to the dominant knowledge system both from within the West and from the South and the grassroots women's resistance to mainstream economic development. In Part Three the chapters move from theory to practice, reviewing women's contribution to the UNCED debate and the state of play in feminist research and politics in sustainable development. Part Four is devoted to one of the most contentious issues in the debate: the interrelationship between population, women and environment. The chapters set out alternative positions which aim to move the debate away from the simple link between population growth and environmental destruction in the South to discussions which are open to the debate's complexity and the importance of examining consumption and lifestyle patterns in the industrialized North.

What emerges from the essays is that we are experiencing a shift in developing thinking on gender, a move from 'WID' (women in development) to 'WED' (women and environment and alternatives to development). The WED debate continues the WID critique of the inadequacies of economic development theory to deal with gender relations. The primary argument of the WID position is that current development policies fail to recognize gender relations despite the fundamental roles women play in maintaining the household in informal, rural and even market economies and in their management of natural resources. WED, instead, mounts a profound critique on the whole development process. Proponents of the WED position, as reflected in the contributions to this book, argue that development theory and practice founded on Western biases and assumptions, excludes both women and nature from its understanding of development and, in so doing, has contributed to the current economic and ecological crisis. Feminist perspectives also question whether Western science, on which development is founded, is the best method for explaining and producing knowledge. Corinne Kumar D'Souza, in the poem which opens the book, suggests that Western science and modernization are deaf to alternative knowledge systems, what she calls the 'wind from the South'. Instead of separating human and natural processes and lining them along the path of progress we should, she argues, understand and express the circles – the organic and complex relationships between people, communities, institutions and ecosystems.

In seeking to understand the current gender bias and the 'linear' mode of development, the WED critique tries to be open to non-Western cultures' understanding of people's interaction with the environment. The writers aim to take into account various contributions to social and cultural production without trying to create a hierarchy of truth of one position over another. Frédérique Apffel-Marglin and Suzanne Simon argue strongly for a reappraisal of the WID position, which they suggest approaches development from the same hierarchical and ultimately arrogant stance as mainstream development, one which furthers the very inequalities it tries to address.

The ambivalence about the benefits of development extends not only to questioning whether economic development as measured by GNP has really benefited the very poor, the majority of whom are women, but also if the whole enterprise of development based on extracting value from natural and human resources is sufficiently caring of the base. The contributors argue that the current development model gives little recognition to the need to nurture and restore human life and ecosystems. The underlying argument is that there is a need to shift from an understanding of development as an efficient way to convert natural and human resources into material wealth, to a perspective which de-emphasizes efficiency and growth and respects the interrelationship between people, their communities and their life-support systems. Hazel Henderson, 'Atu Emberson-Bain and Raff Carmen set out ways to challenge the economism of development, and discuss how better to balance environmental, social, cultural and political concerns. They also point to the need to understand the specificities of gender relations to the environment in different societies. It is by starting from the local understandings of the environment that we can counteract the all-encompassing and grand-sounding notion of global environmental and development concerns. The big picture and big theories of policy and science too often lose sight of the daily realities of people's lives. In particular, the inequitable and conflictual gender relations in, for example, usufructory rights and decision-making in the family, which determine livelihoods, are glossed over in the bureaucratic and economic vision.

To confront and, it is hoped, to bridge this gap between reality and theory, the discussions in the book begin from the authors' experiences, as researchers and as women involved in the resistance to mainstream development. They look at gender-specific relationships to the environment from women's own realities and priorities in the Pacific, in Kenya, in Tanzania, in India and in Europe, in international feminist politics and research institutes, for subsistence, survival and security. Several of the chapters take up women's experiences in the South: Marja-Liisa Swantz draws on her experience in Tanzania; Corinne Wacker from her field work in Kenya; Frédérique Apffel-Marglin on her many years in India; 'Atu Emberson-Bain on her activities and research in her home region, the Pacific; and Julia Martin writes about her teaching experience in South Africa. It emerges that women's daily use of natural resources – managing the forests and water resources, maintaining soil fertility, establishing community support and preserving ecological diversity – means that, for survival, they view natural resources as part of a complex and interrelated ecosystem. Consequently, women often resist the current economic development process which has high environmental and human costs: erosion of the natural environment; displacement of people; loss of knowledge about the local environment; and loss of resources that sustain families, and which undermines self-sufficiency.

As these authors argue, in order to take into account women's diverse experiences across age, class, race and geographic boundaries, we need more than just a change of policy – we need a substantial rethinking and recasting of the development enterprise. Because women's experiences and knowledge have been obscured in the male bias of Western academe, including economic development theory and practice, the task is not simply to add women into the known equation but to work with new epistemologies and methodologies. This implies an open challenge to current knowledge production, one which displaces the neutral male subject of Western science and also dissolves the division between research and practice. Working with current feminist epistemologies, Julia Martin, Corinne Kumar D'Souza and, in a fascinating analysis, Nina Lykke and Mette Bryld propose new ways of knowing, bringing to the foreground the experiences of other subjects than those of Western scientific positivism.

The contributors also challenge the tradition of research as politically neutral and confined within the boundary of the writers' particular expertise. Coming from different disciplinary backgrounds (sociologists, philosophers, foresters, historians, biologists, political scientists, ecologists, economists, anthropologists and literary experts) the authors have a multidisciplinary approach and share a political commitment to research as part of a process of change which will bring women and environment concerns from the margins to a more consolidated position in sustainable development policies. Willy Douma et al and Janet Abramovitz discuss the principles of strategic feminist research, arguing for a participatory model of research and action which seeks to understand people's lives as they live them and to make room for alternative modes of knowing. The chapters contribute to a growing body of feminist methodology and approaches to understanding knowledge systems and power structures in different academic disciplines.

Another common theme of the contributions is the creativity and strength which local, national and international women's groups have found in their communities' resistance to unsustainable practices. In their varied responses to the environmental and economic crises, women, through their interactions and networking, are creating new spaces outside traditional development projects and institutions which inspire alternative paths for sustainable development. Sabine Häusler documents how the WED lobby at UNCED contributed an important input into the sustainable development debate. Though she maintains an ambivalence about the process, she records how throughout UNCED, partnerships were negotiated among women working in government delegations, researchers, NGOs and women's groups, in order to scrutinize and lobby on the key documents and agreements under discussion. Networking was at the core of this process, with many women taking the opportunity to build on strategic interests and to exchange ideas on women and environment issues which, as Frances Connelly argues, built on women's past experience in, for example, the peace movement. The adoption of a Chapter on women (Chapter 24) and the 'mainstreaming' of women's issues throughout

Agenda 21 were interpreted by the women's groups as significant political accomplishments, which Connelly suggests need to be capitalised upon.

As the different positions put forward by Connelly and Häusler reflect, the 'WED' debate acknowledges and thrives not only on the tensions between mainstream development concerns and the women's movement, but also on the tensions within the feminist position. The chapters argue for a shift in dominating knowledge systems as the key strategy for sustainable development, but they do not propose a new unified model in place of the old – rather they ask for a flexibility and openness to working with diverse knowledge and solutions. There is an continuing discussion in the book about which paths to take. It is not possible, nor desirable, simply to give a categorical 'no' to all technology, economic production and modern methods of organizing. But how is it possible to determine what is desirable and appropriate and what is not? Many of the contributors, as those working in the reality of the development crisis, monitor the difficult fit between the vision of an alternative and the demands of the current environmental and economic crisis to find practical and different solutions for those people who are directly affected.

As one of the most fiercely contested areas in development, population brings out acutely the dynamism and complexity of the sustainable debate. Feminists working in the population area are confronted with the enthusiasm with which male-dominated institutions, such as the church and state, and now the development community and ecologists, have taken up the issue. There are also very different positions within the women movement's response. But the perspective taken up by the authors is not to argue for one side or another but to look closely at the analytical links between women, environment and population. It is not possible to act effectively unless the situation is analysed so that the power relations and interests of all the actors are understood. Through analysis, feminists can find an effective way to negotiate better political positions as they interact / protest with the different institutions, actors and interests. As Franck Amalric argues, we cannot divide the world into separate local, national and global spheres of action but must analyse the interlinkages between international intervention, government at the local community level and then at each stage of negotiation if we are to change the myriad inequalities which the population debate covers. Gita Sen, in her discussion of the different actors involved in the population debate (from policy makers to environmental activists) suggests strategic ways in which women's environmental groups can work with other actors. While Helga Moss points to the need to analyse the situation of women in the North as part of a strategic link between Northern and Southern women's networks.

As this book reveals, feminist theory and practice is a fluid political process which, though at times proving difficult and even contradictory for the women and men involved, is a direct response to the dilemmas facing women in their daily interaction with their environments. The book reflects a historical moment where the international sustainable development debate has enabled women and men from diverse cultures and backgrounds to enter into dialogue. In defining a feminist perspective of sustainable development, women can better understand their relationship to the environment as a product of the success and failures of the current play of knowledge / power in the development discourse. But it is important to acknowledge that there are no right or wrong feminist perspectives on sustainable development, nor is there a completely consensual view on how to enter the debate in a constructive and politically useful way. As the extent of ground covered in this book suggests, the debate is not seeking to resolve contradictions and differences; on the contrary, the strength of the feminist position is the openness which its very diversity brings.

Notes

1. I would like to thank the many men and women involved in the Roundtable and the production of this book, in particular the SID staff and members of the SID/WUMEN team in The Netherlands: Sabine Häusler, Ineke van Halsema, Patricia Mohammed and Heleen van den Hombergh; and in Rome: Manuela Pujals for her whole-hearted assistance and support in all stages of the exercise and Lucia Cecchetti for her invaluable help in the preparation of the final papers.

2. Following others, such as Paul Ekins of the New Economics Foundation and Marja-Liisa Swantz (see Chapter 7 of this volume), I prefer to use the expression 'two-thirds world' instead of calling the majority of the world's people the 'Third World'. The term is synonymous (though less geographically misleading) with 'the South' used elsewhere in the book.

PART ONE

Situating the Feminist Position in the Sustainable Development Debate

1

Negotiating Positions in the Sustainable Development Debate: Situating the Feminist Perspective

Wendy Harcourt*

Feminist objectivity makes room for surprises and ironies at the heart of all knowledge production. We are not here to change the world. We just live here and try to shake up non-innocent conversations. (Haraway, 1991: 199)

Introduction

Development = economic growth is at the centre of development discourse. Even though many commentators point out that development is far more than economic growth but extends to social, political, cultural, environmental and gender concerns, economic growth remains firmly entrenched as the stated goal of development[1] from which modern critiques of development begin.

Over the last few years, this approach to development has been criticized and challenged by a number of development economists interested in revising economic theory and methodology to include environmental considerations. They have been joined by development professionals concerned that poverty alleviation and the basic needs approach of development programmes are not bringing about the hoped-for end to mass poverty and environmental deterioration. Women working in development are also part of this debate in their argument that the fundamental gender bias of development thinking and practice prevents gender equity and ignores women's contribution to the economy and their role in the management of the environment. And radicals in both industrialized and developing countries enter into the debate questioning the whole modernization process and Western knowledge systems on which development is based.

* I would like to thank Bina Agarwal, Teresa Brennan, Robert Cassani, Lucia Cecchetti, Geoff Harcourt, Claudio Sardoni, Maurice Williams and Simon Zadek for their encouraging and helpful comments on earlier versions of this chapter.

These thinkers and activists have found their voices in the recent policy debates on environment and development labelled 'sustainable development'.[2] They have used the political platform created by the United Nations Conference on Environment and Development (UNCED) (held in Rio de Janeiro, June 1992) to bring their particular concerns about the thesis that development = economic growth to the public arena.

The debates around UNCED point to the multifaceted problems of environment on the local and global level. Various causal factors are suggested, from patterns of production and consumption in the North to population pressures and industrial development in the South, to noxious chemical processes and to the complex and destructive processes which make up modern lifestyles. But a key factor singled out for examination is the link between environmental degradation and aggregate output growth. As Juliet Schor (1991) argues:

> Although choice of technology and product as well as numerous other factors are key determinants for the extent of environmental degradation, it is difficult to deny the role of growth itself. More production of steel and autos creates more air pollution and global warming, more newspapers and houses lead to the felling of more trees, more food generally implies more pesticides, and increased output in the rise in toxic substance ... the conclusion that growth is environmentally destructive implies that there is some identifiable function between growth and environmental 'change. (Schor, 1991: 75)

In recognizing the implications of this fundamental link for both developing and developed countries, the sustainable development debate proposes a new productive ethic at the heart of development which will value the quality of peoples' relations with each other and with nature. The arguments supporting this proposal have been conducted both on a polemical and on an academic level – translating economic thought and history, social critique and anthropology into a debate which aims to challenge traditional approaches to economics, to change the current practice of development policy-makers and to raise public awareness both inside and outside development institutions about the links between environment and development.

The sustainable development debate[3] marks a shift in development thinking and practice as well an open challenge to traditional economics. Only a few years ago, few development professionals would have looked to ecologists, women's groups, activists and anthropologists as collaborators and sources of expertise to solve what they would have seen as solely economic problems. We are now witnessing a process of ferment and openness to debate which is creating different possibilities for change. This is not to say that new economic ideas are being created but rather that new combinations are being tried out, that people are recognizing the partiality of their knowledge and, in an attempt to create more meaningful strategies for change, are seeking to form alliances across borders which previously would never have been crossed.

This current challenge to the development = economic growth equation provides a promising momentum for feminist methodology, thinking and practice to fulfil a useful role. Feminists can contribute their perspective[4] to this process by analysing the connections and contradictions of these various approaches. Joining the other actors, feminists can seek diverse strategies which respect local positions, diverse perspectives on social and natural environments and eschew the fruitless search for a universal model to explain all human productive and reproductive activity. This chapter reviews some of the positions held by the actors in the sustainable development debate who are seeking to undermine the notion of development = economic growth from the perspective of the environment, power/knowledge production and culture.

A review of these positions is important in the formation of a feminist perspective on sustainable development. In welcoming potential collaboration with other groups in strategies for social change, feminists need to enter into partnerships prepared to challenge the gender bias of the men and women working in these fields and to be very clear about the different situated positions of those involved in shared knowledge production and discursive practices. Secondly, the critique of development = economic growth inherent/implicit in these different approaches offers some useful points of connection for feminist theory and practice.

Real-life economics

The first school of thought represented by Ekins and Max-Neef (1992) redefines economic thinking in terms of how a nation's wealth is managed and distributed for the benefit of its people in relation to long-term human and ecological security. Theorists such as those in Ekins and Max-Neef (1992) seek to place economics as part of a complex set of social and economic interplays which have a direct impact on human and natural resources.[5] The concept of development is expanded to take on issues of environmental degradation, poverty, political participation and popular resistance in a critical examination of the dominant policy objectives of industrial economic activity worldwide. The topics under scrutiny are: whether Gross National Product (GNP) is a reliable gauge to measure social and environmental impacts on a nation's wealth (Soderbaum, 1992: 137); the relationship between the ecosystem and the economy (Daly, 1992a); a search for 'steady state economy' based on 'biophysical' limits and 'ethiosocial' limits to growth within the limits of the ecosystem. (Daly, 1992b)[6]

From a feminist perspective real-life economic arguments present two

major problems. First, they are still confined and expressed within a closed
system which seeks to explain complex problems of sustaining the earth's
resources, containing growth, empowering people and redistributing
wealth in a revised ecological economic version of a universal economic
model in order to explain development (now of peoples, nations and
nature). It is difficult, for example in Daly's explanation of economics as
a quasi-steady-state subsystem of the ecosystem, to see how the specific
environments and people involved in this cycle of throughput of material
can be opened up to other explanations of reality, and in particular gender
relations.

The second problem is that, despite claims to set up a framework which
brings on board a multidisciplinary critique of economics from social and
ecological sciences to grassroots experience, recent feminist scholarship
is passed over and gender is ignored as one of the axioms of economic
behaviour. In this they inherit the gender blindness of traditional economics. But in a study of the social, ecological and ethical dimensions of
real-life processes a consideration of gender relations is essential.

In order to change the gender bias of these critiques of development,
we need to demystify economic language and methodology in order to
disclose the sexism embedded in its practice. Development = economic
growth discounts not only many factors which determine economic behaviour in its claim to transcend culture, power, environmental and class
concerns, but gender relations too. The attempt to express economics in
the form of mathematical models gives it a mathematical sophistication
which is deeply reductionist and totally inadequate for explaining the
ambiguities and contradictions of the complex process of development.[7]
The study of gender relations has implications for the philosophy of
individualism which these economists challenge. The notion of freedom
of choice is not gender neutral. In understanding the disparities between
South and North, poor and rich, we must also recognize that within and
across these categories women have a less advantaged position. In putting
the relationship between economics and environment into a wider social
and cultural context we also need to consider feminist critiques of the
gender bias inherent in development discourse. Beneria (1992),
Boserup (1989), Elson (1991), Henderson (1992), Heyzer (1988), Hill
(1986), Lewenhak (1988), Moser (1989), Vickers (1991) and Waring
(1988).

People-centred economics

Working from outside the development establishment, another challenge
to economic theory is provided by James Robertson who defines principles
of a new economic order to move beyond development = economic growth
and to set out the ground rules for an 'enabling and conserving economy'

to 'invest in people'. (Robertson, 1989) His fundamental question for development economics is: 'how can people be enabled to become more self-sufficient and conserving?' (Ibid., 3) Following in the tradition of great economic thinkers such as Adam Smith and Karl Marx, he challenges the assumptions that self-interest is the driving force of the economy, that people have no desire or sense of responsibility to do intrinsically useful and rewarding work, and that people cannot use their economic powers (purchasing and investing) to make the world a better place. He also seeks to reinstate the informal and household sectors as major economic activities, which he argues could meet peoples' economic needs in perhaps an even better way than the formal sectors. (Robertson, 1989: 32)

What is interesting from a feminist perspective is that Robertson's focus on local-scale development opens up space for women's productive and reproductive activities to be valued. He emphasizes the importance of the community and household economy and defines the housewife as a producer, investor and worker. (Ibid., 35) He suggests that the informal economy, in which women predominate, should be fully valued in an economic and cultural sense, and he explicitly mentions the need for women's equal status in the formal economy and the need to relieve them of their disproportionate share of responsibility and work in the informal economy.

Robertson's vision for future wealth suggests some useful strategies for feminists interested in negotiating better positions for women in the sustainable development debate. In a deceptively commonsense approach to economic activities he takes into account how gender relations operate in the household and informal sectors and underlines the importance of these activities to the wider field of people, not growth-centred development. But a feminist critique could go even further to question the meaning behind the term 'investment' in people – is this not a residue of the language of economic growth? And, like the 'real-life' economists, Robertson proposes a universal model for a people-centred development which, though advocating the need to adapt to different situations, still starts from a Eurocentric view on equity, resources, household and informal economy and applies it to the South with not enough awareness of his own situated position. In doing so, he fails to allow for the differences in family and cultural behaviour in diverse societies. He also fails to note the cultural and social barriers for women in both developing and developed countries to decision-making within the home and their lack of access to resources needed to fulfil their needs (rather than their husband's or children's). Nor can we afford to see the informal sector as non-exploitative, particularly of women and children.

Development as knowledge/power

Another position in the debate is taken up by the contributors to Sachs (1992) who challenge the language and power relations of development discourse. They argue that development should, above all, be about people taking control of their own destinies.[8] They deconstruct development by placing under scrutiny key conceptual tools in economic growth models, such as planning, poverty, progress, resources and population, in order to ascertain the historical and political context of development = economic growth.

The core of their critique is that development in its present economic context has reduced all societies to a single blueprint, which posits modern Western values and lifestyles as the universal goal. In a 'steamrolling of the mind' (Sachs, 1992) development discourse divides the world into the haves and have-nots and is blind to the diversity of other cultures and ways of living. Despite the rhetoric of assistance, development as a world project has promoted economic growth as the only goal of development which, the authors argue, has had demonstrably disastrous effects from the point of view of ordinary people.

From their critical standpoint the policy-makers' contribution to sustainable development debate does little to clarify economic and social practices which would empower people and conserve the natural world. Instead, it is producing what Sachs (1992) depicts as an ever-expanding 'ecocracy' and few if any effective strategies for policy changes. The development profession's emphasis on population growth and poverty as the enemies of natural resource protection, masked in the rhetoric of assistance and global equity, is denounced as founded on the blind and faulty reasoning of the economic growth logic, which attempts to 'develop' nature. (Sachs, 1992: 211)

According to this critique, development planning produces a language of products and markets, traditional versus modern, development versus underdevelopment (Escobar, 1992: 139), which excludes women and nature and compartmentalizes peoples' lives into 'economy', 'health', 'education', 'leisure'. These writers reject monetization of both people and nature, along with the Western biases of mainstream development, in order to give space both to subjugated people and to their knowledge. In terms of gender relations these writers suggest that, not surprisingly given the lack of recognition of women's contribution to the economy, poor women have opposed development practice more actively than have men.[9]

In these writings about sustainable development, women are heard as the voices of resistance and as repositories of creative vision and knowledge which should be valued alongside (if not replace) Western concepts of how to produce and to manage the natural resource base. (Sachs, 1992: 142) In support of the feminist enterprise these writers propose that new development strategies based on more pluralistic and egalitarian practices, sensitive to the role of knowledge, culture and gender, can be involved as 'the links between development which articulate the state with profits, patriarchy and objectivizing science and technology on the one hand and the marginalization of peoples' lives and knowledge on the other become more evident'. (Sachs, 1992: 142)

From these writings we learn how development discourse based on development as economic growth is made to appear as a universal truth in the powerful operation of a knowledge system which subjugates both non-Western ways of thinking and nature. But although these writers look to feminist analysis and to women's groups as sources of strength and alternative vision, they do not look for negotiating positions with the many other groups in the debate. In order to open up their critique to allow a strategic dialogue with other actors in the debate they also need to situate themselves as part of the discourse. They write as outsiders to development discourse, but no such place without identity and power exists, and they too are positioned within and contribute to the sustainable development debate. In recognizing their own historical context and inheritance of the traditional resistance to industrialization, beginning with the French Revolution, Proudhon, the ambiguities of Adam Smith towards consumerism and, of course, Marx (Hirschman, 1992), they could be more open to further avenues for negotiation and change.[10] There is also a disturbing sense of a hidden dualism in these writers' arguments to the extent that, even while calling our attention to dualistic divisions in development discourse, they themselves seem able only to reverse the categories. They evoke concepts of the good, pre-modern, traditional world and the honourable, resisting Third Worlder, and the bad, modern, industrialized world and the thoughtless, greedy Westerner. Given that many of the writers themselves are part of the West – either born or educated there – it does seem curious that they so totally oppose that tradition.

Also, while it is useful to recognize the 'discontents' (Hirschman, 1992) particularly in relation to ecological destruction, increasing poverty and peoples' resistance, we should beware of being over-pessimistic and seeing no role for the West, industrialization or modernity. We are part of an historical moment which is not about to revert to a pre-industrial past. We also risk the danger of idealizing traditional societies' relationship to nature (which is not necessarily non-exploitative and understanding of others) and misrepresenting the heterogeneity of the West. Even using the categories of 'Western' or 'Northern' ignores the different traditions in the West and the mixtures of modernity and culture which make each country unique. In analysing modern development discourse we must be aware that nature and tradition have taken on new meanings, which cannot be neatly opposed to culture and modernity. We are all part of a complex set of transitional interplays between many positions.

Donna Haraway (1991) in her description of the cyborg world indicates
how we are all in some way part of the computerized highly technical
world. Even if we see modernity as destructive to nature and traditional
culture, we are involved in that process, which both repels and attracts us.[11]
It is the contradictions with which we must deal – the hopes as well as the
despair that development and modernity offer us.

The point is not that we have no ethical or moral observations to make,
but that we see how we are implicated in the power relations in which we
are embedded and, through the knowledge of how we are embedded, we
are empowered to create ways of change. This possibility for change
resides not only in the grassroots, but also in intellectuals explaining how
and to what extent women and men of the Third World are subject to and
are developing their own subjectivity in relation to the agenda, priorities
and values of the industrialized North.

Culture, economics and modernization

In order to do this we need to address the issue of culture and development
in relation to the modernization process.[12] Economic development, in
focusing on industrial growth as the quickest form of wealth creation, has
filtered out non-economic concerns and in so doing eventually confirmed
that culture does not matter. In the critique of development as economic
growth a number of writers influenced by anthropology and sociology
enter the critique of industrialization and modernity with an examination
of the relationship between culture, economics and modernization.

According to the writers in Apffel-Marglin and Marglin (1990) and
Mazlish (1991), the move from an agricultural to an industrial economy,
and the accompanying shift of the workplace from the home and the
growth of transportation and communications systems and urbanization,
produced a similar breakdown of connections in different cultures and
historical times. (Mazlish, 1991) They study these effects in relation to the
dominance of economics as a system of knowledge in the modernization
process. They adopt a critical stance towards development, arguing that
we must understand the interrelationship between economics and the
modernization ethic if we are to understand continuing global social
inequities. They ask whether development discourse should be so confi-
dently promoting the Western model of production – where the
productivity of the work is perceived as satisfying individual desires rather
than fulfilling community needs – as a universal model which is the best
option for the organic growth of non-Western cultures.

Marglin (Apffel-Marglin and Marglin, 1990) identifies two distinct
ways of understanding, focusing and expressing reality: episteme and
techne, in order to explain the high value placed on economics as a
knowledge system in Western development.

Economics as part of Western science is an example of episteme, based on logic and rationality, disembodied from doing, essentially book-learning. Episteme is disembodied from its particular contexts; it is an instrumental knowledge which lends itself to the logic of calculation. Techne is embedded in practice. Crafts such as spinning and weaving are examples of techne knowledge which is gained through process and learning-by-doing within a community, passed down from generation to generation. Marglin traces these different types of learning to classical times and argues that Western civilization has learnt to consider episteme as the only pure knowledge, elevating it to a superior knowledge and relegating techne to no knowledge at all.

For feminists, Marglin's explanation of how industrialization has displaced techne in the Western world and is now doing the same in the Third World helps us to see how the work of caring for the environment, and women's role as nurturers, are also undervalued in the logic of development economics. Sustaining local environments is not book work, it is learnt through time, passed on from generation to generation, and cannot easily be brought into the higher rationale of economic episteme. It is, therefore, easier to ignore it altogether, at considerable cost to those who, in traditional societies, were valued holders of knowledge but in the process of modernization have become devalued, 'illiterate', 'non-skilled', 'unpaid', 'non-productive' members of society.

In their descriptions of and reflections on various cultural behaviours, this school of thought questions the devaluing of women's reproductive and productive role and argues that modernization and development, by placing value only on paid productive work and on acquiring resources, have failed to value some of the more fundamentally healthy and creative practices in other cultures which retain a high value of the feminine in society. (Apffel-Marglin, 1992) They are careful not to idealize the oppressive practices of traditional cultures such as female genital mutilation or widow burning (*suttee*) but rather to explain their cultural meaning in order to open up other non-instrumental ways of working for change. A respect for other cultural approaches would prevent development practice imposing new methods that destroy the cultural integrity and harmony of a community in the name of modernization.

Challenging modernity touches on another complex issue for feminism. In the strong anti-development stand of the South, so-called fundamentalist movements have rejected the Western values and identities which tend to be crystallized in the symbol of the South's Westernized woman. Mazlish (1991) comments how in Muslim societies Westernized women 'embody at once all social ills: the super-consumer of imperialist/dependent foreign goods; the propagator of the corrupt culture of the West; undermining the moral fabric.' (Mazlish, 1991: 41) In understanding women's place as subject in the sustainable development debate, we have to be aware of the rich history of women as symbols of cultural biases which reflect male social and political struggle more than women's own reality, but nevertheless have implications for how women can act to change the situation. Outsiders can play a useful role in distinguishing women's own perceptions from cultural expectations. Modernization as a practice of the development discourse can, when respecting other societies and used responsibly, be a liberating discourse. We must be wary of romanticizing traditional cultures but rather aim to make explicit the values and morals inherent in development discourse in order to expose contradictory and explosive issues. There is no true culture or nature to which we can return or preserve. Social and cultural change and knowledge production are ongoing and fluid struggles involving all actors. The important thing is to acknowledge the different positions: it is not just a question of the West versus the others; we will have to negotiate through a far more complex and difficult process if we are to confront and try to resolve social inequities.

For a feminist critique these writings based on observations of Third World cultures and perceptions raise the question of whether modern economics might not learn from other ways of social and economic organization, rather than always assuming a dominance and superior knowledge. Feminist critics place development economics, with its devaluation of nature and its failure to treat other cultures and people with dignity, as just one system of knowledge in the process of modernization, which needs to be examined critically for its continuing worth, given its current poor record at solving the problems it defines and sets out to solve in development. In doing so these writings give economics a cultural context which helps deconstruct its claims to objectivity and truth.

Gender, environment and alternative development: forming alliances

Given the complexity of the dialogue described above, what do these positions in the sustainable development debate mean for a gender analysis of environment and development (the WED debate)?

The real-life and people-centred economists offer a critique of economic growth which is now entering into mainstream development. This opens a space for feminists working in gender and environment issues to negotiate the inclusion of gender relations with economists already concerned to introduce ecological concerns into the mainstream economic paradigm. Their analytical proposals for how to redesign economic theory to include environment and people-centred strategies could be built on and strengthened to remove the gender blindness. Beginning a dialogue with the proponents of this position who are already politically open to hearing challenges to economic development is an important strategy for those concerned with a feminist perspective of the analysis and practice of sustainable development.

Feminists in the WED debate can also learn from those entering the debate from a critique of the power/knowledge position, who are suspicious of the development enterprise. Their questions about the accountability of the policy-makers arguing for sustainable development from a political and historical context are useful. Such powerful critiques of the institutions and practices of development can help feminists more effectively to subvert the development discourse based on development as economic growth. Feminist analysis can add a greater flexibility to the critique by underlining the importance of defining the actors' situated positions and working with the contradictions between the different ways of seeing.

The observations of those writers, working from a cultural critique about the presumed links between development economics and modernization, deepens the critique of economic growth by seeking to displace the authoritative voices of development economics and Western culture. In seeking to dispel the necessity of a mono-cultural development and bringing out the need to respect other cultures, this approach strengthens the aim of feminists concerned with gender and environment issues who are endeavouring to listen and to respect the different experiences of women working in developing and developed countries. They provide important insights for approaching networking and joint projects without assuming Western knowledge to be the dominant and most useful explanation of productive activities. But feminist theory cautions these writers not to romanticize other cultures in a wholesale attack on Western economics and modern culture, pointing out that the symbolic objectification of women in cultural explanations of society can reduce women's capabilities to act.

The feminist position in the sustainable development debate needs to seek out and form such alliances as we work towards explaining reality and finding solutions to the environment and development crisis. These alliances hold out a promise for feminist strategic research on gender and environment and its entry into policy-making, but such alliances remain precarious and in constant flux, displacing and being displaced as they come into contact with the differences and changing interests of the positions. As WED forms strategic alliances, old definitions will need to be abandoned and work done to create new ones in unsettling the understanding of development as economic growth. But, as the above dialogue suggests, the task of transforming economic theory in development is a hard one for those inscribed in the feminist position on the margins of the knowledge production of environment, economics and development.

Notes

1. I define development as a collection of theories (development as economic growth), institutions (Bretton Woods, NGOs), practices (projects, community societies) and procedures (programmes, plans) through which individuals and communities are constituted. Within this field or set of discourses, enmeshed in a web of power relations (North-South, gender), subjects (peasant women, development experts, ecologists, company representatives) are defined. Development, then, is not an accurate description of reality but rather one of the elements through which we construct reality. Neither do we imply that there is any causal relationship between any of the actors involved in a particular negotiation, rather it is the interplay of all the elements of the set of discourses called development which enable us to define what we understand as the subject and problem when we enter into the negotiations. (St Hilaire, 1992: 2-3).

2. Sustainable development is a highly contested term with many attempts to define it precisely (Dover, 1989). We need not be concerned here with the various definitions through in the mainstream debate sustainable development is used to refer to a concern with balancing conservation of economic resources with economic growth based on industrialization and the need to safeguard earth's resources for future generations. See *Development* 1989: 2/3 and 1990: 3/4 for a series of articles contributing to this debate in response to the Brundtland Commission's *Our Common Future* (WCED, 1987).

3. An example of the literature marking the debate amongst economists in the development profession in recent years, some of which I refer to below, is found in the regular section 'SID Debates Sustainability and Development', in *Development* 1991-93; *The People Centred Development Forum*, Korten (ed.); Max-Neef (1991); Robertson (1989); Carley and Christie (1992); Daly (1992a, 1992b); Ekins *et al* (1992); Henderson (1992); Soderbaum (1992); Buarque (1993); Pearce (1993).

4. To define what I mean by a feminist perspective: feminist knowledge production and practice seeks to bring out the different positions of the actors in order to allow for possible connections with others; feminist analysis aims to interpret, not claim, truth. Hence, in development work, feminists are not seeking the correct analysis which will point to the right path for change, but are rather seeking to identify the different paths necessary to change particular situations as defined both by the people living in the area and the outsiders who wish to offer support. A feminist perspective on sustainable development, therefore, tries to establish connections between the different actors as subjects of knowledge about women's relationship to the environment and development practice. This implies fostering what Haraway (1991) calls conversations between subjects, rather than studies of objects by subjects in order to empower those subjugated by oppressive practices by negotiating with other actors workable solutions to the environment and development crisis.

5. I touch on, but do not enter here into, the debate about whether these writers accomplish their ambitious objective to redefine economics. See Harris (1991), who argues that Daly and Rosenstein-Rodan have some valuable and useful

observations on entropy in the interrelationship between economics, natural resources, energy and biological systems.

6. For Daly, sustainable development policies must restate issues of costs and benefits by looking at a range of economic and ecological relationships: 'We are related not only by a nexus of individual willingness to pay for different things but also by relations of trusteeship for the poor, the future and other species' (Daly, 1992a: 190). In his theory of the economy as a 'quasi-steady-state subsystem of the ecosystem', his major point is that the human economy is not exempt from the laws governing natural systems (Daly, 1992b: 215). Daly has inspired many other theorists such as Carley and Christie (1992), who explicitly build on his concept of the planet's carrying capacity and his assertion that economic growth makes us poorer, to outline the political and social choices we have to make in terms of balancing environmental and economic decisions.

7. Following the same logic, we might also query here the usefulness of the project attempted by development economists interested in ecological issues to make environment into an economic concept. Economics, as Keynes himself pointed out, is a tool for explaining human economic activities and not intended to be stretched to explain all human activities.

8. Interestingly, in the development policy-making community, the position held by the contributors to Sachs's book would once have been dismissed as idealistic or as thinly veiled support for communists or at least an anti-capitalist (US) stand. Now, in the post-Cold War era, we can start to move away from assuming monolithic political allegiances and on to assessing another level of political issues, many of which are sketched by these authors.

9. Development Alternatives for Women for a New Era (DAWN) proposed in 1984 (Sen and Grown, 1984) that a feminist critique of development can begin from the perspectives of the poor women from the South. DAWN and other women researchers and activists fly in the face of the development establishment's assumption that women are more traditional and therefore more conservative.

10. Perhaps their message would be more effective if they applied some of the historical irony Hirschman mentions in his discussion of the resistance, criticism and anxieties aroused by industrialization.

11. For example, Norberg-Hodge (1992) writes in despair of the cultural destruction of the Ladakhi peoples in their recent confrontation with the developed world. But she notes how much they themselves want modernization even if she profoundly regrets the loss of a uniquely sustainable society and culture. At the same time, it is those very development processes which have allowed her to be there studying and learning from Ladakh and sharing those discoveries with others.

12. Since World War Two, not the pre-colonial era when culture was central to the development 'mission'. (Sachs, 1992)

References

Apffel-Marglin, Frédérique (1992) 'Women's Blood: challenging the discourse of development', in *The Ecologist*, vol. 22.

Apffel-Marglin, Frédérique and Stephen Marglin (eds) (1990) *Dominating Knowledge: Development, Culture and Resistance*. Clarendon Press, Oxford.

Beneria, Lourdes (1992) 'Accounting for Women's Work: The Progress of Two Decades', in *World Development*, vol. 20, no. 11, November.

Boserup, Ester (1989) *Women's Role in Developing Economies*. Earthscan, London.

Buarque, Cristovam (1993) *The End of Economics: Ethics and the Disorder of Progress*. Zed Books, London and New Jersey.

Carley, Michael and Ian Christie (1992) *Managing Sustainable Development*. Earthscan, London.

Daly, Herman E. (1992a) *Steady-State Economics*. Earthscan, London.

—— (1992b) 'Allocation, Distribution and Scale, Towards an Economics that is Efficient, Just, and Sustainable', in *Ecological Economics*, no. 6, December.

Dover, Stephen (1989) 'Sustainability, Definitions, Clarifications and Contexts', in *Development: Journal of the Society for International Development*, no. 2/3, September.

Ekins, Paul, Mayor Hilliman and Robert Hutchinson (1992) *Wealth Beyond Measure*. Gaia Books Ltd., London.

Ekins, Paul and Manfred Max-Neef, (eds) (1992) *Real-Life Economics: Understanding Wealth Creation*. Routledge, London and New York.

Elson, Diane (1991) *Male Bias in Development*. Manchester University Press, Manchester.

Escobar, Arturo (1992) 'Reflections on "Development". Grassroots Approaches and Alternative Politics in the Third World', in *Futures*, June.

Haraway, Donna (1991) *Simians, Cyborgs, and Women: The Reinvention of Nature*. Free Association Books, London.

Harris, J.M. (1991) 'Global Institutions and the Ecological Crisis', in *World Development*, vol. 19, no. 1.

Henderson, Hazel (1992) *Paradigms in Progress: Life Beyond Economics*. Knowledge Systems, Inc., Indianapolis.

Heyzer, Noeleen (1988) *Daughters in Industry*. Asian and Pacific Development Centre, Kuala Lumpur.

Hill, Polly (1986) *Development Economics on Trial*. Cambridge University Press, Cambridge.

Hirschman, Albert (1992) 'Industrialisation and its Manifold Discontents, West, East and South', in *World Development*, vol. 2, no. 9.

Lewenhak, Sheila (1988) *The Reevaluation of Women's Work*. Croom Helm, London, New York, Sydney.

Max-Neef, Manfred (1991) *Human Scale Development: Conception, Application and Further Reflections*. Apex Press, New York and London.

Mazlish, B (1991) 'The Breakdown of Connections and Modern Development', in *World Development*, vol. 19, no. 1.

Moser, Caroline O. (1989) 'Gender Planning and the Third World: Meeting Practical and Strategic Gender Needs', in *World Development*, vol. 17, no. 11.

Norberg-Hodge, Helena (1992) *Ancient Futures: Learning from Ladakh*. Rider, London.

Pearce, David (1993) *Economic Values and the Natural World*. Earthscan, London.

Robertson, James (1989) *Future Wealth: A New Economics for the 21st Century*. Cassell, London.

Sachs, Wolfgang (ed.) (1992) *The Development Dictionary*. Zed Books, London and New Jersey.

Schor, Judith (1991) 'Global Equity and Environmental Crisis: An Argument for Reducing Working Hours in the North', in *World Development*, vol. 19, no. 1.

Sen, Gita and Caren Grown (1987) *Development Crises and Alternative Visions*. Monthly Review Press, New York.

Shiva, Vandana (1989) *Staying Alive*. Zed Books, London and New Jersey.

Simmons, Pam (ed.) (1992) 'Feminism, Nature, Development', in *The Ecologist*, vol. 22, no. 1, January/February.

Society for International Development (1989) 'Sustainable Development from Theory to Practice', in *Development* (1989: 2/3)

—— (1990) 'Human-centred Economics: Environment and Global Sustainability', in *Development* (1990: 3/4)

—— (1992) 'Developing Environmental Sustainability', in *Development* (1992: 2)

Soderbaum, Peter (1992) 'Neo-classical and Institutional Approaches to Development and the Environment', in *Ecological Economics*, no. 5.

St Hilaire, Colette (1992) 'Canadian Aid, Women and Development: Re-baptizing the Filipina', in *Philippine Development Briefing*, no. 3, December.

Vickers, Jeanne (ed.) (1991) *Women and the World Economic Crisis*. Zed Books, London and New Jersey.

Waring, Marilyn (1988) *If Women Counted*. Harper and Row, San Francisco.

World Commission on Environment and Development (1987) *Our Common Future*. Oxford University Press, Oxford.

2

Feminist Orientalism and Development

Frédérique Apffel-Marglin and Suzanne L. Simon

The shift[1] from a 'Women in Development' (WID) discourse to a 'Women, Environment and Development' (WED) discourse which took place in the late 1980s and early 1990s, is significant in that it opens up a space for questioning the developmental enterprise itself. It also signals a more critical attitude towards modernity and the modernizing process. From our viewpoint this shift is most welcome, opening up possibilities for the voices of non-modern, non-commodified and usually non-Western women to be heard in a new way; for their knowledge and ways of life to be taken seriously as potential alternatives to modernity and the commodification that comes with it. In other words this shift opens up a road to diversity and pluralism rather than representing the highway to a single destination: modernity.

Here, at the threshold of this new WED discourse, in our opinion it is timely and necessary to abandon some of the historical baggage that the WID discourse carried. It seems to us that this historical baggage is in direct continuity with a colonial discourse, carried forward in the WID discourse mostly undetected, clothed in a language that gives the illusion of discontinuity. Without a clear identification of this historical continuity, this baggage is in danger of contaminating the new WED language. To achieve such a break we need to make the continuity explicit and to identify how it manifests itself. Furthermore, we need to identify accurately what assumptions underlie these colonial legacies, particularly assumptions about the nature of personhood and of women's bodies.

In Part I of this chapter, we intend to reveal the historical continuity between the perception of the 'Third World Woman' in the WID discourse and the perception of the colonized woman by Victorian feminists and colonialists. The image of the 'Third World Woman' is a contemporary version of the 'uncivilized' colonized woman. The way in which many modern Westerners have perceived non-white women is largely a function of an unconscious valorization of a type of personhood functional to industrial capitalism, that is, to modernity. The 'modern' individual has a certain conception of the body (Duden, 1991), and understands women's generative capacity in terms of biological processes, perceived and described by the use of industrial and productive metaphors. (Martin 1987) Much feminist scholarship has revealed that such understandings of personhood and 'female bodily processes' do not carry historico-cultural assumptions and, therefore, cannot have universal validity. (Bordo, 1989; Duden, 1991; Franklin, 1993; Haraway, 1989, 1991; Harding, 1986; Hubbard, 1990; Jordanova, 1989; Keller, 1992; Martin, 1987; Strathern, 1992.)

With the shift from a WID to a WED discourse, the issue of the relationship between human beings – and women in particular – and the non-human world becomes central. A modernist understanding of women's generative capacity in principally biological terms implies a fundamental rift between women's 'natural' – that is, biological – processes and their 'cultural' – properly symbolic – capacities. It is here that the modernist dualism between nature and culture is located. In this dualism lies the estrangement between what a modernist consciousness considers 'properly human capacities' and the non-human world. In our view, the issue of generative capacity is central to approaching broader environmental concerns. As long as it is subsumed under the category of biology, the rift between the human and the non-human world (the latter being an object to the former) cannot be breached. If we are to move from an exploitative relationship toward the non-human world to one in which generative and regenerative processes subsume both the human and the non-human world, we need simultaneously to deconstruct some of our basic modern categories as well as to listen to the voices of non-modern peoples with new ears. To that end, Part II of this chapter attempts to present one example of a non-modernist way of being in the world, of being a person, in which the rift between nature and culture is unknown. This is a world in which women's generative activities are not divorced from their socio-cultural activities; a world where both men and women engage in generative and regenerative activities; a world where generation and regeneration are at the centre of cultural and societal concerns.

I

Victorian colonialist feminists

In colonial narratives, women were typically represented as essentially passive. (Etienne and Leacock, 1980) Colonized women were seen as helplessly and passively suffering from the backwardness, savagery and wretchedness of their own cultures. In Hindu and Muslim societies particularly, women were seen to suffer behind the veil from segregation, isolation and seclusion. In the case of Hindus, *sati* was highlighted as emblematic of women's dismal position in society. (Ware, 1992; Ahmed, 1992; Chaudhuri and Strobel, 1992; Mani, 1989) The treatment of women was the measuring rod or 'index of civilization' of a particular society, measured against the standard of British Victorian womanhood which stood at the apex of an evolutionary incline.[2]

Leila Ahmed (1992) has shown how in colonial Egypt the veil became the symbol of women's oppression in Westernized narratives and came to stand for the backwardness of the society as a whole. In the rhetoric about the veil, colonialists and Victorian feminists combined to conflate women and culture. The comparison of womanhood in 'civilized' Britain and in colonized Egypt made it possible for someone like Lord Cromer (then Governor of Egypt) to oppose Victorian feminists at home while simultaneously using Victorian feminist arguments in respect of Egyptian women to argue for the wholesale overhaul of Egyptian ways of life. As Leila Ahmed puts it:

> ... what was created was the fusion between the issues of women, their oppression, and the cultures of Other men. The idea that Other men, men in colonized societies or societies beyond the borders of the civilized West, oppressed women was to be used, in the rhetoric of colonialism, to render morally justifiable its project of undermining or eradicating the cultures of colonized peoples ... [W]hatever the disagreements of feminism with white male domination within Western societies, outside their borders feminists turned from being the critic of the system of white male dominance to being its docile servant. Anthropology, it has often been said, served as the handmaid of colonialism. Perhaps it must also be said that feminism, or the idea of feminism, served as its other handmaid. (Ahmed, 1992: 154-5)

In India, *sati* played a similar role to that of the veil in Egypt. Lata Mani (1989, 1992) in her historical study of *sati* during colonial times, shows that the colonial discourse on *sati* represented Hindu women as essentially passive. Women who committed *sati* were either heroized as faithful widows and obedient keepers of tradition or seen as passive victims who needed to be saved. Official rhetoric made a distinction between 'good' and 'bad' *sati*. 'Good', in this official rhetoric, was *sati* performed voluntarily by the widow in blind obedience to Brahmanic scriptures; 'bad' was *sati* performed under coercion to secure financial or other material gains for the survivors. Colonial officers categorized the former as legal and the latter as illegal. Colonial officials called upon pundits to provide scriptural authority and vouch for the 'authenticity' of the act. These procedures amounted to the constitution or 'invention' of tradition in the 19th century. (Mani, 1989: 113) Colonizers' ostensible effort to preserve the dignity of women performing *sati* was actually made through an equation of women and tradition/culture, since it necessitated the identification of what constituted 'authentic' Indian culture. This attempt to distinguish between authentic and inauthentic *sati* was based on the colonizers' classificatory act of decreeing brahmanic scriptures and their brahmin interpreters as the locus of 'authenticity', projecting Christian and Western notions of canonical scriptures on to a Hindu context. Colonial officials perceived themselves as democratizing the scriptural authority of the pundits by making visible to the masses the scriptural basis of *sati*. But such notions are foreign in a Hindu context where local oral traditions can and do supersede scriptural prescriptions. There are no canonical scriptures binding on all Hindus, nor is there a unified, centralized religious priesthood. Furthermore, local practice, even if not codified in any text, can, and typically does, have more authority than pan-Indian texts. This was made clear to Apffel-Marglin during a conversation about *sati* with K.C. Rajaguru, in one of India's main pilgrimage centres (Puri, in Orissa) shortly after a *sati* had been performed in a Rajasthani town, in 1987. K.C. Rajaguru (who died in 1992) was the highest authority supervising all rituals in Jagannatha (one of the greatest pilgrimage temples of India) as well as the spiritual preceptor of the king of Puri and the head of the assembly of brahmin pundits (Mukti Mandapa Sabha) who interpret the 'sacred law texts' (*dharmasastras*). Rajaguru said:

> In our area this *sati* custom has never existed. In some parts of India it existed and still exists. But nowadays it is more important that the widow become as *brahmacarini* (an ascetic). Our *sastras* (texts) say that if the husband dies prematurely the wife has three choices: 1. she can become *sati*; 2. she can become *brahmacarini* (ascetic); 3. she can remarry. It is not our tradition here to do *sati*. Our widows become *brahmacarinis*.

Asked about the 1987 *sati* in Rajasthan and the pronouncements of the Puri Sankaracharya (one of four in India but *not* an Oriya) in support of *sati*, Rajaguru said:

> At the *sati* in Deorala [Rajasthan] there was drumming; they forced her; she was shouting 'save me, save me!' and they threw her into the fire. Do you think that is according to the *sastras*? The *sastras* would never support this. It should never be done ... Sankaracharya should never have uttered the sentence he did. What happened in Deorala should never be done.

At this point, his 53 year old eldest daughter confirmed that: 'The tradition of *sati* never existed in this region. It is not our custom. Our widows become *brahmacarinis*.' Apffel-Marglin's subsequent enquiries in Puri as well as in villages in Puri district substantiated what Rajaguru and his daughter had said.

From this conversation it is very clear that sacred texts do not wield ultimate authority and that local practice is determinant. British notions of authentic/inauthentic were colonial creations.

The civilizing mission of colonial officials included safeguarding a tradition perceived by them as threatened by corruption and secularization, as well as protecting weak, obedient and passive women from coerced *sati*.

This amounted to what Eric Hobsbawm (1983) has called the 'invention of tradition'. More specifically, this representation of Indian women, in Lata Mani's words:

> ... has been fertile ground for the elaboration of discourses on salvation, in contexts of colonialism, nationalism, and, more recently, Western feminism. For the most part, all three have constructed the Indian woman not as someone who acts, but as someone to be acted upon. (Mani, 1989: 397)

To this we must add Victorian feminists, the historical precursors of contemporary Western feminism. The role of a prominent Victorian feminist in the Ilbert Bill controversy of 1883 is a case in point. This Bill would have extended Indian courts' territorial jurisdiction and legalized the subjection of European women to the Indian court system. Two gender themes dominated the controversy surrounding this Bill. Colonial women and men perceived Indian men as effeminate, obviously unfit to judge British women. There was also concern that if such legislation were passed it would threaten the security of the 'pure and defenceless white women in India'. (Sinha, 1992: 99-101) Annette Ackroyd, speaking against the Bill, said:

> In this discussion the ignorant and neglected women of India rise up against their enslavement in evidence against their masters. They testify to the justice of the resentment which Englishwomen feel at Mr. Ilbert's proposal to subject civilized women to the jurisdiction of men who have done little or nothing to redeem women of their own race, and whose social ideas are still on the outer verges of civilization. (Quoted in Sinha, 1992: 110; see also Ware, 1992: 147 for a similar discussion)

It was bad enough that ignorant and uncivilized Indian women were enslaved by their men but that civilized British women should be judged by such men was clearly outrageous! As in Egypt and in the US (see bell hooks, 1981), Victorian feminists shared the racist outlook of the men in their society.

Annette Ackroyd went to India to establish a girls' school in order to instruct young Hindu women on the virtues of 'practical housework, and the formation of orderly and industrious habits' (Beveridge, 1947: 92) as well as other more scholastic topics. For colonized Indians caught between 'two civilizations',

> The education of her women is the only solution [for] the women who live behind the veil in India, or who, though without, are utterly untouched by modern education and modern ideas are still the vast majority [for whom

the] never failing theme of education as the root of all progress [is the solution]. (Cowan, 1912: 14-15)

Such sentiments became a dominant theme of the Brahmo Samaj, a Hindu reform movement embodying one indigenous response to British perceptions of 'Hinduism'. The Brahmo Samaj advocated the British model of womanhood as a model to be emulated. Its leader in the 1860s and 1870s, Keshub Chunder Sen, addressed British women in 1870 as follows:

I now have the honour to make an urgent yet humble plea to you English-women – I may say English sisters. I sincerely and earnestly call you to do all in your power to effect the education of Hindu women ... My business this evening is to tell you that in her distress India bids you come over and help her. Governments are trying to do what improved legislation can to crush and exterminate bad customs. Philanthropic men have gone there to promote a liberal education amongst males, and now if English-women are ready to vindicate what are called women's rights in England, if they have to make platform speeches, let them show that their views and sympathies are not confined within the limits of this small island. (Beveridge, 1947: 84-5)

By the end of the 19th century, the education to be brought to Indian women from England had become a means to educate women better for the industrial workforce. Furthermore, John MacKenzie (1984) has argued that imperial propaganda deployed through the schools and other institutions from the latter third of the 19th century, well into the 1950s and 1960s, played an important role in fashioning a particularly British sensibility. The ideological cluster in this propaganda consisted of militarism, patriotism, worship of military and national figures, as well as the racism of Social Darwinism. Such an ideological cluster reinforced and was reinforced by widespread British notions of racial and national superiority and progress, particularly in contrast to the state of the 'backward', colonized races. MacKenzie argues that such propaganda was deeply responsible for fashioning British sensibility in popular culture, a sensibility that justified colonization in the name of a moral duty to civilize. British Victorian feminists, as we have seen, had fully participated in this imperial culture.

The Third World woman and the WID discourse

Just as Victorian culture was shaped by imperial propaganda, the 20th century has been shaped by the more subtle, humanistic, imperial propaganda of development. The feminism that informs the WID discourse descends directly from Victorian colonial feminism. To illustrate this, one can begin by noting the similarity between Keshub Chunder Sen's speech (quoted above) and the following contemporary statement on the role of educating women in development:

> Women are indeed the second sex in the poor countries of the world. They are less educated than men, have fewer occupational options, and earn less when they work ... poverty is very much a woman's issue, at least in part BECAUSE of their double roles. Women both affect and are affected by the development process ... In fact, the 'woman's issue', once thought of as no more than a welfare issue, affects the prospects for efficiency, growth, and development in the economy as a whole. (Buvinic, Lycette and McGreevey, 1983: 3, 13)

In recent women-in-development narratives, tradition and social constraints are identified as barriers to women's access to the market. Social constraints must be removed in order to make women more visible, inaugurate their modernization and their integration into industrial capitalism. This amounts to creating economically productive, independent units.

The date of the development 'discovery' of Third World women's poverty as well as their role in economic productivity corresponds to the 1970 publication of Ester Boserup's *Women's Role in Economic Development*. Since then, development has sought increasingly to bring Third World women within its focus. Invisibility and Tradition are evoked as a hindrance to development, a constraint and a symptom of traditional subordination. Perhaps most importantly, women are conceived of as primarily poor. The automatic equation of women with poverty justifies the development desire to transform all Third World women into 'economically productive', autonomous, independent subjects.[3] The very basis of the WID discourse rests on the same colonial perception of the victimization of women.

The women-in-development vision posits an essentialized universal subordination of women, and development as the vehicle for eradicating male dominance. The following passage from Gita Sen and Caren Grown's book (1987)[4] on the subject illustrates this:

> The transformation of the structures of subordination that have been so inimical to women is the other part of our vision of a new era. Changes in law, civil codes, systems of property rights, control over our bodies, labor codes, and the social and legal institutions that underwrite male control and privilege are essential if women are to attain justice in society ... At its deepest level it is not an effort to play 'catch up' with the competitive, aggressive, 'dog-eat-dog' spirit of the dominant system. It is, rather, an attempt to convert men and the system to the sense of responsibility, nurturance, openness, and rejection of hierarchy that are part of our vision ... feminism has as its unshakable core a commitment to breaking down the structures of gender subordination as a vision for women as full and

equal participants with men at all levels of societal life. (Sen and Grown, 1989: 79, 81)

The universal subjugation and oppression of women is the basis and the justification of these writers' claims that societies and cultures must be transformed in order to accommodate the liberation of women. The 'oppression', and consequently the need for a liberation of women, serves as justification for the development intervention and the transformation of entire ways of life, indeed, of the entire Third World. The women-in-development rhetoric's insistence in locating the 'oppressed Third World woman' at the very bottom of the heap – that is oppressed by race, gender and class – lends further justification to such an argument for symbolic and structural transformation of societies in order to allow the Third World woman to rise from the depths of poverty and oppression.

In development rhetoric, poverty shares the status of the veil, *sati*, or genital mutilation in much of Western/ized feminist rhetoric; symbols of oppression, tradition and patriarchy, these are practices and forces to be eradicated. Once again, the equation of women with culture and with poverty, and poverty with economic backwardness, utilises women's position in society to measure that society's progress, as an index of its civilization/modernity. And once more, the standard against which Third World women's position is judged is that of the 'emancipated' (formerly the 'civilized') woman in First World countries: the autonomous, economically independent woman, fully integrated into a commodified world.

When women's own self-perception concerning their well-being is not that of the autonomous, independent self, but rather a self embedded in kinship (and other social) webs, as well as in the local landscape, the women-in-development logic leads to invalidating these perceptions as not being true to reality. Such logic thereby confers prerogative on the development experts' construction of 'reality'. As Amartya Sen states:

> It has often been observed that if a typical Indian rural woman was asked about her personal 'welfare', she would find the question unintelligible, and if she was able to reply, she might answer … in terms of her reading of the welfare of her family. The idea of personal welfare may not be viable in such a context …
>
> This empirical problem of perception and communication is indeed important. [But] it is far from obvious that the right conclusion to draw from this is the non-viability of the notion of personal welfare …
>
> … and the lack of perception of personal interest combined with a great concern for family welfare is the kind of attitude that helps to sustain the traditional inequalities … It can be a serious error to take the absence of protests and questioning of inequality as evidence of the absence of that inequality … Third, personal interest and welfare are not just matters of perception; there are objective aspects of these concepts that command

attention even when the corresponding self-perception does not exist ...
There is a need to go beyond the primitive feelings a person may have on
these matters, based perhaps on unquestioning acceptance of certain traditional priorities ... [P]erceptions must not be confused with the person's
well-being, or alternatively, taken as evidence of the non-viability of any
perception of well-being. (Sen, 1990: 126-7)

According to this argument, a woman's perception of her self-interest
as inseparable from that of her family or community is highly suspect due
to the possibility of inequalities within the family or community. What is
disturbing in such an account is the assumption that the source of inequality resides in 'tradition', which tends to be equated with 'backwardness'
and 'constraints', whereas modernity, education, in sum the integration of
women in industrial capitalism, is assumed to be liberating. Some WID
scholars, however, have identified another major source of the victimization of women in the very development process itself. (Bunch and Carillo,
1990: 74-7; Sen and Grown, 1987: 15-16, 25-6, 28; Buvinic and Yudelman, 1989: 36) But this does not lead Amatya Sen to question development
itself, only to exhortations for 'better' development; when writing of
women's oppression, the role and the process of development itself is not
invoked. The ahistorical category of 'tradition' used by Amartya Sen
becomes the repository of all the forces contributing to women's oppression; there is no attempt to inquire into the historical interplay between the
processes of integration and changes in attitude toward and practices
concerning women that these very processes may have ushered in.

Additionally, Sen undermines the knowledge that any Third World
woman may possess about her own situation. Any words that fail to
acknowledge oppression and gender inequality are reportedly the product
of a mistaken and distorted perception, the products of 'primitive feelings'.
Essential to this argument is the narrative of: 'We know what is best for
them in spite of what they may say for themselves.' Women's own
perceptions and ways of knowing are identified as an obstacle to development which must be removed or transformed if their socio-economic
development is to succeed. Cognitive authority, once again, resides with
the expert who has access to 'objective reality' and not with the women
themselves. Thus the expert's voice replaces (and eliminates) the women's
voices.

The content of the women-in-development discourse differs from that
of the feminist colonial discourse, but what has remained constant in both
discourses is the binary opposition between the civilized/emancipated,
autonomous Western woman and the oppressed/backward non-Western
woman bound by a transcendant, ahistorical 'Tradition'. Such binary
oppositions are possible only with the Western subject as the primary
reference point. As Chandra Mohanty points out, the representation of

'Third World' women in much scholarly, feminist discourse is largely a product of the 'self-representation' of the historically mediated and culturally specific experiences of women in modern industrial societies. In Mohanty's words: 'Beyond sisterhood there are still racism, colonialism, and imperialism.' (Mohanty, 1991: 68)

In the 19th century the colonized woman was the object of the British feminists' 'civilizing' activities; in the late 20th century, the post-colonial woman has become the object of a *planned* 'liberation' called development.[5] The terms of such liberation are set by the dominant discourse of feminism and women-in-development. The 'Third-World woman' is a creation of Western/ized feminists that amounts to a discursive colonization at the level of knowledge and knowledge production. Such a creation suppresses the heterogeneity and historical particularity of non-Western, non-modern, non-integrated women simultaneously reproducing the prevailing notion that they are voiceless, passive and unable to speak truthfully or objectively about themselves. (Mohanty, 1991: 71-2) Critics of the women-in-development discourse are dismissed as irrational, romantic, nostalgic and simplistic; a deft move at the level of discourse that entrenches the hegemony of the dominant discourse by delegitimizing all challenges as inferior knowledge. The image of the 'Third World oppressed woman' 'exist[s] in universal, ahistorical splendor, setting in motion a colonialist discourse which exercises a very specific power in defining, coding, and maintaining existing first/third world connections.' (Mohanty, 1991: 73)

This view of global oppression, furthermore, prioritizes constructs of gender based on experiences of gender in modern industrial economies. It confers priority on social, economic and legal equality. Such a construction is the outome of a long process of the enclosure of commons, begun in Britain in the 15th century, continued throughout the colonies and in post-colonial societies.[6] The process of enclosure and industrialization resulted in the dislocation of the individual from community ties and from ties to the landscape and the non-human world. Out of this process emerged the individual as a bounded unit, separate from and in competition with other similar individuals, as well as pitted against an inert, machinelike 'environment' from which s/he has to extract resources. Additionally, within the field of development, the First World woman emerges as the masculinized 'mythical norm', so aptly described by Audre Lorde as 'white, thin, young, heterosexual, christian, and financially secure'. (Lorde, 1984: 116)

II

Before attempting to present a non-enclosed, non-modern conception of the individual, of women's bodies, and of people's relationship to the non-human world, it is necessary to examine critically this 'mythical norm'. In particular, this will allow us to bring into focus the relationship between the 'mythical norm' and an exploitative stance toward the non-human world.

Individualism and the enclosure of women

The emergence of a unitary and proprietary self, owning its labour force and able to sell it on the market, results from the enclosure of the commons and the industrial mode of production.[7] The body, the part of humans that modernity assigns to the natural/biological realm, came to be seen in the same light as nature.[8] Just as nature had become inert, unthinking and unfeeling and like a great machine, the body also came to be thought of, as well as experienced, as a machine. This machine is powered by the energy of the passions, which, when controlled by Cartesian rationality, performs the tasks necessary to the industrial mode of production. Descartes did not advocate repressing the passions, but rather harnessing them for the powering of thought. (Taylor, 1989: 150) It is thus enclosure and industrialization that created the modern individual, the atom of society, maximizing his/her self-interest. With this modern individual came the whole language of modern liberal humanism: rights, equality and autonomy. It is a reality and a language functional to industrial capitalism making of both self and society an adjunct to the market.

The reproductive capacity of women's bodies, however, did not enter the market in the same way as did the reproductive capacity of men's bodies. For women to control their labour in reproduction by means of their rationality and will would re-duplicate a relationship, between rationality and the body, central to commodified labour. This would raise the spectre of the commodification of reproduction and logically entail alienating the products of such labour through wages. This was unacceptable, since men saw themselves as co-owners of the product of women's reproductive labour. The solution was the domestication of women and the ideology of domesticity, keeping women and their labour safely in the domestic sphere and out of the commodified sphere. It also made women dependent on men's earnings and on the public sphere generally. Reproduction became the natural/biological working of machine-like bodies and a sphere inaccessible to women's minds and wills. It became a sphere under the control of a masculinized medical science. (Martin, 1987; Hubbard, 1990) With enclosure and industrialization, women's bodies doomed them to what became seen as the 'mere reproduction of life' – an activity devoid of consciousness, rationality and will.

In Simone de Beauvoir's *The Second Sex* – a canonical text for many Western feminists – this view is presented not as the result of specific historical and cultural developments in the West but as universal, ahistorical fact:

> On the biological level a species is maintained only by creating itself anew; but this creation results only in repeating the same Life in more individuals. But man assures the repetition of Life while transcending Life through Existence [i.e. goal-oriented, meaningful action]; by this transcendence he creates values that deprive pure repetition of all value. In the animal, the freedom and variety of male activities are vain because no project is involved. Except for his services to the species, what he does is immaterial. (de Beauvoir, 1961: 59)[9]

In other words, women, like animals, are engaged in 'the mere repetition of life'. For women, the implication of these views of de Beauvoir are fully articulated in an essay by anthropologist Sherry Ortner (who provided the clarification of 'Existence' in the above quotation):

> In other words, woman's body seems to doom her to mere reproduction of life; the male, in contrast, lacking natural creative functions, must (or has the opportunity to) assert his creativity externally, 'artificially', through the medium of technology and symbols. In so doing, he creates relatively lasting, eternal, transcendent objects, while the woman creates only perishables – human beings. (Ortner, 1974: 75)

As the expression 'mere reproduction of life' along with the view that 'woman creates only perishables – human beings' make abundantly clear, the domain of nature has lost all value and been totally severed from the realm of the mind, of culture.

Because, with enclosure and industrialization, the reproductive force of women's bodies led to their domestication, feminist movements in industrialized countries have seen women's entrance in the public sphere as liberating, that is, as freeing women from their subordination in the domestic sphere. These feminists have universalized categories such as 'biology', the 'domestic', 'public sphere', 'rationality', the 'individual' and many others. Instead of realizing the historical and cultural specificity of these categories, they have projected them on to the rest of the world and all women. Such a position, however, does not question the logic of enclosure and of commodification. Neither does it question the construction of bodies as machines devoid of consciousness nor the existence of proprietary and unitary selves, who own and control their machine-like bodies. It does not question the view of nature as a great machine, or the view that the human mind is totally separated from the non-human world.

In the latter years of the 20th century, with mounting environmental disasters, the faith of adherents of women-in-development in the benefits of the worldwide spread of enclosure and industrialization reveals itself as more the continuation of the colonial enterprise than the vanguard of a liberating army. Proponents of development, like their forebears who set out to civilize the world, must surely emerge as caught in a peculiarly modern collusive madness. As Theodore Roszak puts in, in his book *The Voice of the Earth*:

> Sick souls may indeed be the fruit of sick families and sick societies; but what, in turn, is the measure of sickness for society as a whole? While many criteria might be nominated, there is surely one that ranks above all others: the species that destroys its own habitat in pursuit of false values, in wilful ignorance of what it does, is 'mad' if the word means anything. (Roszak, 1992: 68)

On the threshold of a new departure from WID framework, WED should be wary of introducing unwanted historical legacies into its conceptual framework under the apparently innocent guise of such phrases as 'the Third World woman' or 'the autonomous, productive, independent woman'.

Regeneration and the ecological self

In commons (non-enclosed) regimes, the self is not bounded by the skin, but is rather embedded in relationships to others and to the non-human world. The body is not a machine; rather it is the dwelling place of spirits and deities and made up of the same elements that make up the non-human world. For example, in one of the indigenous Indian medical systems, Ayurveda, a central therapeutic concept is that of *ritu-satmya*, 'appropriateness to the season'. Health is understood as a proper balance with the non-human world, and illness as lack of balance. This balance is maintained by the way in which individuals appropriate their environment within themselves:

> The doctor's task is thus to formulate an alimentary, gymnastic, climactic, etc. regimen in such a way that it will be appropriate both to such and such a phase of the sickness and to such and such a season, and thus restore accord between the patient and his life environment, an accord that the sickness has broken. (Zimmermann, 1980: 101)

This accord between people and the non-human world is an embodied one, in that the bodily fluids of persons are made from the humours, flavours and qualities of the atmosphere, the climate, the landscape which an individual appropriates through eating the foods and medicinal plants growing in the landscape she or he inhabits. Zimmermann here relies on one of the classical Sanskrit treatises on Ayurveda, namely the Caraka Samhita (4th century AD). In contemporary vernacular contexts, similar views are expressed differently by peasant women and men. In 1990, on the occasion of the festival of the menses celebrated in coastal Orissa, a woman, Sisulata Devi, spoke to Apffel-Marglin as follows:

> For these four days of the festival husband and wife will not sleep together. Those men who stay in the village leave the women alone. That is because [the goddess] is at her periods. We have this condition (of menstruating) from her and because of that the men leave. The women stay in the village ... This festival is almost like our menstruation; we do not bleed but we follow the same rules as during our menses since we are of the same kind as Her. She is a woman and we are all women. We are portions (*ansa*) of Her.

The local goddess – Haracandi – is a portion of the earth, the earth of that locality, that region. A man at the festival, Bhikari Parida, expressed it thus:

> Women are reflections of the Mother and of the Earth (*pruthibi*). The Mother, the Earth and women are the same thing in different forms. During the four days of the festival, the Earth, the Mother, is bleeding ... We think that women are bleeding too, not really but symbolically (*sanketika*).

The nature of the identity between women and the earth is clearly not symbolic or metaphorical. The word 'symbolically' (*sanketika*) is used to clarify what is meant by saying that women bleed during the festival of the menses. That is they do not 'really' bleed; they simply follow the rules of menstruation, as Sisulata puts it. But when she and Bhikari Parida speak of the bond between women and the earth the language is different. Women are 'portions' of the earth; the earth and women are the same thing in different form. The bond between women and the earth is substantive, not symbolic; it is embodied in the form of the Goddess. It would be a sad impoverishment to think of the Goddess as a symbol of the earth or of women.[10] Such a mode of understanding the Goddess reduplicates the dualism between consciousness and the mind on one side and the truly real, the world, on the other side. The Goddess is a form in which elements of consciousness and elements of the world coalesce. It is an image which allows the interpenetration between subjective consciousness and the world. (Hillman, 1992: 7; Grillo Fernandez, personal communication) In other words, it a conception in which the subject-object and the nature-culture dualisms dissolve.

The Goddess embodies the reality that women and the earth are one, and at the same time shows that the generation and regeneration of the world is a human, a natural and a divine activity in which consciousness and the world interpenetrate. In this world the dualism between biology/

nature on the one hand and culture on the other, vanishes, and with it the view of women as 'the mere reproducers of life'.

The separation between men and women during the festival of the menses echoes the separation between the earth and the clouds in this hot and dry season of the year. Men are the virile clouds that fertilize the earth. The actions of humans harmonize with the actions in the non-human realm so as to bring accord and thereby health and the regeneration of life. Just as the fallow period of the earth during the hot, dry season is necessary to the following fertile, rainy period, the women's fallow period at their menses, when they stop all productive activities, is necessary to the following fertile period when they resume productive activities and unite with their men. As the earth regenerates its strength during its fallow period, so do women and the whole community.

The regeneration of the community is effectively achieved through this festival. The communities contribute equal quantities of cash and food for the feasting that takes place during the four days of the festival. The villages are multi-caste, the cultivator caste being the most numerous. During the festival, conviviality and equality are actively fostered by all villagers, regardless of caste, sleeping and eating together in large communal tents. As a man from one of these villages put it:

> Coming to this fair, to the place of the Mother ... we feel that we are all Her children and that we are the same. ... Here all the men feel as brothers since She is the Mother ... There is no feeling of inferior and superior ... We try to keep peace and order in this place. Nobody has bought this land to become master over another; the sacred grove belongs to everybody. With all the tents in it, it looks like one big village ...

The festival takes place in a sacred grove where a temple to Goddess Haracandi is located. Men from some 60 villages around the sacred grove come and pitch communal tents for the festival. Women celebrate in the villages where they take over all public spaces.

The regeneration of the community is brought about not only by deliberately creating equality and conviviality, but also more literally. One of the major topics of conversation between the men at the festival is marriage. All the villages which participate in the festival are part of a marriage exchange circle. The marriageability of a daughter depends in great part on the reputation of her village. The behaviour of the men of that village at the festival directly affects the marriageability of its daughters. These villagers practise village exogamy (they marry women from other villages). The festival is a major occasion for finding out who is marriageable and for evaluating the worth of a village as a potential home for one's daughter and as the place of one's future in-laws.

The Goddess's sacred grove is the place where the community regenerates itself. It is common land, where all the male villagers live in common. Generation and regeneration bring about the continuity of a life undivided between nature and culture. The activities of women in generating, cooking, caring for the cattle and whatever else they do are as vital to the generation and regeneration of their life world as is the work of the men. Human activities are not subordinated to the market and to production. Rather, they are part of larger cosmic activities of generating and regenerating the world.

Conclusion

Seen through the lens of the language of the autonomous, productive, 'liberated woman', these Oriya women would no doubt emerge as constrained by tradition and probably patriarchy as well. If, however, we are seriously concerned about ecological degradation, as well as clear about the relationship between the modern unitary bounded self with its instrumental relationship to its body and an exploitative stance toward the non-human world, these Oriya women and men emerge differently. We begin to discern a world in which the generation and regeneration of both human and non-human life are at the core of human activities, of both men and women. Women are no longer the 'mere reproducers of life'. The body and nature are no longer to be acted upon instrumentally by humans; they are no longer the source of human and natural resources and raw material. The body, the land and the community are all embedded in the same processes of generation and regeneration that necessitate the work of both men and women. The core concern of these communities is not the increase of their productivity, as the following remark by one of the farmers makes clear: 'I come here to pray the Mother to give me just enough, not too much and not too little.' One woman told Apffel-Marglin, during her latest visit to her village in 1992, that if one does not have a daughter and is therefore unable to perform the 'gift of a maiden' (*kanya dan*), then one will be cursed by being in the state of *antiba*, a state in which nothing is ever enough, which means one will always experience a state of insufficiency, of unsatisfied wants or desires. When one's desires are unlimited one is cursed with insufficiency, *antiba*. What the neo-classical economics paradigm takes as a given, namely the unlimited nature of wants, is, in this non-commodified world, considered a curse. This is, indeed, a far cry from economistic assumptions.

One of the features most pregnant with consequences for ecological as well as gender issues is the fact that there is no division here between reproductive and productive labour. Both men and women are engaged in generative and regenerative activities; these activities are at the level of the person, the immediate kin group, the village and the region where many villages form a marriage circle. Generating and regenerating are activities involving both men and women; they are also activities conducted syn-chronically with the rhythms of the seasons. This synchrony is not an 'imitation of nature' but rather emerges from a way of being in the world which makes no radical division between the human and the non-human world. Human welfare and the welfare of the land are related by the consubstantiality between them.

We have tried to show how non-Western women have been perceived by colonialists, Victorian feminists and some of their contemporary de-scendants, a perception that arose from a modernist construction of the person and of women's bodies in particular. In Part II, we tried to relate these conceptions to modernist assumptions about the relationship be-tween the human and the non-human world. Finally, we briefly sketched an alternative way of life in which nature and women's bodies are not treated as resources but rather are not differentiated from socio-cultural processes.

In other words, if one fails to question the modernist construction of personhood and of women's bodies – as Ortner and de Beauvoir do – one is led to reject women's generative capacity as the 'mere reproduction of life'. This has led many feminists towards a masculinist and modernist conception of what constitutes 'liberation'. It has also made it more difficult to integrate ecological issues with gender issues. By questioning such constructs, one is instead led towards a profound reformulation of the concept of 'reproduction' as well as of the relationship between nature and culture.

Notes

1. On the shift from a WID to a WED discourse and its implications see the Introduction and Chapter 1 of this book.

2. Suzanne Simon wishes to thank Helan Page for stimulating discussions on these issues in her class.

3. On the use of 'poverty' in development discourse generally see Majid Rahnema's entry on it in *The Development Dictionary* edited by Wolfgang Sachs, Zed Books, London, 1992.

4. As Gita Sen's essay in this volume shows, she has since participated in the shift from a WID to a WED discourse.

5. On 'planning' in development see Arturo Escobar's entry in *The Development Dictionary*.

6. On development as enclosure see 'Whose Common Future?' in *The Ecologist*, vol. 22, no. 4, Aug-Sept. 1992.

7. On the relationship between the commoditization of labour and the emer-gence of the unitary colonizing self see F. Apffel-Marglin with P.C. Mishra 'Woman's Blood: Challenging the Discourse of Development' in *The Ecologist*, Vol. 22, Jan-Feb. 1992. See also F. Apffel-Marglin 'Gender and the Unitary Self:

Locating the Dominant when Listening to the Subaltern Voice' in Gloria Goodwin Raheja (ed.) *Oral Tradition*, special edition on Gender in South Asia, forthcoming.

8. The most well-known marker for this change in world view is Descartes' work.

9. In her book *Inessential Woman*, Elizabeth Spelman showed how Simone de Beauvoir slipped from considering the situation of white bourgeois women like herself, to all women. She shows how de Beauvoir's unconscious move was motivated by male intellectuals' taunts to women intellectuals about their incapacity to universalize.

10. Frédérique Apffel-Marglin is grateful to Eduardo Grillo Fernandez for raising this point with her in a personal communication. Grillo Fernandez has written extensively on the indigenous Andean world, mostly Quechua and Aymara. One of his key phrases that articulate the relationship between native Andeans and the world is that they converse with the non-human world, talking to stones, forests, streams and soil. The phrase that best captures their relationship to the world is '*criar y dejarse criar*'; this is difficult to translate, but an approximation would be 'to raise the world [as one raises children and crops] and let oneself be raised by it'. See, among others, Eduardo Grillo Fernandez *et al. Desarrollo o Descolonizacion en los Andes?* (1993).

References

Ahmed, Leila (1992) *Women and Gender in Islam*. Yale University Press, New Haven.

Apffel-Marglin, Frédérique (forthcoming) 'Rationality, the Body and the World: From Production to Regeneration' in F. Apffel-Marglin and S.A. Marglin (eds) *Decolonizing Knowledge: From Development to Dialogue*. Oxford University Press, Oxford.

Apffel-Marglin, Frédérique with P.C. Mishra (1992) 'Woman's blood: Challenging the Discourse of Development', in *The Ecologist*, vol. 22.

—— (forthcoming) 'Gender and the Unitary Self: Locating the Dominant when Listening to the Subaltern Voice', in Gloria Goodwin Raheja (ed.) 'Gender in South Asia', special edition of *Oral Traditions*.

Bordo, Susan (1989) 'The Body and the Reproduction of Femininity: A Feminist Appropriation of Foucault', in Jaggar and Bordo (eds) *Gender/Body/Knowledge*. Rutgers University Press, New Brunswick.

Boserup, Ester (1970) *Women's Role in Economic Development*. St. Martin's Press, New York.

Bunch, Charlotte and Roxanna Carillo (1990) 'Feminist Perspectives on Women in Development', in Irene Tinker (ed.) *Persistent Inequalities*. Oxford University Press, Oxford, pp. 70-82.

Buvinic, Mayra, Margaret Lycette, and William McGreevey, (eds) (1983) *Women and Poverty in the Third World*. Johns Hopkins University Press, Maryland.

Buvinic, Mayra and Sally W. Yudelman (1989) *Women, Poverty and Progress in the Third World*. Foreign Policy Association, New York.

Chaudhuri, Nupur and Margaret Strobel (1992) *Western Women and Imperialism: Complicity and Resistance*. Indiana University Press, Bloomington.

Cowan, Minna G. (1912) *The Education of the Women of India*. Fleming H. Revell Co., London.

De Beauvoir, Simone (1961) *The Second Sex*. Bantam Books, London.

Duden, Barbara (1991) *The Woman Beneath the Skin*. Harvard University Press, Cambridge, Mass.

Escobar, Arturo (1992) 'Planning', in Wolfgang Sachs (ed.) *The Development Dictionary*. Zed Books, London and New Jersey, pp. 132-45.

Etienne, Mona and Eleanor Leacock (1980) *Women and Colonization*. Praeger, New York.

Franklin, Sarah, *et al.* (eds) (1993) 'Procreation Stories', in *Culture as Science*, vol. 17, Summer.

Grillo Fernandez, Eduardo *et al.* (1993) *Desarrollo o Descolonizacion en los Andes?* Proyecto Andino de Tecnologias Campesinas, Lima.

Haraway, Donna (1989) *Primate Visions*. Routledge, New York.

—— (1991) *Simians, Cyborgs, and Women: The Reinvention of Nature*. Routledge, New York.

Harding, Sandra G. (1986) *The Science Question in Feminism*. Cornell University Press, Ithaca, N.Y.

Hillman, James (1992) *The Thought of the Heart and the Soul of the World*. Spring Press, California.

Hobsbawm, Eric and Terence Ranger (eds) (1983) *The Invention of Tradition*. Cambridge University Press, Cambridge, U.K.

hooks, bell (1981) *Ain't I a Woman?* South End Press, New York.

Hubbard, Ruth (1990) *The Politics of Women's Biology*. Rutgers University Press, New Brunswick.

Jordanova, Ludmilla (1989) *Sexual Visions* University of Wisconsin Press, Madison.

Keller, Evelyn Fox (1992) *Secrets of Life, Secrets of Death*. Routledge, New York.

Lorde, Audre (1984) *Sister Outsider*. South End Press, New York.

MacKenzie, John M. (1984) *Propaganda and Empire: The Manipulation of British Public Opinion*. Manchester University Press, Manchester, U.K.

Mani, Lata (1989) 'Contentious Traditions: The Debate on Sati in Colonial India', in Kumkum Sangari & Sudesh Vaid (eds) *Recasting Women: Essays in Colonial History*. Kali for Women, New Delhi.

Martin, Emily (1987) *The Woman in the Body*. Beacon Press, Boston.

Mohanty, Chandra Talpade (1991) 'Under Western Eyes', in Chandra T. Mohanty, A. Russo, Lourdes Torres (eds) *Third World Women and the Politics of Feminism*. Indiana University Press, Bloomington.

Ortner, Sherry (1974) 'Is Female to Male as Nature is to Culture?', in Michelle Rosaldo and Louise Lamphere (eds) *Woman, Cuture, and Society*. Stanford University Press, California.

Rahnema, Majid (1992) 'Poverty', in Wolfgang Sachs (ed.) *The Development Dictionary*. Zed Books, London and New Jersey, pp. 116-31.

Roszak, Theodor (1992) *The Voice of the Earth*. Simon & Schuster, New York.

Sachs, Wolfgang (ed.) (1992) *The Development Dictionary*, Zed Books, London and New Jersey.

Sen, Amartya (1990) 'Gender and Cooperative Conflicts', in Irene Tinker (ed.) *Persistent Inequalities*. Oxford University Press, Oxford, pp. 123-49.

Sen, Gita and Caren Grown (1987) *Development, Crisis, and Alternative Visions.* Monthly Review Press, New York.

Sinha, Mrinalini (1992) 'The Politics of Gender and Race in the Ilbert Bill Controversy, 1883-1884' in Nupur Chaudhuri and Margaret Strobel (eds) *Western Women and Imperialism: Complicity and Resistance.* Indiana University Press, Bloomington, pp. 98-118.

Spelman, Elizabeth (1989) *Inessential Woman.* Beacon Press, Boston.

Strathern, Marilyn (1992) *Reproducing the Future.* Routledge, New York.

Taylor, Charles (1989) *Sources of the Self: The Making of the Modern Identity.* Harvard University Press, Cambridge, Mass.

Ware, Vron (1992) *Beyond the Pale: White Women, Racism and History.* Verso Books, London.

Zimmermann, Francis (1980) *La Jungle et le Fumet des Viandes: Un Thème Ecologique dans la Médecine Hindoue.* Gallimard, Paris.

3

Mining Development in the Pacific: Are We Sustaining the Unsustainable?

'Atu Emberson-Bain

Mining development, politics and gender: making the connections

The mining industry encapsulates some of the fundamental problems associated with development in the Pacific region and, in particular, offers useful insight into the unsustainability of the dominant growth-led development model. It also provides a challenging area for gender analysis. Research into the effects of mining on Pacific island societies is still in its early stages, and relatively little is documented about its impact on women's health and social and economic status. It is, however, already evident that mining development reveals important links between global and macro structures and processes, on the one hand, and negative local-level socio-economic and environmental change on the other. It highlights the spuriousness of distinctions between the private and public domains and testifies to the links between household, economy and global politics. It is a complex system that appears to place women as a sub-group at the bottom, subjected to a range of controls over their sexuality, mobility, reproductive and productive labour, and access to such vital resources as land.

One aim of this chapter is to draw out some of these connections as part of building an analysis of the social impact of mining. It is argued that inequitable gender relations of patriarchy appear to be a central feature of the unsustainability of mining development, whether this is taking place in the independent Pacific states of Fiji (gold), Papua New Guinea (PNG) (gold, copper), and Nauru (phosphate) or the French-controlled colonial territory of New Caledonia (nickel). In this context, patriarchy is treated as a holistic concept that simultaneously addresses the more localized unequal distribution of power embedded in gender relations and the wider relations of dominance and exploitation that sustain the industry. There is an urgent need to think seriously and critically about whether mining development, as it is at present defined, can possibly hope to promote equitable and sustainable human development in the Pacific region.

For feminist writers, there might be a clear political or moral imperative for writing women (their active role as well as experiential knowledge) into the social history of mining. But there is also what might be termed an inherent logic in addressing the gender issue. The importance of examining the specificity of women's condition and developing a gender analysis rests in their ability to enhance our understanding of the social impact of mining, or, alternatively, of the process of social change in those countries drawn within the mining nexus. In turn, these tasks are highly relevant to any serious attempt to avert or reform the most problematic features. Part of this exercise must be to look both at the contribution of women to mining development and at their community-based actions against the industry.

In her work on rural women in South East Asia, Noeleen Heyzer (1988: 63) observes how gender-based hierarchies, evident in women's limited access to resources and participation in the development process, and their disadvantaged position within the gender division of labour, have meant that rural women have been more harshly affected by the negative effects of the development process. The example of mining development in the Pacific region throws up some interesting parallels, especially in those areas which traditionally vested women with ownership and control of land (Bougainville and Lihir in PNG, and Nauru), or at least with independent access to food-producing land (Ok Tedi, PNG). In general, available evidence suggests that women have reaped fewer of the rewards/benefits of mining while bearing the brunt of some of the most dislocating and problematic aspects of it. As traditional custodians of the home and family, their marginalization has naturally reverberated on the livelihoods of their children and others within the household.

The invisibility of women in most research within the historiography of mining and the limited attention that has been paid to its impact on their lives probably reflects the perception of it as a 'male' industry. Such a view may also explain why women have been excluded from the public domain of community discussions and decision-making about mining development where these have occurred. Yet the male-centric definition of mining is misleading and fails to account for the central role that women have played in mining development as well as the numerous ways in which their economic and social status have been detrimentally affected by it. The contribution of human labour power to the process of profitable mineral exploitation has nowhere in the world consisted simply of male mineworkers. In the mining economies of the Pacific, no less than their counterparts in Southern Africa, the unpaid labour of women has been a crucial factor in maintaining low-cost labour systems for the mining industry.

Women's labour for the industry has taken various forms outside paid employment. It includes their unpaid household management, food production and social security support to dependants in village economies stripped of their young, able-bodied males; their paid sexual labour services (prostitution) in bachelor mining outposts; and their unpaid social and biological reproductive labour in mining centres that have opted for family settlement. Every mine labour process has in one way or another been dependent on and subsidized by women's productive, sexual and reproductive labour. To depict the mining industry as a male enclave of the labour market or indeed a male industry is therefore, for all these reasons, to misrepresent the real situation. It is important that any study seeking to understand the social impact of mining in all its complexity, including the dynamics of exploitation and power within the labour process, should account for its gender component.

A central feature of the unsustainability of mining development appears to be its patriarchal nature. Patriarchy in Pacific mining economies is mediated through a range of processes, not only through gender relations within the domestic arena (including men's appropriation of female labour) and a gender division of labour which prescribes for women a subordinate and exploited role in mining labour systems as unpaid workers. Patriarchy also maifests itself within the corporate mining establishment; in the machinery (including the military arm), policy and operations of the state in defence of mining capital; and in the subordination of dependent Pacific mining economies to colonial (as in New Caledonia) or neo-colonial forces of control within the global political-economic system. Part of the global system is the nuclear and conventional arms industry, into which the mining industry feeds directly through the extraction and processing of nickel (New Caledonia) and uranium (Australia).

Finally, as a form of economic imperialism that has plundered the human and natural resources of small Pacific island states, the patriarchal nature of mineral exploitation expresses itself in the disempowerment of local communities, and particularly the women within them. This process has been a complex one (for example, it has not necessarily compromised the interests of traditional elites) and it has not always been explicit. Historically, colonial capitalism in the Pacific, as indeed elsewhere in the Third World, sometimes treads a covertly destructive path by articulating traditional social formations with the intruding capitalist economy rather than totally destroying them. Such a process involves the selective exploitation of traditional organizational and belief systems. The mining labour systems of Fiji and PNG, for example, depended to differing degrees on traditional village economies and social systems for the maintenance and reproduction of cheap, male, migrant labour. In Fiji's mining town of Vatukoula, the early integration of traditional chiefly elites into the labour recruitment process and the 'management' of native labour also deliberately served as a buffer against the forces of social change. (Emberson-Bain, forthcoming)

Mining, an asset for whom?

Disempowerment of communities drawn within the mining orbit has not, however, stopped short of structural and ideological change. Before colonial conquest, the imposition of a cash economy and the establishment of Western capitalist 'development', Pacific island economies were largely self-sufficient. Sustainable or 'rational' land management systems existed, as did food production and consumption patterns based on the principles of communalism and reciprocal exchange. They secured a health and nutritional status for the indigenous inhabitants widely believed to be superior to that prevailing today. (Thaman, 1991: 83) In keeping with the general pattern of colonial capitalist expansion, however, mining development systematically appropriated and/or degraded the resources – land and labour – that were the cornerstones of these sustainable economies. Labour and land resources were typically redirected from food production and other activities aimed at meeting basic needs and towards competitive production for overseas markets. The undermining of the communalist ethics inherent in most Pacific societies compromised the mechanisms for redistribution and reciprocity which traditionally guarded against disparities in wealth and power. The erosion of women's land rights and the reinforcement of male authority and patriarchal values typical of the cash economy and private property have been features of this transition in certain places. They appear to have been a noticeable outcome of mining development in the matrilineal societies of Bougainville, Lihir and Nauru.

It is important to note that matrilineal systems which transferred land rights through Pacific women did not necessarily confer significant levels of economic independence, power or authority, or reduce their social subordination to men. (Slatter, 1991) In Nauru, for example, women's matrilineal status was traditionally circumscribed by their limited access to positions of political leadership (Pollock, 1991) and by (patriarchal) controls over their sexuality in relation to marriage. It is nevertheless notable that the matrilineal land system, according to Pollock, provided the vehicle through which women 'indirectly controlled much of the subsistence economy'. (Ibid: 97) In Bougainville, moreover, matrilineal principles of land inheritance were supported by uxorilocal residence and gave women a social position of some importance. Overall, gender relations tended to be marked more by 'complementarity' than the 'hierarchy' typical of PNG's highland societies. (Wesley-Smith, 1991) Women's land rights, moreover, seem to have given them a significant amount of decision-making authority over the use and distribution of land, although their views were generally expressed indirectly through male spokespeople (such as a brother or uncle). The failure of the mining compensation system to account for the custom of matrilineal inheritance, or to respect women's status as 'mothers of the land' (Interviews, Solomon Islands, 1993; Okole,

1990: 16-24) and the complete marginalization of women from land-owner/company negotiations have not only eroded women's status but jeopardized the stability and well-being of Bougainville society as a whole.

Pollock has argued that on Nauru 'women's control' within the phosphate economy has not been usurped; that along with men, women have been recipients of an independent source of cash income from mining; and that the distribution of mining royalties to landholders has continued to be based on matrilineal principles. (Pollock, 1991: 98, 104) While this may be so, it needs to be noted that in spite of their status as landowners, women appear to have been unable to influence negotiations over compensation for mining or to participate in the management of their resources. Further, the destruction of the island's subsistence (Topside) economy by phosphate mining appears to have undermined an important basis of women's status within the traditional division of labour, including their economic and social independence. (Weeramentry, 1988: 182-4) The loss of the Topside has disrupted women's role as food providers and craft makers, eroded the prestige they enjoyed as transmitters of cultural knowledge (through the production of craft valuables), and forged a more dependent, domesticated lifestyle which has contributed to a decline in their health. At the Ok Tedi mine in the Star Mountains, on PNG's border with Indonesian-controlled West Papua, Wopkaimin women who traditionally engaged in gender-specific (female) food collection, consumption and housing similarly also appear to have lost important aspects of their former economic and social independence. As a result of mining, they are dependent on their husbands for food and shelter. (Hyndman, 1991: 83-4; Emberson-Bain, 1992a)

There is a special significance to the land losses and degradation resulting from mining that has caused an aggravated dimension to Pacific peoples' deprivation and sense of powerlessness, as well as underpinned the conflict that has erupted. Traditional Pacific values have no parallel in Western capitalist notions of land as an alienable and disposable material commodity. In Pacific cultures, the productive use, distribution and control of land are not only crucial to physical survival, they are integral to Pacific social formations, including kin, gender and class-based relations. Land has a distinctive non-material or spiritual value that enshrines an unseverable sacred link between the dead (ancestors) and the living. Land is generally perceived as inalienable (disposal or proprietorial rights do not extend to permanent alienation, let alone destruction). Communal rather than private tenure predominates, and there is no tradition of proprietorial rights being vested exclusively in single males. Moreover, the claim of the state, in both its colonial and post-colonial forms, to ownership of (mineral) wealth beneath the surface, and the distinction between surface and subterranean land rights used to justify this appropriation, has no cultural legitimacy. As a Bougainville health worker and mother describes it: 'Many Bougainvilleans regard land as a fragile thing. I mean it is also something that is very valuable to them ... because if there was no land, there was no water, there was no bush ... there is no life.'

A final feature of the political economy of mining that points to the disempowerment of indigenous communities (workers and landowners) has been the close, albeit sometimes tenuous, relationship between Pacific (colonial and post-colonial) states and corporate mining interests. State (including equity) interest in the mining sector and collaboration with mining capital have been demonstrated in official acquiescence in the dispossession of traditional landowners, environmental degradation, the investment of public revenue in mining, concessions to foreign mining companies and the use of the state security apparatus in their 'protective' interest, even to the extent of violently suppressing community resistance. As the recent military/police offensives against Bougainville landowners and Fiji mine strikers show well, colonialism is by no means a precondition of state violence. Indeed, the disturbing links between militarism and mining are becoming increasingly apparent in independent PNG, where Australian-backed military operations have been aimed at protecting both a lucrative source of state revenue and the interests of a major Australian mining company, whose shareholders stand to lose most from the closure of the rich Panguna mine, one of the world's largest copper producers.

Gender bias in the mine labour market

Structural biases in the mine labour market are also based on gender, with barriers to women's employment excluding them from one of the few material benefits that can be derived from large mining projects. Male dominance of commercial spin-offs like business/co-operative ventures, where these have occurred, as in Bougainville, (Wesley-Smith, 1991, 22-3: 18) also emphasizes women's greater economic marginalization relative to men. In small mining towns like Vatukoula, where opportunities for non-mine related work seldom exist, the overwhelming preference for males has implications for women's educational/literacy status by reducing the perceived 'need' to educate girls, particularly when money is short. This in turn strengthens women's economic and social dependence on men, and reinforces traditional expectations that marriage and motherhood are their primary social functions. Women comprise a very small proportion of the paid mine work-force in PNG and Fiji, and virtually none at all in Nauru and New Caledonia. Of the 20,740 women classified as wage/salaried employees in official PNG statistics, there are only 243 in the mining sector (including quarrying), representing four per cent of the total 6,326 employees in mining. In 1987, women claimed just three per cent (2,524,000 kina) of the total mining wages and salaries bill (81,570,000 kina). (PNG Census)

The gender bias of the mine labour market reflects the general dominance of patriarchal values as well as the industry's own traditions and rationale, both of which prescribe an essentially domestic and reproductive (or prostitution) role for women. The strongly Catholic society of Lihir in PNG, one of the more recent mining prospects to get off the ground, exemplifies the role that traditional ideologies play in restricting women's access to mine employment. Women's mobility, control of their own fertility and participation in the public domain of community discussions and decision-making (including debate and negotiations about mining proposals) appear to be severely restricted. There are strong pressures on women to be exemplary homemakers, in particular food producers and caretakers of children, and social mores insist that 'women must have as many children as possible' (currently an average of twelve). Male-perpetrated violence represents an accepted means of punishing those whose domestic skills are found wanting. (Mandie-Filer, 1989: 397-412)

In Fiji, patriarchal values find expression in the law through prohibitions on underground mine work and restrictions on night work. Ostensibly based on 'protectionism', the restrictions on women's employment at the Vatukoula mine mean that they are largely confined to certain types of lower-status, lower-paid surface jobs. In the past, work opportunities for ethnic Fijian women did not extend beyond very low-paid domestic work in the houses of European management, and in the early years a semi-illicit prostitution trade. Today, women are still employed as cheap domestic servants (earning as little as FIJ $20-30 per week without holiday or sick pay rights) but they are also found in the research, geology, administration and stores sections on the surface, as well as in the mill as rock-sorters.

The exploitative conditions of work for women millworkers expose the spuriousness of the protectionist argument. Around 25 rock-sorters enduring a dusty, extremely hot and poorly lit working environment, work all three shifts (day, evening and 'graveyard'). They are required to spend the entire eight-hour shift, apart from a 30-minute lunch break, standing bent over a conveyor belt and are expected to perform strenuous manual work such as shovelling soil and rock. The women are paid at the minimum unskilled rate of $1.55 an hour, although their job requires them to make quick distinctions between gold-bearing rock and mullock. For those with families, the working day begins around 4 am to enable cooking for the family and other domestic work to be done. (Interviews, Vatukoula, 1993)

It is uncertain whether greater employment opportunities for women would necessarily enhance their economic independence and social status. At the Lihir and Vatukoula mines, at least, there are indications to the contrary and these may point to a more general pattern. Because of the social and cultural context within which women enter the labour market, employment opportunities can (and do) represent a mechanism for intensifying the exploitation of their productive labour. Lihir women earners have no rights of disposal over their own incomes since these are (unlike those of men) considered to be 'family property', expected to be surrendered to their parents if they are single and divided between their husbands' and their own families if they are married. Further, in the absence of any change in the sexual division of labour, including the cultural pressures on women to bear many children, greater opportunities for employment sentence them to an unusually burdensome 'double shift'. Greater male violence is also perceived by Lihir women to be a consequence of their employment because of the feelings of insecurity and loss of control that their employment outside the home invokes in the men. (Mandie-Filer, 1989: 406, 412-14)

Picking up the pieces: women and unsustainable livelihoods

It is at the local level that the full impact of mining-induced dependence and underdevelopment is felt. The land losses and environmental abuse, the diversion of labour and other forms of socio-economic dislocation have placed traditional systems of food production under considerable stress, and generally undermined the sustainability and self-reliance that existed before mining. They have had grave implications for the nutritional and health status of families, especially children, encouraging a greater dependence on store-purchased goods of poor nutritional value. The histories of several indigenous communities in the Pacific tell gruesome tales of dispossession, degradation and/or resettlement.

It is at the micro level of the household, in particular through analysing the experiences of women, that many of the negative features of mining can be clearly observed. In their traditional role as unpaid reproductive labour, women in mining communities feel the harsh effects of the industry most acutely. It is they who bear the brunt of the loss of land resources and environmental degradation, the withdrawal of (male) labour, or the subjection to low (male) wage systems. All these processes directly impinge on women's capacity to provide nourishment and care for their families and have direct implications for their work burden and health. The depletion and contamination of sources of firewood and water, the loss of farming land and fishing grounds, and the inadequacy of household earnings, raise the labour intensity of women's work, for example in the distances that have to be travelled on foot and the time spent in food gathering or cultivation, or collecting firewood.

Certainly, at the Vatukoula mine, the evidence suggests that the majority of Fijian households survive on the backs of women, that is, through the crucial contribution they make to supplementing their husbands' earnings by growing food, fishing, gathering firewood (in lieu of buying kerosene) and where possible manufacturing and selling mats. The arduous nature of mine work and the 24-hour shift system that operates are responsible for having shifted most of the burden of garden work on to women. Subsistence fisheries, which are now a regular feature of the working day of miners' wives, involve long hours of standing waist-to shoulder-deep in cold river water. The working day for miners' wives typically begins between 4 am and 5 am and usually includes at least one visit to the garden (to weed, collect food, plant) and/or a fishing excursion, the collection of firewood and the usual 'female' jobs of cooking, washing, ironing, cleaning and child care. Gardens, like fishing grounds, can be several miles away. (Interviews, Vatukoula, 1993)

In general, Pacific women also have to shoulder the burden of social conflict and violence associated with mining, whether this occurs at the level of the household (in respect of marital and wider kin relations) or the wider community. Male alcoholism, sexual and domestic violence, male fighting, prostitution (with its attendant health risks) and teenage pregnancies typify some of the problems evident in the mining centres of PNG, though it is difficult to generalize about the scale and intensity of their impact. Certainly, congested and culturally alienating mining settlements have not offered an environment conducive to maintaining traditional mechanisms of social control or social mores, which give women some rights to privacy (Vatukoula, Ok Tedi). According to Hyndman (1991: 84), availability of beer has led to the establishment of competitive night-time male drinking gatherings at the Ok Tedi mine which have encouraged violent drunken behaviour, including rape and other serious assaults on women.

Mine employment has also introduced a new dimension to the traditional controls on women's sexuality through the displacement of traditional valuables, such as pigs, by cash as the form of bride price which traditionally compensated a bride's family for the loss of her productive and reproductive labour power and which had to be effectively reimbursed if she left her husband. It has paved the way for a more competitive, entrepreneurial marriage market managed by men and a surging inflation in bride price that seriously constrains women's ability to withdraw from an unhappy marriage. On the island of Misima, heavy beer consumption by male mineworkers has also resulted in a higher incidence of domestic violence. In Fiji, male violence in the home and disputes (including fights) between women in the settlements are both said to be fairly widespread. Marital tensions are commonly attributed to the shortage of money for food and school fees, or the hefty part of the wage packet sacrificed to drinking binges on pay day. (Hyndman, 1991: 84-5; Emberson-Bain, 1992a and interviews 1993; Gerritsen and McIntyre, 1991: 47-8)

Since 1989, the military offensives by the PNG state against the people of Bougainville have encapsulated in its most extreme form the violence and underlying politics of mining capitalism. The war has taken a heavy toll on women and men's livelihoods. Virtually all Bougainvilleans have experienced the loss of, or separation from, close family; thousands of homes and sources of livelihood have been destroyed; and a four-year economic and medical blockade has terminated supplies of food, medical provisions, fuel and clothing, and services like hospitals and schools. For women, the war has killed or taken their husbands away, broken up their marriages (as long separations have led to men taking up with other women), and left those who have managed to flee from the fighting into the mountainous jungle to build their own houses as well as to look for food and protect their young children. The blockade has killed many women in childbirth and the absence of vaccines has meant no innoculations against killer infant diseases such as measles, TB and whooping cough since 1989. As the primary care providers, women are responsible for cultivating extra food gardens to meet the needs of the war-ravaged community, including those engaged in combat, refugees from the military-controlled areas, and the sick and elderly, and for manufacturing products such as salt and soap which are no longer available in the stores because of the blockade. Last, and perhaps most devastating of all, women have had to endure the most degrading and terrifying instrument of war: systematic (and sometimes multiple) rape by members of the invading military forces. (Emberson-Bain, 1993a, b)

Community resistance to mining

Mining development in the Pacific is becoming increasingly steeped in controversy and conflict, in particular bitter opposition from local communities who have been affected most directly and adversely by it. Women have been active in community-based opposition to mining, notably in worker struggles in Fiji (Emberson-Bain, 1992b and forthcoming) and landowner struggles on Bougainville. Bougainvillean women were on the front line of the earliest clashes with the Australian mining company CRA, and since the outbreak of the crisis, the leadership of a new landowners' association has reinstated the matrilineal principles of organization. (Okole, 1990; Moody, 1991) While not engaged in active combat within the Bougainville Revolutionary Army, women play a supportive role through their reproductive labour. Moreover, the origins of the armed struggle appear to owe something to their pressure on the men: '*Em nau graun i bagarap mipela ol meri i bin no laikim kopa main long kamap, na mipela i no sainim agrimen. Na yiupela ol man yet i sainim. Na yiu lukim bagarap i kamap, bai yiu makim wanem nau?*' ('Our land is now destroyed because you signed the agreement ignoring what the women wanted. Now that there has been all this destruction, what are you going to do about it?')

Such popular protests are distress signals which highlight the extent to which ordinary Pacific islanders, the powerless and the poor, have been alienated by this form of 'development'. They underscore the depressing reality that mining by large-scale transnational capital, commonly supported by national political elites, is arguably proving to be one of the most destructive and violent forms of Western-style development in the region. The living human scars of this rapacious industry are starkly visible in the suffering endured by the war-torn people of Bougainville, but it needs to be remembered that the pervasive violence of mining (in the broader sense of the term) was recognized 20 years ago at the dawn of the mining 'development' experience. (Hannett, 1975)

Conclusion

The impact of mining on Pacific island economies, environments, food systems, cultures and women has been considerable, in some respects catastrophic. Moreover, while economic benefits have accrued at the national level, the limited, unequal and gender discriminatory nature of their distribution at the local level is a conspicuous anomaly. So is the appropriation or destruction of irreplaceable resources such as land and river systems which has impoverished communities and which must ultimately raise serious doubts about the potential mining has to offer as a form of sustainable development.

On a broader plane, the evidence of Pacific mining bears witness to the shortcomings of continuing to measure development by quantitative variables such as GNP or export earnings. It supports the theory that class, gender and other sectional interests underpin growth-led development to the detriment of the poor, and that development strategies that focus blindly on growth will almost certainly exacerbate existing levels of poverty, deepen income inequalities and breed greater social alienation.

Many questions need to be asked to take us beyond this fundamental point of departure from dominant development thinking. It might be self-evident for development critics that growth-led development is inherently unsustainable, but under what circumstances can market-oriented capitalist 'development' grounded in the principles of private accumulation ever be sustainable (assuming a working definition of sustainability that implies quality in people's lives and some form of social equity)? Are not all forms of such economic activity (including commercial resource extraction such as mining) irreconcilable with development? Can one pursue capitalist development, whether or not it is growth-driven, and hope to achieve an equitable distribution of resources or to 'arrange' sustainable livelihoods for the poor along the way? As an extractive export-oriented capitalist industry, can mining be expected to bring sustainable livelihoods even with the introduction of more stringent legislative controls, greater community participation and direction, and other reforms?

The emerging trend in official thinking in the Pacific appears to be that the challenge facing regional governments is to balance the two 'absolutes' of environmental protection and 'the imperatives of economic development' (defined as economic growth) to ensure that growth-led development is 'carried out in an environmentally sound and sustainable manner'. (Emberson-Bain, 1992c) To some extent, therefore, there is recognition of the conflict of interest between the physical environment and economic growth strategies. But is it enough to inject a dose of environmental (or indeed gender) sensitivity into mining development plans, or to pay lip service to customary systems of resource management and knowledge about the environment, when the exploitative and destructive (that is patriarchal) structures of the industry remain intact? Are such measures not ultimately little more than cosmetic changes if they fall short of challenging these structures? In sum, can mining development really be 'reformed'? Such questions go to the heart of a broader ideological debate, but they need to be asked if only to pose the further and more fundamental question of whether there will not be serious limitations to building 'alternative' development strategies on existing (and largely discredited) foundations.

The problems for devising alternative development strategies seem to lie not only with deciding on the philosophical principles but with the more practical question of implementation. Within the Pacific context, advocating participatory, community-based development as a basis for alternative development, for example, requires careful thought about the kind of structures and processes that would permit such local-level empowerment. Gender hierarchies within Pacific communities are one form of stratification that has to be circumvented, and the empowerment of women is an obvious goal. But gender is not the only problem. Social class distinctions, mediated through fairly rigid traditional chiefly systems in some parts of the Pacific (including the mining economies of Fiji, Nauru and New Caledonia) are also a major determinant of access to resources, decision-making authority and power at both local and national levels; and they represent another potential (cultural) impediment to constructing participatory development. In the domain of national politics, moreover, the close ties between political elites and corporate (mostly foreign) mining interests have enabled the latter to be very effective in resisting institutional controls on their activities (through environmental safeguards, for example).

There are evidently many imponderables. But there are some clear messages too. Populist resistance to mining on such a scale as has already occurred in the Pacific provides an important reminder of the priority that should be given not only to evaluating the local-level impact of proposed mining development projects in the future but also to giving serious and urgent attention to the problems and perspectives of the poor. The marginalization of Pacific communities, especially women, from planning, policy and decision-making about mining, and the repression of those who have protested, are testimony to their powerlessness. Finding ways to empower these people so that they are able to fend off the most harmful and destructive features of mining, to have a greater influence over mining policy and, ultimately, to help shape a more socially equitable and sustainable form of development, albeit within the limitations noted above, is certainly a challenge for Pacific feminists and development NGOs.

Given the political realities of the region, including its integration within the global economy, it may be unrealistic to contemplate anything more than reforms to curb the worst excesses of mining. An instructive starting point might be to look to the rich body of cultural knowledge about the environment (including women's specialized knowledge and skills about resource management and conservation) that enabled Pacific and other indigenous peoples to provide for their subsistence needs for centuries. Curiously, while the environmentally-sound features of traditional management systems are openly recognized by Pacific governments, such systems are celebrated for their instrumental value to growth-driven development rather than being seen as viable and more sustainable alternatives to it. (Emberson-Bain, 1992c) Making a more sincere effort to recapture the equitable, self-reliant and sustainable features of pre-capitalist Pacific societies would require relearning some old and forgotten lessons. It could mean 'ending up' where the ancestors of today's Pacific Islanders 'began' before 'development' came along.

References

Emberson-Bain, 'Atu (1992a) 'Perilous Pursuits: The environmental and social impact of the mining and nuclear industries in the Pacific'. Paper presented to Social Science Research Council, New York/DAWN Workshop on Population and the Environment, Mexico.

—— (1992b) 'Fiji: Poverty and Post-Coup Pressure' in David Robie (ed.) *Tu Galala: Social Change in the Pacific*. Bridget Williams Books Ltd/Pluto Press, Australia.

—— (1992c) 'The Pacific Way? A Review of the Pacific Island Development Countries'. Report to the United Nations Conference on Environment and Development (UNCED) DAWN Pacific Regional Meeting, December.

—— (1993a) 'Catching a Common Vision? Mining, Development and the Perspectives of Pacific Women'. Research paper for the International Women's Development Agency (IWDA), Melbourne.

—— (1993b) 'Bougainville: Women's Voices from a Pacific War Zone'. Documentary radio programme.

—— (forthcoming) *Labour and Gold in Fiji*. Cambridge University Press, Cambridge, UK.

Gerritsen, Rolf and M. McIntyre (1991) 'Dilemmas of Distribution: The Misima Gold Mine, Papua New Guinea', in J. Connell, and R. Howitt (eds) *Mining and Indigenous Peoples in Australasia*. Sydney University Press and OUP, Sydney.

Hannett, L. (1975) 'The Case for Bougainville Secession', in *Meanjin Quarterly*.

Heyzer, Noeleen (1988) 'Productive Labour: Rural Women in South East Asia', in *Development* 2/3.

Hyndman, David (1991) 'Zipping down the Fly on the Ok Tedi Project' in J. Connell and R. Howitt (eds) *Mining and Indigenous Peoples in Australasia*. Sydney University Press and OUP, Sydney.

Mandie-Filer, A. (1989) 'The Problem of Lihir Women', in C.S. Filer and R.T. Jackson (eds) *The Social and Economic Impact of a Gold Mine in Lihir*. Revised and expanded. Lihir Liaison Committee, Konedobu, PNG.

Moody, Roger (1991) *Plunder! The Rise and Fall of the World's Most Powerful Mining Conglomerate*, Partizans, London.

Okole, Henry (1990) 'The Politics of the Panguna Landowners' Organization', in R.J. May and Mathew Spriggs (eds) *The Bougainville Crisis*. Crawford House Press, Bathurst, New South Wales.

PNG census data

Pollock, Nancy (1991) CEDAW, 'The Status of Women in Nauru'. Country Overview Paper for the South Pacific Seminar on the United Nations Convention of the Elimination of all forms of Discrimination against Women (CEDAW).

Slatter, Claire (1991) 'Situation Analysis of Pacific Children: A Regional Perspective'. UNICEF Pacific Office, Suva.

Thaman, R.R. (1991) 'Evolution and Change in Pacific Island Food Systems'. Background Paper No. 3 in M.L. Bakker and R.R. Thaman (eds) 'Population, Food and Development, Suva, USP/SPC/UNFPA Regional Symposium, 1990 Proceedings.

Weeramentry, C.G., R.H. Challen and G. Degidoa (1988) *Republic of Nauru Report: Commission of Inquiry into the Rehabilitation of the Worked-Out Phosphate Lands of Nauru*. Australia.

Wesley-Smith, Terence (1990) 'The Politics of Access: Mining Companies, The State, and Landowners in Papua New Guinea', in *Political Science* vol. 42, no. 2, December.

—— (1991) 'Changing relations of production in Bougainville', in *The Contemporary Pacific* 4, (2), September.

4

The Logic of Economics vs. the Dynamics of Culture: Daring to (Re)Invent the Common Future

Raff Carmen

Scarcely twenty years were enough to make a billion people define themselves as underdeveloped. (Ivan Illich, 1981)

Underdevelopment is something that forces you at an early age to think someone else's thoughts and to feel something your own heart does not feel and to somehow being unable to stand on your own two feet. They train you to be paralyzed, then they sell you crutches. (Eduardo Galeano, 1993)

Blinkered vision, aborted take-off

The modern development project, in an impasse since the 1970s, is in full retreat. The grand Rostowian metaphor which promised an orderly planned progress taking underdeveloped societies out of their initial lethargy through consecutive stages, from take-off to eventual self-propelled growth, culminating in a millennium of global and universal mass consumption, never credible at the best of times, has evaporated. Its memory, though, lingers. Its vehicle, the panglossian vocabulary of conquest and success, now out of step with reality on the ground, is still very much in place. One could compare the global development project to that of Howard Hughes' 16-engined wooden seaplane project, launched with much razzmatazz in 1947: the giant wooden plane never managed to lift its enormous weight out of the water and ended up in a shed on the waterfront, a mere footnote to aviation history. Though in retrospect it is clear that the design was flawed, the materials used obsolete and the era of giant seaplanes past, the sheer stubbornness and spending power of an eccentric billionaire were nevertheless able to keep the project artificially afloat for a considerable period of time. But nothing could prevent it from going down in the pages of history as the 'Hughes' Spruce Goose'.

The 'Truman Project' (same vintage, same country of origin), the leitmotif running through all the pages of Sachs (1992),[1] similarly failed to engineer, to use its own metaphor, the promised self-sustaining flight, definitely not on the scale nor in the manner predicted: the much-vaunted 'trickle-down' mechanism of the 1960s, if it ever existed, turned out as a de facto and steady trickle-up, in absolute terms, of resources and wealth from the underdeveloped to the overdeveloped. So many vested interests and reputations ride on this now ageing project that its demise appears unthinkable to those who most benefit from it. True, a global nuclear holocaust – all in the name of progress and peace – was avoided (by a whisker) during the long paranoid cold war years. The conflicting ideologies of institutionalized Marxism and capitalism, it is now found, were, all along, in fundamental agreement about the nature and goals of development. 'Forty years of development projects have passed' remarks Nyoni, 'without any substantial change in the condition of the poor. Something must be very wrong'. (Nyoni, 1987) Max-Neef (1991), even more forcefully, has it that 'the cause of poverty is development'.

Hidden, also, from the glare of the headlines, is the festering, protracted holocaust which kills more than 40,000 children daily, the equivalent of a Hiroshima every week. (Nerfin, 1987)

The social construction of meaning

With the cancelling of the take-off and the shelving of the once omnipresent five-year development plans, the present amalgam of crisis management, containment policies and palliatives, feeding off a diet of debt repayment schemes, poverty alleviation measures and structural adjustment planning (SAPs), appears, at best, a thin excuse for what was once the largest enterprise of optimism and hope on a world scale.

Nonetheless, the glossary of success, production, expansion, big push, modernization, technology transfer, rapid industrialization, progress, and last but not least, GROWTH continues to be legal tender. The same is true of the vocabulary borrowed from the handbooks of martial arts and hunting: mobilization, targeting, strategic planning, campaigning, combating, extermination, extinction and eradication.

The power and glamour of keywords continues to fascinate. Keywords are to modernity and its culture of success what vernacular speech is to the common-sense experience of the word of everyday life. Vernacular speech belongs to people who speak their own minds, who, in orature, orality and oracy reveal the hidden source of their popular knowledge and wisdom which even pre-dates written newcomers such as the Quran, Bible or Vedas. It is a free, commonly-shared type of vernacular knowledge which still survives in the West African griot, even though the griot's artistry is reduced to just another digit in UNESCO illiteracy statistics.[2]

Keywords, on the other hand, are bits of compartmentalized, sanitized, commoditized, subjugated knowledge, repackaged for the purposes of market demand and supply. Keywords are not the purpose of market demand and supply. Keywords are not owned but acquired through the medium of professionals who speak for us and to us. (Illich, 1983) The underdevelopment keyword 'trains you to be paralyzed, then they sell you crutches'. (Galleano and Bonaso, 1993) The stark reality is that development as commonly construed by the West has meant underdevelopment for women and, consequently, for children and communities as well. (Stamp, 1989: 19) Twenty years were all it took to make one billion people define themselves as underdeveloped. (Illich, 1981)

Monopolized professional knowledge, regardless of protests to the contrary, is biased in that it artificially separates what belongs together, reduces what is whole, objectifies what properly belongs to the subjective, sanitizes what comes naturally, institutionalizes what is vernacular, universalizes what is particular, and targets and reifies (from the Latin *res*, that is, makes into a thing) what is value-specific, non-quantifiable and autonomous.

Poverty, so we are told, can be eradicated, alleviated, crushed even, while it is quite obvious that what we are talking about are poor people who ought not to be crushed or eradicated. (Carmen, 1993)[3] Negative thinking produces negative vocabulary which in turn inhibits people's own agency.

According to Illich there is a fundamental rupture between all preceding conceptualizations of society and the present one which, to a large extent, rests on the possessive right of the individual to freedom from any relations with others except economic ones. A second characteristic is the exclusion of gender from social theory and practice. Only the individual who is both possessive and gender-less can fit the assumption of scarcity on which any political economy must rest. (Illich, 1983: 10) This analysis is echoed by Stamp, who points out that no political economy is gender-neutral. (Stamp, 1989) In development terms, a Fourth World (consisting mainly of women and their children) ensuring the survival of a Third World is essential for the maintenance of the present, First World-dominated, international world order.[4]

The Judeo-Christian ancestry of the myth of progress

The ancestry of the modern myth of progress is unmistakably Judeo-Christian. It finds its legitimation – whether justified or not – in the original divine command of Genesis: 'Increase and multiply, and fill the earth and subdue it.' (Genesis 1: 28) The Myth of Progress is but an extension of Bacon's 'Masculine Birth of Time', which promises a 'blessed race of heroes and supermen' who will dominate both nature and society. Nature, from now on, is no longer to be 'Mother Nature' but female nature, conquered by an aggressive masculine mind. (Shiva, 1989: 17) The hegemonistic prerogatives of conquering exploitative capitalism thus dovetailed with the original myth which appeared to license the conversion of living, nurturing Nature into inert, manipulable and exploitable matter (commodities).[5]

Male bias is at the very core of *homo oeconomicus'* androcentric concept of society and of his global project. Macro-economics is driven by and intimately wedded to the Western male imperative of monopolization of resources and power by state and market, to the detriment of the equally valid and necessary rights of and contribution by the citizen (Nerfin, 1987: 171), in particular the female citizen. So much so that Vandana Shiva refers to development as 'the Project of Western Patriarchy'. (Shiva, 1989) What needs investigation and analysis are not merely (male)-biased so-called outcomes or processes (Elson, 1991) but the source from which those biased outcomes and processes spring, that is, the quintessentially male, inherently ethnocentric and economistic development construct itself. Feminist analysis of bias, to be at all effective, owes it to itself to be radical (from the Latin *radix*, root).

Semiology: challenging interiorization of values and domestication of concepts

Language is a product of culture. It is also generator of culture. The discourse of the dominant culture permeates the language of everyday life so powerfully that even those who suffer the adverse effects of the dominant ideology end up using its language as if it were their own. Semiological analysis retraces the process of the social construction of meaning by studying signs (language, idiom and codes) in their holistic context. It investigates what, on the surface, appears to be obvious and common sense. This retracing helps to elucidate how people make sense of their experience and the way in which they express it.

Economic logic loves to display the achievements of efficiency and effectiveness wrought by the combination of money, labour and machines, in a climate of artificial scarcity, and its capacity to satisfy the thus created wants and needs with a virtually inexhaustible horn of plenty (at a price). Logic is not synonymous with wisdom: what economic logic conveniently and consistently discounts is entropy. The discounting of the fact that the last link in the economic growth cycle is not consumption, but waste, exposes the earth to being turned into a self-centred pile of trash. (Illich, 1992: 29) Alternatively, and equally absurdly, half a dozen supplementary planets would eventually be needed as both mining and dumping grounds.

Interiorization of values is the subconscious mechanism by which the mind allows itself to be colonized by values and meanings which may be contrary to the subjects' true identity and, ultimately, better knowledge and interests. An extreme version of this is self-colonization, a conscious reneging, invariably by a privileged minority, on local thinking and culture (wa Thiongo, 1986), allowing continued penetration of imported and alien values. Domestication of concepts upholds and maintains a body of knowledge which relies on co-opted keywords and inverted meanings.

Alternative development?

Development economics, large-scale economics, that is, that branch of learning entrusted with the task of determining content and strategy of national and international economies in the First World, and which dresses up as development economics in the Third World, has traditionally been – and to a large extent remains – the sole arbiter of development idiom and content. In that sense, development is the keyword *par excellence*: it has been trademarked and turned into an *appellation contrôlée*, that only a particular brand of products, coming from a central distribution point, is exclusively entitled to bear in its crest.

In the face of such overwhelming odds, diverging or competing views on the nature of development have no choice but to resort to qualification: 'alternative', 'human-scale', 'sustainable', 'another', are some of the more common descriptive stratagems to which the representatives of dissent resort. The very use of such adjectives – while the master terminology remains all the time eerily exempt from any need to specify – constitutes an implicit internalized acknowledgment of the presumed universal validity and legitimacy of the trademarked term, an implicit confession, also, that the alternative, so labelled, is either unauthentic, second-rate, illegitimate, purist, utopian or marginal, or all of these taken together. The real utopia, that is, a development which is patently unsustainable and happening on an inhuman or de-humanizing scale, adjustment-with-a-human-face (UNICEF, 1987) notwithstanding, is thus confirmed as valid, authentic and legitimate. Another consequence is the reduction of major disciplines, such as education, to the status of sub-disciplines, as is manifest in the often-heard expressions 'education for development' or 'communication and media for development', 'the contribution of health-care, culture, literacy, poverty alleviation to development' or 'Women in Development' (WID): as if education, literacy, health or women were *here* and development over *there*.

While, from an ethical viewpoint, the economics-serving-people principle ought to be paramount, it is the logic of people-serving-the-economy (and state) which carries the day. In Mies' view, it is essential for the categories of capitalist patriarchy to be transcended for a new space in which women, men and nature are neither exploited nor destroyed, to emerge. (Mies, 1986: 23)

The reclamation of vocabulary

The use of disembedded keywords has traditionally been one of the many mechanisms by which the illusion of objectivity and neutrality is fostered and ethical judgment is frustrated: people, that is, historically and socio-logically situated, gendered persons, are consistently referred to in development parlance as beneficiaries, targets, clients, (un)employed, human capital, human resources, assets, production factors, commodity or surplus producers, variables, welfare seekers and recipients, labour and workers. Food is translated into number-crunching nutrition variables. Life derives its meaning, not from quality (of life), culture, leisure or creativity, but from narrow and qualitatively meaningless life expectancy indicators. Homes become provision of housing in the economist's dictionary, while poor women and men are conflated into poverty indicators. Orates, as already pointed out, are defined as illiterates. Hunger, rather than pangs in the stomach and blight of the soul, is defined in the esoteric terms of Food Availability Decline (FAD), Food Entitlement Failure (FEF), Resource Bundle Deficiency (RBD) or/and Endowment Failure (EF) (World Bank, 1986; Sen, 1981), thereby epistemologically inhibiting reference to human causation or counteractive autonomous human agency.

The hallmark of dominant, socially-constructed knowledge is, furthermore, its predilection for negatives. A classic example of negative speak is the title of a book which for many years has acted as a textbook in Community Development and Development Education studies: *Attacking Rural Poverty: How Non-Formal Education Can Help.* (Coombs and Ahmed, 1974) This title contains no less than three negatives, while the suggestion that non-formal education might help does little to ease the overall impression of gratuitous tinkering at the margin.

Even though the formal sector often provides public or modern-sector employment to no more than a fraction of nationals,[6] dominant terminology relegates the bulk of the productive population to the informal sector, variously designated also as home industry, street economy, domestic service industry, domestic enterprise (women's!) economy, slum, traditional, artisan, non-cashcrop, black marketeering, bazaar, and waste recycling. Female is re-codified and neutralized as non-male. A black female doubly so, by the invisible norm of colonial whiteness. (McLaren and da Silva, 1993: 58)

What-is is defined by what-it-is-not

What people are and are capable of doing is obliterated by what they are not or what they happen not to be doing. Reclaiming our vocabulary has

little in common with the type of pedantic word-games which give
semantics a bad name. Words, as arbitrary codes, are themselves unim-
portant: it is the meaning, the culture and ideology they carry which can
turn words into formidable-to-insurmountable first hurdles. Is, for example, underdevelopment merely the obverse of the development coin, a
mere (temporary) lack of what the developed already have? Or is underdevelopment the reverse side of overdevelopment, which, combined,
translate into maldevelopment, that is, universal global failure? (Amin,
1990) While overdevelopment and maldevelopment are hardly ever heard,
development discourse relies heavily on underdevelopment terminology
and its derivatives. Using development in isolation from any reference to
overdevelopment/maldevelopment perpetuates the myth that the underdeveloped one day will, and can, be like us, the developed countries (DCs).
By contrast, maldevelopment means that both the so-called developed and
the so-called underdeveloped are in need of development. The implications are all-important. Threshold theory, developed by Max-Neef's
CEPAUR research group in Chile, holds that there is, up to a certain point,
a positive correlation between an increase in GNP, conventionally measured, and the quality of life of people. If, however, GNP continues to grow
beyond a certain threshold, the quality of life starts to deteriorate.
CEPAUR findings converge with those of Daly and Cobb (1989: 28), who,
in isolation from CEPAUR and starting from totally different methodologies, developed a Quality of Life Index (QLI), which was applied to the
USA economy for the period 1950 to 1989. Their research showed that,
from 1950 until about 1975, the growth in GNP in the USA ran in almost
perfect parallel with the QLI. But, starting from 1974–75, growth continues, while the Index starts coming down.

> If the rich countries have reached the threshold point and there are, on the
> other hand, poor countries which have not reached the threshold point, it
> means that there are certain countries that should stop growing, so that
> others can achieve the growth which they still need. Because, if the former
> continue to grow, it is absolute waste. It does not add anything, except
> create even deeper problems. So it is good business to stop growing. (Daly
> and Cobb, 1989)

Autonomous development: human agency as top resource

The cornerstone of both conventional and radical concepts of development
has always been the perception that the state (public policy), aided and
abetted by the market, is the ultimate liberator, equalizer, purveyor and
distributor of the benefits of development. Nerfin (1987: 172) starts from
the empirical observation that 'the powers that be, governmental and

economic, have more often than not proved unable by themselves to offer solutions to the crisis and even less to the search for alternatives. They are more part of the problem than part of the solution.' The once all-powerful state is now, more than ever before, beset by crushing problems, from international debt-repayment schedules which swallow, in some cases, virtually the entire domestic product of a country, to hyperinflation which makes a mockery of the sophisticated, hyperefficient, civil-servant-led economy. Goran Hyden (1988: 145) speaks of the overburdened state, a phenomenon which has led, in both the erstwhile Second World and in most Third World nations, to a flowering of parallel economies (the barter economy of yore) as well as to parallel organizations and popular movements. The forfeit of the state has meant the emergence of an enabling environment which opens up a new chapter in the development saga, by giving, at long last, due recognition to the resourcefulness of people, to the supremacy of society over state and to the predominance of the means over the end (human welfare).

The if-you-are-good-now-you-will-be-rich-2000-years-from-now-type of promises have lost their last shred of credibility for those whom Frantz Fanon already referred to as *les damnés de la terre* (the wretched of the earth). (Fanon, 1967) Huidobro speaks of the gradual creation of a new type of society, also capitalist, or rather sub-capitalist, the capitalism of poverty: 'we are expendable, so they have decided to let us die'. (Huidobro, 1992) Priority concern with the Basic Needs of the poor (BNA), a 1970s sequel to the inoperative trickle-down development dogma, was mildly revolutionary, but still well within the paradigmatic framework and operational grasp of development economics, which is quite effective when it comes to dealing with the subjective-particular. For a host of reasons, attention is now shifting to the subjective-universal, that is, the axiological (value-specific) categories of need which have traditionally been ignored or shunned by the objectivist disciplines. Unlike consumption-needs and wants, potentially infinite but always limited in supply, Fundamental Human Needs (FHN) are finite, few and the same in all cultures and in all historical ages.

CEPAUR lists nine such Fundamental Human Needs (with a possible future tenth – Transcendence – as yet not considered universal, to be added at a later stage): Subsistence, Protection, Affection, Understanding, Participation, Idleness (not laziness), Creation, Identity and Freedom. Needs are not just about deprivation. Needs are, also, at the same time, challenge and potential. 'To the degree that needs engage, motivate and mobilize people, they are a potential, and eventually become a resource.' (Max-Neef *et al.*, 1989) Resource, it should be noted, derives from the Latin verb *surgere* which evokes the image of a surging spring which rises again and again, in generous bursts of continuous, recreative activity. The need to participate is also a potential for participation, just as the need for affection is potential for affection. An ancient Wolof (West Africa) proverb has it that the lack of means is already a means. While the animal in us needs to be fed, clothed, sheltered and medically kept on its feet, the human in us needs to be fulfilled by creative acts. Development, in as much as it provides formal education, functional literacy, modern technology or sophisticated forms of allopathic medicine, does not in any way add to or subtract from this most fundamental of human endowments.

Subverted development concepts and corrupted meanings have not come about spontaneously, nor are they blind data, an irreversible *fait accompli*, still less an inescapable fate or uncontrollable act of god, but, imminently, the end-product of a man-made process. All this can, therefore, be counteracted, be undone by informed human agency.

Agency is ability to act or intervene, this being a precondition of creative knowledge. (Freire, 1987: 11) Human agency, ability to act autonomously in and through history, is at the opposite end of a continuum made up of passivity, receptivity, automatism, adventitiousness or seren-dipity. Agency critically challenges interiorization of values and domestication of concepts, which leaves Pandora's box wide open, free to spill out its calamitous, culture-destructive content. In the end, so the narrative goes, only hope remained: the core of the last, vestigal glimmer of hope must be human agency.

Agency acquires its historical grounding in informed individual and collective emancipatory, and therefore humanizing acts, by which an unsustainable and untenable dehumanizing worldview is constantly being challenged and transformed. At the cutting edge of this agency are those citizens (*wananchi*, the Swahili equivalent, that is, children of the Earth) who 'perceive that the essence of history is the endless effort for emanci-pation by which [they] grope towards mastery of their destiny. An effort which is, in the final analysis, coterminous with the process of humaniza-tion of [wo]man.' (Nerfin, 1989: 172) Agency leads the way out of the shadows of invisibility and 'culture of silence' which 'prohibit[s] [people] from creatively taking part in the transformations of [their] society and therefore prohibit[s] [them] from being'. (Freire, 1985: 150)

The fundamental flaw in mainstream development thinking, all the adjustments, revisions, reforms and reappraisals since the disorienting 1970s and the lost 1980s notwithstanding, is that the development profes-sion has traditionally and conveniently overlooked the vital truth that the domain of economics cannot ever be separated from that of politics, nor education from either.

Education 'for' or 'as' development

Education is either the vehicle of domesticated knowledge and skills and of static culture, a human resources reservoir-cum-conveyor-belt feeding into 'the Engine of Growth' (education 'for' development), or synonymous with knowledge creation, a 'permanent search of people, together with others, for their becoming more fully human in the world in which they exist' (education 'as' development). (Freire, 1973: 94)

The present crisis is such that local communities have no other option than to attempt to protect themselves on a self-empowering, DIY basis, even though, paradoxically, they have even less power than the state in the face of the onslaught by world economic forces.

> [These policies] have resulted in a war on the rural poor, a war that shows no signs of abating. The rural poor must therefore be empowered not only to fight back, but to regain ownership and control of the resources that were originally theirs. (Kahn and Bhasin, 1986)

Countervailing, autonomous people's agency manifests itself in social movements, self-help organizations, base groups, local community organizations and international networks, as exemplified by IBFAN (International Baby Food Action Network) or the 6 Ss[7] in West Africa. (Allain, 1989) They represent, in contemporary forms, a social power which in history has always filled the void where state and social and cultural actors were unable or unwilling to act.

Development, thus understood, is a process by which members of a society, starting from the most disenfranchized (rather than the other way around), increase their personal and common capacities critically to reflect, decode and read their world and organize accordingly for a sustainable improvement of their own lives and those of their children's children. Cultural and educational dimensions of development are just as important – at a different level – as the economic dimension which traditionally has held pride of place. The Romans expressed this interdependence and hierarchy of priorities in their *primum vivere, deinde philosophare* (while the body is a primary concern, the ultimate purpose of a healthy body is not the body, but a philosophy of life). The process through which the fundamental needs of large, marginalized sections of the population are discovered is laborious and continuing: no educational models to help those communities to discover their needs are at present in existence. There exists, however, a body of theory and an ideology which are sympathetic to those concepts. There exists, also, a vast body of practice, mainly unrecorded and unresearched.

Freire (1989), in collaboration with Antonio Faundez, explores the process and methodology of a knowledge-creating education which sets itself the task of knowing how to provide solutions to questions which have never before been posed by the participants.

PAR: the permanent creation of knowledge

Creating knowledge, in dialogue with others, is eminently the task of the organic intellectual, that is, of the thinking and organizing person, such as union leader, facilitator, internal animator, female activist or networker. Unlike professional researchers, such persons are not normally counted as legitimate knowledge producers (researchers) or intellectuals.

Legitimate knowledge production is presumed to happen in ad hoc institutions by a select certified few, who, in laboratory-imposed isolation, research for us and deliver the results to us. It is they, too, and the institution, who determine what are (and what are not) legitimate research areas. Knowledge production responds to the logic of economic scarcity which readily turns the commons into commodity. Owning and controlling knowledge becomes a power issue: knowledge is power. So much so that Budd Hall asks whether we 'have ... created a structure for the production of knowledge ... that makes it impossible for a farmer living in Bwakira Chini, Tanzania, to contribute to the world's state of information?' (Hall, 1979: 397)

PAR (Participatory Action Research), a collective enterprise of participatory knowledge creation in which members, in particular when belonging to groups, themselves get involved as active and competent subjects, challenges the orthodox protocols of knowledge production which concentrate on research objects, data, givens. The change (transformation) brought about by PAR in turn becomes the incentive for further research: a dialogical, emancipatory movement ensues between researching and the results of the research.

PAR does not require certification following years of preliminary training. Its qualitative methodologies and value-specific philosophy challenge the type neutralism-objectivism which is a sophisticated form of partisanship and partnership: whose side are you on?

Ideally, the organic intellectual, as the name itself suggests, reclaims the name and the right to be an intellectual and is, organically, part of the powerless and/or displaced groups struggling for survival and emancipation. This reclamation manifests itself, for example, in engaged theatre (popular theatre) and popular education. (Kidd, 1983 and 1982)

Management ought not to belong exclusively to a literate, First-World-trained elite. There exists a Third World management theory and practice by, with, for and of LLLs (people with Lower Levels of Literacy), which originated among the Latin American Peasant Leagues and has now spread to the Caribbean and Africa. Clodomir Santos de Morais is to (Third World) management/organization what Freire is to (Adult) education. (Santos de Morais, 1976)

As for those intellectuals coming from the outside ('External' OIs), they are expected to be committed participants and learners, organically integrated in the process that leads to militancy rather than detachment. Which means that the fact of their being middle-class academics does not constitute an absolute cause for exclusion. Their involvement situates itself on a continuum from those in intellectual work only, to those engaged, at the same time, in a considerable amount of manual/social work.

I think that it is in this spirit that Nel Brooks welcomes Freire's comments on the subject of the involvement of men in women's causes:

> If the women must have the main responsibility in their struggle, they have to know that their struggle also belongs to us, that is, to those men who don't accept the machista position in the world. The same is true of racism. As an apparent white man, because I always say that I am not sure of my whiteness, the question is to know if I am really against racism in a radical way. If I am, then I have a duty and a right to fight with black people against racism. (McLaren and da Silva, 1993)

Asserting the right to reinvent the common future

For decades development has been concentrating on drawbacks, on constraints, on what is not working and why, on eradication, elimination and combat (of poverty, ignorance and disease), using people as targets and doing things for them, on mobilizing them for other people's causes, or allowing them to participate in other people's (agencies') initiatives and projects. (Oakley, 1991)[8] Pradervand draws attention to the human factor (human agency) at work in Africa, as it is at work in other continents, and how a growing number of farmers, prominently among them women, refuse to continue to consider themselves as victims of circumstances that are oppressive, unjust or difficult to bear. A fundamental change is triggered in both individuals and groups the day they simply refuse to consider themselves as victims and say: 'we are responsible for our life and circumstances'. This is 'the best-kept secret in the development arena'. (Pradervand, 1990: 17)

Sankara, the young and tragic president of the country he rebaptized 'the land of the proud and upright people', Burkina Faso, (Sankara, 1989), started from the principle that all forms of development based on exogenous aid are enslaving.

> All Aid policies are designed to disorganize us, to 'de-responsabilicize' [from the untranslatable *de-responsabilizer* in the original French] us and to reduce us to slavery. We have decided to take the risk of embarking on a new path so as to be comfortable in our own skins. By doing so, we have rejected, abruptly and terminally, any type of outside 'diktat' so as to create the preconditions of our human dignity. ... We demand the right to 'invent our own future'. (Sankara, 1990)

From the Latin American vantage point Galeano (1993) concurs:

> We have to regain our dignity. The dignity of being ourselves. Not to repeat the past, but to invent the future. Not because of what we were, but because of what we will be. The reality is what is ahead, not the one we already know.

Notes

1. 'The idea of Development stands like a ruin in the intellectual landscape. It shadows and obscures our vision.' This is a direct reference to Harry Truman's inauguration speech of 20.1.1949 in which the countries of the Southern Hemisphere were first declared the underdeveloped regions of the world.

2. 'Spilling from the griot's head came an incredibly complex Kinte clan lineage that reached back to many generations: who married whom, who had what children … '. (Haley, 1977: 629)

3. Conferences on the subject of 'poverty eradication/alleviation' made Max-Neef wonder whether he was not sometimes 'participating in a rather obscene ritual'. (Max-Neef, 1989: 10)

4. Paul Harrison (1992) recently argued that in the wake of the collapse of the Eastern Bloc (Second World) the designation 'Third World' is far from obsolete. It is even less so when we realise that there is a 'Fourth World' which keeps the Third World on its feet and fed.

5. Moreover: 'There could be hardly a more important distinction than between primary and secondary goods, between renewable and nonrenewable.' (Schumacher, 1987: 41)

6. Thomas Sankara used to point out that, as President of Burkina Faso, he was one of the 0.035 per cent of Burkinabe who was in remunerated 'formal' sector employment.

7. 6 Ss = *Se Servir de la Saison Seche en Savanne et au Sahel* (Making use of the dry season in the Savannah and the Sahel).

8. I published a critical review of this book in DSA Forum UK, no. 41, 1992. The 'Project' keyword, identified in the books as 'a basic instrument of intervention', is heavily prominent throughout this book.

References

Allain, Annelies (1989) 'IBFAN: On the Cutting Edge', in *Development Dialogue*, no. 2. Dag Hammarskjold Foundation (DHF), Uppsala.

Allen and Thomas (1992) *Poverty and Development in the 1990s*. Oxford University Press, Oxford.

Amin, Samir (1990) *Maldevelopment: A Global Failure*. Zed Books, London.

Carmen, Raff (1993) *Poverty and Poverties: Some Semiological and Ethical Considerations*. DSA Rural Development Symposium on Rural Poverty Alleviation, Manchester, 25-26 March.

Coombs, P. and M. Ahmed (1974) *Attacking Rural Poverty: How Non-Formal Education Can Help*. Johns Hopkins University Press, Maryland.

Daly, H.E. and J. Cobb (1989) *For the Common Good: Redirecting the Economy Towards Community, the Environment and a Sustainable Future.* Merlin Press, London.

Elson, Diana (1991) 'Male Bias in Development Outcomes', in Diana Elson (ed.) *Male Bias in the Development Process.* Manchester University Press, Manchester.

Fanon, Frantz (1967) *The Wretched of the Earth.* Penguin, Harmondsworth. (*Les damnés de la terre.* Maspero, Paris 1961).

Faundez, A. and P. Freire (1989) *Learning to Question.* Continuum, New York.

Freire, Paulo (1973) *Education for Critical Consciousness.* Seabury Press, New York.

—— (1985) *The Politics of Education: Culture, Power and Liberation.* Macmillan, London.

Freire, Paulo and Donaldo Macedo (1987) *Literacy: Reading the Word and the World.* Routledge, London and New York, pp. 11-12.

Galeano, Eduardo and Miguel Bonaso (1993) 'The Last Chance Café', in *South Visions of Tomorrow.* Channel 4 TV programme, UK, 12 April.

Gramsci, Antonio (1971) *Selections from Prison Notebooks.* International Publishers, New York.

Haley, Alex (1977) *Roots.* Picador, London.

Hall, Budd (1979) 'Knowledge as a Commodity', in *Prospects*, IX, no. 4.

Harrison, Paul (1992) 'Calling it the Third World Without End', in *Guardian*, UK, 19 February.

Huidobro, Eleuterio Fernandez (1992) 'Uncertain Future', in *Bandung File*, Channel 4 TV programme, UK, February.

Hyden, Goran (1988) *Recovery in Africa.* Swedish Ministry for Foreign Affairs, Stockholm.

Illich, Ivan (1981) *Shadow Work. Vernacular Values Examined.* Marion Boyars, London.

—— (1983) *Gender.* Marion Boyars, London.

—— (1992) 'Beauty and the Junkyard', in *Guardian*, UK, 12 July.

Kahn, N. and Kamla Bhasin (1986) 'Sharing One Earth: Responding to the Challenge of Rural Poverty in Asia', in *IFDA Dossier*, nos. 53 and 54.

Kidd, J.R. (1982) *The Popular Performing Arts.* CESO, The Hague.

—— (1983) 'Popular Theater and Struggle in Kenya: the Women of Kamiriithu', in *IFDA Dossier*, no. 33, January.

Marshall, J. (1991) 'Her Words on His Lips: Popular Education in South Africa', in *ASPBAE Courier*, no. 52, October, Canberra, Australia.

Max-Neef, Manfred *et al.* (1989) 'Human Scale Development', in *Development Dialogue*, no. 1 DHF, Uppsala.

Max-Neef, Manfred, in conversation with Satish Kumar (1991) 'How Much is Enough?' in *The Schumacher Video Series.* Phil Sheperd Production, London.

—— (1991) 'Visionaries: Small Solutions to Enormously Large Problems', *Channel 4 TV programme*, UK, November (transcript).

—— (1982 and 1992) *From the Outside Looking In.* DHF, Uppsala, 1982, Zed Books, London and New Jersey, 1992.

McLaren, P. and Tadeu da Silva (1993) 'Decentering Pedagogy', in McLaren and

Leonard (eds), *Paulo Freire: A Critical Encounter*. Routledge and Kegan Paul, London.

Mies, Maria (1986) *Patriarchy and Accumulation on a World Scale*. Zed Books, London and New Jersey.

Nerfin, Mark (1989) 'Neither Prince nor Merchant Citizen: an introduction to the Third System', *Development Dialogue*, no. 1, Uppsala.

Nyoni, Sithembizo (1987) 'Indigenous NGO's: Liberation, Self-Reliance and Development', in *World Development*, vol. 15, supplement.

Oakley, Peter (1991) *Projects with People*. International Labour Office, Geneva.

Pradervand, P. (1990) *Listening to Africa: Developing Africa from the Grassroots*. Praeger, New York.

Sachs, Wolfgang (ed.) (1992) *Development Dictionary*. Zed Books, London and New Jersey.

Sankara, Thomas (1989) *Sankara Speaks* (trans. by Samantha Anderson). Pathfinder Press, New York.

—— (1990) Transcript of Channel 4 TV *Bandung File* Programme (UK), November.

Schumacher, F. (1987) *Small is Beautiful*. Abacus, London.

Sen, A. (1981) *Poverty and Famines*. Oxford University Press, Oxford.

Shiva, Vandana (1989) *Staying Alive: Women, Ecology and Development*. Zed Books, London and Kali for Women, Delhi.

Stamp, Patricia (1989) 'Technology, Gender and Power in Africa', in *Technology Study* 63 E, IDRC, Ottawa, Canada.

UNICEF (1987) *Adjustment with a Human Face*. Clarendon Press, Oxford.

wa Thiongo, Ngugi (1986) *Decolonizing the Mind*. Heinemann, London.

World Bank (1986) *Poverty and Hunger*. World Bank, Washington DC.

5

Beyond GNP

Hazel Henderson[1]

Introduction

The emerging 'Earth Ethic' blurs old boundaries and shows how GNP-measured 'progress' ignores other realities. For example, the fate of the world's children, the fate of the Earth and the future of the human family are, of course, inextricably linked. Yet the prevalent mindset in today's world systematically denies many such linkages and the seamless web of relationships by which humans live with each other and Nature. Some examples of such denials of reality include the contentions of the United States Government that 'no linkage' exists between disarmament and development, as the reason that the US did not participate in the 1988 UN Conference on Disarmament and Development. Denial of such obvious linkages is not merely a strategic stance governments use, but is part of a much deeper mindset that predominates in governments, business, the media, academia and most modern institutions, which allows and even encourages fragmented perspectives that prevent us from remembering that the world we inhabit is whole. The effect of this in journalism and other media is the compulsive reporting of events, however trivial, at the expense of examining the deeper processes and trends that underlie them. The reportage of the tragic conflict in the 1991 Gulf War lost sight of the deeper causes and focused on the daily military briefings where the minutiae of every sortie and engagement were amplified *ad nauseam* and the countries involved became the 'theatre'. This sanitizing of the war and celebrations of the victory masked the ghastly realities of at least 150,000 Iraqi deaths, the huge civilian casualties, the ecological devastation of Kuwait, the plight of the Kurds, the failure to dislodge Saddam Hussein and the persistence of the repressive Kuwait monarchy – leaving many Americans in a state of moral schizophrenia.

Concerning the children: keeping our promises

In September 1990, another leap in awareness was achieved when 71 Presidents and Prime Ministers were manoeuvred into the first World Summit for Children, signalling an emerging paradigm of acceptance of the interconnections of life by taking public responsibility for the condition of the world's children. Throughout history, children had been viewed as small adults and willing workers, then made 'serfs' in the early industrial factories and sometimes wards of the state, as traditional, extended, and then even nuclear families were shattered by the advance of industrial progress. Children fell between all the stools in the fragmented, Cartesian world: whether as pawns in family custody battles or neglected by both the family and the state. At the World Summit for Children, a new commitment was made: to try to end child deaths and child malnutrition on today's scale by the year 2000 and to provide basic protection for the normal physical and mental development of all the world's children. The Summit exposed the 'quiet catastrophe': not only the 40,000 child deaths each day, but the 150 million children who live on with ill-health and poor growth (UNICEF, 1991), the hundred million six- to eleven-year-olds who are not in school. At last, these shocking statistics were publicly linked at the highest levels to the fact that the means of ending this quiet catastrophe are now both available and affordable. This linkage also signalled that the rationalistic, narrow, 'left-brain' approach was expanding to include once again, the more 'right-brain' moral and intuitive grasp of whole systems needed to address the world's intractable *problematique*: environmental destruction, poverty and social neglect amid rising populations and shrinking resources, with soaring debt accompanying growth of GNP in more and more countries.

The World Summit for Children, however, took the giant step of linking many of the formerly disparate parts of the story, thus laying the groundwork for their historic promise and their Plan of Action by the Year 2000. Another vital linkage was highlighted between population growth and infant mortality, which reversed the Malthusian view that mortality rates must balance birth rates. Rather, the reverse is true regarding child mortality: when children survive with such cheap, simple remedies as oral rehydration therapy (ORT) for diarrhoea, birthrates can be reduced. *The State of the World's Children*, 1991 notes that the total cost of such inexpensive prevention and treatment programmes is $2.5 billion annually (what Soviet citizens spend each month on vodka, or the annual US advertising expenditure on cigarettes). The pay-off is saving the lives of nine million children. Such grotesque figures and anomalous comparisons show clearly the difference between money and wealth, and point to the absurdities of defining 'progress' by GNP-growth. In the United States, the 'richest' country, one in five American children lives in poverty; more than ten million children have no health insurance; half a million drop out of school each year and the US is 22nd among nations in child mortality rates and 29th in low birth-weight babies.

This is all part of the real decline in the US during the 1980s, masked by the rising GNP and stock market. Meanwhile, the 'downward mobility' of American workers, whose real incomes have not increased for a decade, accelerated. As reality broke through in the 1990s, a permanent underclass was 'discovered'; even *Business Week* (1989) commented on the widening gap between rich and poor and in August 1991 ran a cover story, 'What Happened to the American Dream?', exploring the plight of the 'Under-30s', who are finding home ownership out of reach, where even two-job families cannot make ends meet and where few expect to earn as much as their parents.

All these painful linkages of previously separate sets of data are another step to making our understanding of the world whole again – just as the pictures of the Earth from space show us this truth. It is not surprising that the grassroots movements to heal the Earth and to care for the world's children are more effective in pressing these agendas on politicians than are specialists and academics. The powerful, reintegrating, passionate concern showed by grassroots groups, whether the Chipko movement in Asia and the Greenbelt movement in Africa to protect and restore forests, or the worldwide efforts to encourage the media to write stories about the plight of children, have helped elevate children, as well as the environment, in global priority-setting. Yet another linkage in the picture of the world's problems is that complex set of issues surrounding the role of women which is forcing another rethinking of the 'development' debate. (Waring, 1989; Vickers, 1991a; Pietilä and Vickers, 1990)

Many developing countries almost gave up on the North-South dialogue of the past decade, as their proposals for a New International Economic Order were ignored. The South Commission, co-chaired by Julius Nyerere, former President of Tanzania, and President Carlos Andrez Perez of Venezuela, charted a new course at its meeting in Kuala Lumpur in 1987. The Commission resolved to redefine 'sustainable, equitable, people-centred development' without the help of traditional, Eurocentric industrial development theorists. The term 'sustainable development' has gained wide acceptance since it was advocated in *Our Common Future* by the World Commission on Environment and Development, chaired by Gro Harlem Brundtland of Norway. Much imaginative work to put into operation these new concepts of development is under way, such as that in Venezuela. In fact, China's ten years of improving living standards are not reflected in its GNP, and prove that per capita-averaged income and current national accounts conventions are by no means the best indicators of overall welfare or progress. However, China has lagged behind the USSR in democratic reforms. Both countries follow in the spirit of Karl Marx's original invention of the word 'socialism,' that is, a more inclusive, systemic view, beyond economics, despite operational failures.

Broader views of development are essential because from this context comes the criterion of sustainability, that is, providing equitably for the needs of the present generation without jeopardizing the needs of future generations. Thus, today's task of redefining development is much more than simply avoiding the boom-bust cycles of market-dominated, capitalistic economies, or the rigidities of Soviet, Stalinist-style central planning, but also to correct the excessive pollution and depletion of the Earth's resources that both these development models cause, now damaging the opportunities for the South. In the United States and other mature industrial societies the excesses of mass consumption have brought moral crises: from eroding ethical standards, drug abuse, crime, illiteracy, widespread homelessness and hunger to an increasing gap between rich and poor, as well as splintered families and communities.

The basic problem is that the ideology of industrialism, crystallized in economic theory, is an unscientific basis for sustainable, equitable development. An expanded theoretical framework is needed, based on broader, interdisciplinary concepts. (Henderson, 1992) Some economists are currently exploring chaos models, and models developed from the life sciences, in the hope of overhauling their discipline. The need for a 'positive' normative goal-oriented approach to managing an economy was stressed by few economists – notable exceptions being Robert Heilbroner and Adolph Lowe (Vickers, 1991).

Once we rise above economism and its false universalism, we can see how many intractable debates between economists, such as those about planning vs. markets and competition vs. co-operation, and so on, can be overcome. The key issues are less whether countries are market systems or centrally planned, as many economists still believe, but rather, the extent to which they function cybernetically, that is, incorporate at every decision level the necessary feedback loops from those people and resource systems affected by the original decisions. (Henderson, 1992)

Seeing the economy whole

Unfortunately, as technology becomes more complex and social and technological interlinkages increase, managerial scale and scope must also increase to attempt to control this complexity. Each order of magnitude of technological and managerial scale in the market sector calls forth an equivalent order of magnitude of government regulation (particularly in democracies where citizens demand it politically).

From a general systems theory perspective, all economic systems are sets of rules, devised to fit the specific culture, values and goals of each society. Thus, even so-called free market or *laissez-faire* economies are designed by humans and legislated into existence, while prices and wages reflect the values of each society and its state of knowledge of its real situation in the physical world. In fact, the notion of 'objectively set', 'free market' prices is revealed as a myth (albeit a politically useful one) since all markets are in one way or another created by human agency, rather than any 'invisible' hand. Resource allocation methods, whether planning, prices, regulation, rationing, barter or reciprocity, are only as good as the state of human knowledge.[2]

This decision-theory view of economic systems as 'games' with human rules, that is, as management systems employing many feedbacks and strategies, allows an overview of planning, market and other tools of policy. As already mentioned, both competition and co-operation are equally useful strategies which must be continually balanced in all societies. Systems scientist Stafford Beer has been designing such models for many years and is currently applying them under a United Nations grant in Uruguay.

Ecological and natural resource decisions and prices are only as good as human scientific knowledge and must be based on sound science in systematic, dynamic models. Many systems theorists, including Fritjof Capra, Leonard Duhl, and the World Health Organization itself, have proposed substituting 'health' as a basic criterion for development, that is, healthy land and water, healthy cities, healthy public policy – all with healthy people as the goal. (Macy, 1991) The Chinese government in a joint project with the World Resources Institute is focusing on a key cause of environmental destruction, the waste of resources, and how they can be conserved by correcting prices to include social costs incurred. Full-cost pricing will provide a more accurate market allocation method, although additional accounting for environmental and social costs will produce an inflation effect, since most countries have been overstating productivity for decades. For example, the National Academy of Sciences 1991 Report, *Policy Implications of Greenhouse Warming*, calls for 'full-cost pricing' to assess fossil fuel use more accurately and mitigate greenhouse gas emissions. In response the Oil, Chemical, and Atomic Workers Union (OCAW) pointed out that the report did not go far enough in calculating full-cost prices, since it omitted the costs of retraining and unemployment benefits for those workers laid off from such pollution industries. (Public Health Institute, 1991)

The GNP-growth models of economic development, derived from macro-statistics and 'business climate' models (such as those of the US-based accounting firm Grant Thornton, prepared for its clients in their corporate location decisions), now clearly marginalize local areas, businesses and workers in the informal as well as the formal economy, not to mention further exploiting local environments and natural resources. At prevailing international interest rates, banks linked to the global economy with branches in local communities simply 'vacuum' out local deposits and throw them into the global electronic funds transfer systems. As discussed, this aggravates local deficits of currency for local trade and investment and reinforces the marginalizing effect of the 'business climate' approach to GNP-measured economic growth.[3] I have termed this a latter-day 'plantation model,' by which I mean that a local area must

compete with other local areas to 'lure' a large enterprise to locate a plant
to employ local people. To do this, the community must put itself up for
auction by offering tax holidays, cheap land, cheap labour, low tax rates,
few environmental regulations (or regulations of any kind) and be un-
friendly to labour unions. This disempowering and foolish strategy is best
underscored by the fact that in the US, for example, at least 25,000 local
municipal and state governments and business development groups put
out glossy brochures extolling this type of 'business climate' – all chasing
some 500 location decisions annually. Today's global economy makes it
worse.

The grassroots approach

As people try to make whole their fragmented perception, they begin to
see that the 'luring outside investors' approach to development is becoming self-defeating and ever more risky. Today, for a whole generation of
technologies, the innovation-to-obsolescence life-cycle can be three years
or less. Thus, focusing on the 'home-grown economy' is a safer approach.
This basic strategy offers a minimal 'safety net' until such time as the
world trade roller-coaster is tamed by new global agreements, for example
those towards which the G-7 countries are already moving (in spite of their
'free market' preferences).

The commonality in the new approaches in the US, one of the world's
most mature industrial societies with one of the highest per capita averaged
income and GNP levels, is the now widely shared insight that sustainable
development must begin locally from the grassroots and basic agriculture,
rather than the failed trickle-down model of industrialism. A good example
of the grassroots approach is the Sarvodya Shramadan movement in Sri
Lanka, which fosters development in the Buddhist tradition as 'awakening
of all' in over 8,000 villages, which themselves are incorporated as
'enterprises'.[4] The industrial model saw rural communities and farmers as
backward people to be mobilized into industrial production. But, as has
been discovered in most countries, there are few such easy short cuts to
sustainable development, which involves steady efforts and prevention of
harmful, unanticipated consequences which are often expensive to remedy, or even irreversible.

The US Office of Technology Assessment (OTA)[5] released a study in
June 1988 on *Grassroots Development in Africa*, which surveyed efforts
to enable the poor to participate in the process of development. OTA
assessed 19 countries in which such projects had been funded by a new
agency set up by the US Congress, the African Development Foundation
(ADF). Between 1984 and 1987, the ADF awarded grants to 114 projects,
ranging from $700 to $250,000, two-thirds of which were for agricultural
activities and potable water, raising vegetable crops for local consumption,

improving animal health, renting tractors, helping set up co-operatives, and the like. OTA's study confirmed the validity of ADF's assumptions concerning participation as the key to healthier forms of social and sustainable development. The World Bank is examining other grassroots development models such as Bangladesh's Grameen Bank, and the New York and Amsterdam headquartered network of Women's World Banking, with local affiliates in 55 countries. Another co-operative model is that of Seikatsu in Japan – a highly successful multi-million dollar buying club organized by women. (Yokota, 1991)

A now widely perceived key to sustainable development seems to involve what the World Bank refers as to as 'capillary lending,' where channels are sought to pass through large sums of money to many village organizations – bypassing government and political influence in capital cities. Thus, it is questionable whether the World Bank can yet recycle recent Japanese surpluses effectively.

Seeing the informal sectors

All these new grassroots lending policies, both in industrial societies such as the US, Canada, and many European countries, and in developing countries, again prove that old left or right ideologies associated with economic models are obsolete. For example, the World Bank is pressured from both left and right to stop its massive, inappropriate projects geared to host-country governments and infrastructures, which have led to some $30 billion of over-investment in centralized energy projects on a world basis. Conservatives demand the grassroots, private sector approach in the name of the free market, while liberals want less environmental damage and maldistribution of income. Still the blindest spot is hardly addressed: the informal economy of unpaid productivity, work still uncounted in any national accounting models. These informal sectors still provide the basic safety nets in all societies, even those in the US, Canada and Western Europe. Sociologists (rather than economists) collect these data, using methods of counting productive hours worked, whether paid or unpaid. Most of these studies, in France, Sweden, Canada and the United Kingdom, show that roughly 50 per cent of all productive work is unpaid, while other studies show that fully 80 per cent of all the world's capital formation and investment is monetarized, a fact that millions of subsistence farmers, rural entrepreneurs and most of the world's women know only too well. (Giarini, 1980)

Accounting for unpaid production is a way to address price inflation and pinpoint specific ways to keep prices in line with true value. A good example of the problem of per capita averaged income statistics based on only monetarized production is evident in Japan. The UK journal, *The Economist* (1988), pointed out that the Japanese GNP-averaged per capita income is the equivalent of $19,200 per year (ahead of the US's $18,200). But when the Organization for Economic Cooperation and Development (OECD) worked out what the money actually buys in each country, that is, its purchasing power parity, Japan looked poorer. Each individual Japanese had only $13,100 compared with the $18,200 for each individual American. The difference, of course, involves the various quality-of-life indicators.

However, while purchasing power parities are an important new social indicator, they still do not get at the full range of social costs and benefits in each country. In Japan, *The Economist* pointed out, extra consumer goods are consumed in ever more unpleasant surroundings – and even New Yorkers have ten times as much green space per capita – and while Japanese life expectancy is in the 80s, homes are prohibitively expensive due to exorbitant land prices, and standard commuter trips to work in cities are over an hour each way. In the UK 'real' purchasing power has remained flat over a decade, while nominal wages have increased. One of the key tasks is to examine the unpaid, informal sectors, and where necessary, create barter systems locally, so that real welfare may be increased without increasing wages and inflation. A recent example of such community-problem-solving includes the 25 per cent vouchers that merchants sell in Berkeley, California, so that people can give them to panhandlers and the homeless sure in the knowledge that they will be exchanged for food, not liquor or cigarettes. Another is from the tightly-knit community of Great Barrington, Massachusetts, where the proprietors of a typical small business encountering the 1991 credit crunch decided to expand their delicatessen by selling 'Deli-Dollars' for nine dollars each, which could be redeemed for meals at ten dollars in six months time. Such low-cost ways of financing small businesses are legion.[6] The interchangeability of money and information is a key to building local 'information societies' based on barter and skills-exchanging networks, in the same way that barter systems are employed when countries wishing to trade with each other do not have foreign exchange for this purpose, for example the barter trade between China and the ex-USSR. 25 per cent of all world trade is now conducted in such barter, or counter-trade, systems. Similarly, countries in the South could set up highly sophisticated computerized counter-trading networks to create multiple South-South trade systems, bypassing the current financial and trade channels.

The blindness of national accounting

The pressing need to overhaul national accounting as currently defined by the UN System of National Accounts (UNSNA) is underlined by Chilean 'barefoot economist' Manfred Max-Neef, winner of the Alternative Nobel Prize, who notes that 'nearly half of the world's population and over half the inhabitants of the Third World are statistically invisible in economic terms'. Hernando de Soto (1980) documents the extent of Peru's informal sector, which accounts for 38.9 per cent of of Peru's GDP, while Marilyn Waring (1989) dissects the UNSNA statistics to show how they reinforce the domination of women in most countries. President Perez of Venezuela offers a new paradigm for development indexes based on his concept of 'integral development' and deals fundamentally with quality of life rather than quantities of goods and services produced. The Perez formula includes: satisfaction of basic needs and treating people as indivisible beings; self-reliance where possible; and sustainability defined as equitable distribution within in-built environmental standards.

A comprehensive review of existing economic indicators and their reformulation is under way in the UK, under the auspices of the New Economics Foundation, directed by Victor Anderson. Research in the Netherlands is proceeding along similar lines, based on the work of Roefie Hueting, Wil Albeda and others, including accounting for natural resource stocks and the non-monetarized work in the informal sector. Many researchers in Europe, including the UK's Gershuny and Robertson, Sweden's Ingelstam and Ackerman, Italy's Giarini, Canada's Dyson and Nicholls, and Germany's Huber have studied the non-monetarized informal sectors of production, but as yet these are not included in national accounting in any integral way. Italy's Orio Giarini (1980) believes that it will be necessary to incorporate the non-monetarized sectors in order to understand the post-industrial services economies now emerging in Europe and North America. James Robertson (1983) reaches the same conclusion. He has coined the term 'ownwork' for the increasing numbers of part-time or self-employed autonomous workers in the UK and North America. Indeed, as noted earlier, self-employment is on the rise in the US, the UK and other mature industrial countries – sometimes as a result of risk-taking and often due to corporate 'downsizing'.[7] Both Robertson and Giarini agree that this type of work must be accorded much higher status, part-time work too must gain more prestige, and encouraging these new services sectors and their expansion will complement the formal, monetarized sectors. (Henderson, 1988; Shankland, 1988)

Concerning the media: redefining progress

We need to remember that our mass media are the nervous system of our body politic and that here, too, there are serious paradigm problems. The problem with economic news today is that most of it comes from economists; and economists are trained to deal with statistics, not with people.

To give a true and whole picture of world or national development, the media need to go beyond numbers to serous consideration of what constitutes human development. Journalists need to think about development and human needs in the context of other disciplinary frameworks, because the economic framework is inadequate. If I were an editor of a network news programme covering economic issues, I would be exploring all the other figures that would be much better indicators of human well-being. For example, I would want to know what the World Health Organization had to say about comparative life expectancy and childhood mortality in various countries. And then I would check with the UN Environment Programme on how well various countries protect citizens' water and air quality. I would go to Amnesty International and look at comparative data on political freedom, and to educational organizations for literacy rates and other measurements of individuals' development.

All these indicators of societal progress are readily available, it is just that most editors overlook them or consider them less important than GNP statistics. Even more significantly, editors should understand that economists are not collecting this information. They need to consult multidisciplinary researchers, including anthropologists, ecologists and sociologists. In fact, sociologists often collect the most significant economic data in a society, because they study the number of productive hours people actually work, whether paid or unpaid. They measure time spent parenting, volunteering in a community, homemaking and in subsistence agriculture, as well as paid labour.

In fact, to spot and to interpret trends, editors must think through what kind of existing quantitative statistics actually measure whether a society is making progress. In almost every case, economic data have very little relevance, and per capita income, which is what the GNP is all about, proves a very weak indicator of the quality of life. In fact, trying to run a complex society on a single indicator like the Gross National Product is like trying to fly a 747 with only one gauge on the instrument panel. There would be nothing there to tell you whether the wing flaps were up or down, whether the fuel tank was full or what the altitude was. In effect, you would be flying blind. Or imagine if your doctor, when giving you a check-up, did no more than check your blood pressure!

Of course, on television and in most general media you find almost nothing but the standard measures which, thanks to inflation and currency fluctuations, are meaningless. Perhaps the most serious paradigm problem with US media is their dedication to commercialism. Funded as they are by advertising, it is hard to see how messages about conserving, and reducing consumption, are going to get through. Many of our drug problems and other dependencies are exacerbated by constant messages which tend to feed these addictions.[8]

Notes

1. © Hazel Henderson 1991, reproduced with permission from Hazel Henderson, *Paradigms in Progress: Life Beyond Economics*, ch. 4, Knowledge Systems Inc., Indianapolis, 1992.

2. See Bruyn (1991), who explores the growth of awareness of problems caused by blind adherence to profit and markets.

3. 'Business climate' models include those developed by accounting firms for their corporate clients, such as those of Grant Thornton Inc. of Chicago. These are now giving way to more realistic models by other firms, such as SRI International of California and the Corporation for Enterprise Development of Washington DC.

4. Further information can be obtained from Sarvodya-U.S., 1 Madison Avenue, New York, NY 10100.

5. I served on their Advisory Council during its start-up years from 1974 until 1980.

6. Further information can be obtained from the Self-Help Association for a Regional Economy (SHARE) in Great Barrington, Massachusetts.

7. See the boom in guidebooks to help 'electronic cottagers' make their home-based enterprises successful, for example the works of the 'gurus' of home business and self-employment, Paul and Sarah Edwards.

8. The Centre for the Study of Commercialism in Washington addresses these issues head-on, as does the crusading magazine *Media and Values* in Los Angeles.

References

Bruyn, Severyn T. (1991) *A Future for the American Economy: The Social Market*. Stanford University Press, California.

Business Week (1989) 'America's Income Gap', 17 April; (1991) 'What Happened to the American Dream?', 19 August, p. 80.

de Soto, Hernando (1980) *The Other Path*. Harper & Row, New York.

The Economist (1988) 'Feeling Poor in Japan', 11 June.

Edwards, Paul and Sarah Edwards (1991a) *The Best Home Businesses for the 90s*. Tarcher Press, Los Angeles.

—— (1991b) *Getting Business to Come to You*. Tarcher Press, Los Angeles.

—— (1991c) *Making It On Your Own*. Tarcher Press, Los Angeles.

Giarini, Orio (1980) *Dialogue on Wealth and Welfare*. Pergamon Press, London and New York.

Henderson, Hazel (1988) *The Politics of the Solar Age: Alternatives to Economics*, ch. 13. Knowledge Systems Inc., Indianapolis.

—— (1992) *Paradigms in Progress: Life Beyond Economics*. Knowledge Systems Inc., Indianapolis.

Macy, Mark, (ed.) (1991) *Healing the World ... and Me*. Knowledge Systems Inc., Indianapolis.

Pietilä, Hilkka and Jeanne Vickers (1990) *Making Women Matter: The Role of the United Nations*. Zed Books, London and New Jersey.

Public Health Institute with the Oil, Chemical and Atomic Workers Union (1991) *Global Warming Watch*, vol. 1, no. 4. New York, August.

Robertson, James (1983) *Future Work*. Gower Publishers, Aldershot.

Schreurs, Styntje, Arleen Richman and Ton de Wilde (1991) *Opening the Marketplace to Small Enterprise*. Kumarian Press, West Hartford, Connecticut.

Shankland, Graeme (1988) *Wonted Work*. Bootstrap Press, New York.

UNICEF (1991) *State of the World's Children*. United Nations, New York.

Vickers, Jeanne (1991a) *Women and the World Economic Crisis*. Zed Books, London and New Jersey.

Vickers, Jeanne (ed.) (1991b) *Rethinking the Future: The Correspondence between Geoffrey Vickers and Adolph Lowe*. Foreword by Robert Heilbroner. Transaction Publishers, New Brunswick.

Waring, Marilyn (1989) *If Women Counted*. HarperCollins, San Francisco.

Yokota, Katsumi (1991) *I Among Others* (English edition). Seikatsu Club Seikyo Kanagawa, Yokohama, Japan.

PART TWO

Gendered Alternatives to Dominating Knowledge Systems

6

The South Wind: Towards New Cosmologies

Corinne Kumar D'Souza

To all those who listen to the Song of the Wind:

In a different place, in a different time, Black Elk heard the Song of the Wind.
'I saw myself on the central mountain of the world, the highest place, and I had a vision because I was seeing in the sacred manner of the world,' he said.

Remember, he said, he was seeing in the sacred manner of the world. And the sacred, central mountain was Harney Peak in South Dakota. 'But,' Black Elk continued to say: 'the central mountain is everywhere.'

From my central mountain, the point where stillness and movement are together, I invite you to listen to the wind;

More specially to the wind from the South: the South as third world, as the civilizations of Asia, Africa, Latin America; the South as the voices and movements of people, wherever these movements exist;

the South as the visions and wisdoms of women:

the South as the discovering of new paradigms, which challenge the existing theoretical concepts and categories, breaking the mind constructs, seeking a new language to describe what it perceives, refusing the one, objective, rational, scientific world view as the only world view: The South as the recovery of other cosmologies, as the discovery of other knowledges that have been hidden, submerged, silenced. The South as an 'insurrection of these subjugated knowledges'.

The South as history; the South as mystery.

The South as the finding of new political paradigms, inventing new political patterns, creating alternative political imaginations. The South as the revelation of each civilization in its own idiom.

The South as a new universalism.

And in our searching for a new understanding of the South, it promises to bring to the world new meanings, new moorings. It could be the birthing of new cosmologies.

The South then as a new cosmology.

I invite you to listen to the wind. More especially to the wind from the South: the South as the Third World as the civilizations of Asia, Africa, Latin America; the South as the voices and wisdoms of the women.

Let us listen to the third world: its subjugation by a world view that was European, Western; at its subsumation by a world order that destroyed its different rhythms, denied its roots. In the name of 'universalism', the West exported its theoretical models, its development and its science, its war and its weapons to the Third World, colonizing its economics, determining its political processes, suffocating its cultures, silencing its civilizations.

Let us look at the women, who in the dominant world view are unknowable, invisible; the categories and concepts do not include women; all of history excludes them. The 'universal' mode strengthened the existing institutions, developing new ideologies which defined and confined woman to her place in a patriarchal world. Every civilization, every system of knowledge, came to be defined by this paradigm. Concepts of gender have been deeply woven into the fabric of this cosmology.

A world view and world order therefore, that was Eurocentric vis-à-vis the cultures and civilizations of the South, the Third World; androcentric vis-à-vis the South, the women. Let us make connections.

We must search outside the dominant discourse of knowledge, of politics, discovering the cosmologies of those who have been on the edges; to find fresh spaces, to generate new imaginations, to invent new political patterns, to create, perhaps, new possibilities of change for our times.

'the other wind rises in all its
grandeur, specific and universal,
a civilization unfolds within its
own conception ..., with its own
scale of values, its own philosophy,
its own ideology'

It is from the edges that the women are speaking:

Listen to the women
Listen to the wind

And from the wind, let me take a poem: it was written by a poet from Guatemala.

I once saw them bury a dead child
In a cardboard box
This is true and I don't forget it
On the box there was a stamp
General Electric Company
Progress is our best product

Knowledge, my friends, is power. As experts and policy makers, and in the world of academia, you know this truth too well. The powerful are always less curious than the powerless; and that is because they think they have all the answers. And they do. But not to the questions that the powerless are asking. They have no answers to the millions killed in wars, to the genocide in Sri Lanka, in former Yugoslavia; to the rape of women in war, to the genocide of women; no answer to the millions who live below the poverty line. They have no answers to the victims of technical fixes – of Green Revolution, depo-provera; they have no answers to the hibakusha of Hiroshima, no answers to Three Mile Island, Chernobyl; to the Pacific Islanders, to the children of Rongelap; no answer to the 45 million child workers in India; no answer to the children tortured in the jails all over the world, no answer to the hungry children in Ethiopia, no answer to that dead child in the cardboard box.

And it is to these questions of the powerless that we must turn. Much will depend on how we continue even to ask the questions. In asking the old questions, using the old categories, relying on the old frameworks, enveloping ourselves in grand theories, we will only be underlining the answers we think we know, preventing the possibility of discerning fresh insights, of breaking new ground. Perhaps we should no longer be afraid to ask the non-questions, to analyse what are considered the non-data, the non-rational, the non-scientific. Perhaps we must begin to search outside the 'dominant discourse', beneath the required level of scientific knowledge, beyond the established parameters of knowledge, discovering the disqualified knowledge and world views of those who have been on the periphery. We must recognize the knowledge of cultures and civilizations that are non-Western, the social knowledge of those who are on the edges, tribes, indigenous peoples, daliths, women. We need to discern in their mythologies, in their metaphor, in their motif, other world views. We must move away from traditions of the dominant discourse and find ourselves in that terrain which has been denigrated by that discourse – the Eastern, the black, the indigenous, the woman. To discover the hidden knowledge of the South in the South; of the South in the North. To listen to the wisdom of vernacular, local, knowledge against all that is dominant and hegemonic. Perhaps we may then move to creating new political visions which are more holistic visions which respond to the complexities of reality more critically, more creatively. For political paradigms of the right

or the left have not given us the answers. Both were bound to a scientific
and mechanistic world view, both to the industrial mode, the global market
and its consumer ethic, both to national security state forms, to wars, to
violence, and to the culture of weapons. The modern idiom of politics is
the Eurocentric world of nation states: centralized, bureaucratized, milita-
rized and nuclearized. The nation state in its homogeneity of the polity has
subsumed all cultural diversities, all civil differences, into one uniform
political entity.

The scientific world view

There exists in this universal world view a deep commitment to a cosmology which is scientific. Underlying its fundamental categories is a
construction of knowledge that is rational, objective, neutral, linear and
also patriarchal. Cosmologies which did not fit into the framework, whose
basis was the certainty of scientific knowledge, were dismissed and
ridiculed. The cosmologies of 'other' civilizations were submerged; the
knowledge of 'other' peoples, of 'women', destroyed. There emerged only
the one, monolithic scientific paradigm in all its rationality and objectivity
which dominated all civilizations, with a patriarchal order which denied
all women.

The Founding Fathers of modern science from the seventeenth century
onwards described the universe as a well-organized machine. Their paradigm catagorized the world in mathematical terms. To Galileo, Nature
spoke in quantifiables; Newton could explain all in fundamental measur-
ables; Descartes' philosophy was mathematical in its essential nature. The
laws of the physical sciences were extended to developing the laws of
society, and only that which could be quantified, measured and empirically
determined was of any value and consequence. 'This tendency to model
scientific concepts and theories after those of Newtonian physics has
become a severe handicap in many fields, but more than anywhere else,
perhaps, in the social sciences.' (Capra, 1982) By adopting this Cartesian
framework, the social sciences reduced complex phenomena into collect-
able, manageable and, more importantly, controllable data, developing a
'whole vocabulary of power, purposes, values and identity ... ' which
could be 'rammed into measurable forms.' (Hales, 1982) What happened
then to facts that would not fit into the existing scientific frames? What
became of phenomena that could not be measured by the different scientific methods? What happened to work that could not be tied to wages and
a market economy? All that is scientific, we are told, is certain, evident
knowledge; all else must be rejected, and only those things should be
believed which are perfectly known and about which there can be no
doubts. By separating and then eliminating all the qualities of life from the
quantities of which they are a part, the architects of the machine world

view were left with a cold, inert universe made up entirely of dead matter. This cosmology laid the basis for a thorough 'desacralization of all forms of life during the ensuing industrial age'. (Rifkin, 1984) Nature became an object; a mere mechanism; Nature was nothing but insensate matter organized in accordance with mechanical laws; all living creatures were seen as Descartes' 'soulless automata' ushering in an epoch of unbridled economic, environmental and human exploitation. Darwin extended the idea of a mechanical universe to a mechanical theory of the origin of species. 'Darwinism and its theory of natural selection provided the best cosmological defense of industrialism ... Social Darwinism served as the main piece for the politics of the Industrial Age.' (Rifkin, 1984) The power and privileges of the powerful, the elimination of the weak and powerless could be rationalized by appealing to the universal laws of nature. Marx and Engels then extended Darwin's law of evolution to the law of evolution of society and of human history. Darwin, Marx and Engels and all the other 'Fathers' shared the same cosmology; man was the centre of the cosmos; they acknowledged the same theory of Nature as the basic premise of the industrial mode. Nature was to be used. Utilitarianism was its idiom; they were convinced that the universe worked according to definite laws; and so, too, did society. A cosmology that exalted competition, power and violence over tradition, ethics and religion. A scientific world view that has become the universal.

A scientific world view that also heralded the 'masculine birth of time'. Modern science evolved at a particular historical conjuncture – the rise of industrial capital and the market economy, the philosophy of possessive individualism and utilitarianism, the polity and politics of the nation state. But if 'modern science evolved in and helped to shape a particular social and political context, by the same token it evolved in conjunction with and helped to shape a particular ideology of gender ... gender ideology was a crucial mediator between the birth of modern science and the economic and political changes of the time.' (Keller, 1989) Bacon often used metaphors of gender to describe the new science as power, 'a force virile enough to penetrate and subdue Nature', to bind Nature to man's service and make her his slave and thus achieve 'the dominion of man over the universe'. Bacon's purpose was not to know nature but to control her, to gain power over her. Nature is mysterious, passive, inert, female, and the talk of the new scientists was to dominate her, to manipulate her, to transform her. Earlier world views, according to modern scientists, could only 'catch and grasp at Nature', but never 'seize or detain her'. The new world view abounded in sexual metaphor and patriarchal imagery. Bacon sought a 'chaste and lawful marriage between Mind (masculine) and Nature (feminine)'. A marriage that was not a union of mind and matter but one that established the 'empire of man over nature'. 'Masculine philosophers either conceived of Nature as an alluring female, virgin,

mysterious and challenging' or in their minds killed off Nature entirely,
writing of it as 'mere matter, lifeless, barren, unmysterious, above all
unthreatening, but still female'. (Easlea, 1983) The maleness of Mind and
the femaleness of Matter has been significant in the construction of gender
in relation to the dominant ideals of knowledge.

This construction of knowledge brought new meanings to the world.

Science and its world view may, through its laws, explain the appearance,
even the structure of phenomena, using its tools of quantification and
objectification, but does not and cannot capture their essence. It reduces
the history of whole peoples into frames of progress, into lines of poverty,
into models of development; it writes the history of whole epochs, leaving
out the women who are half of human experience, and in so doing can
never reach the depths of the different rhythms of cultures, never grasp the
meaning of the different spheres of civilizations, never understand the
different cosmologies of the women, the daliths, the indigenous, the
marginalized, the silenced.

It refuses history; it refuses mystery.

The modern scientific world view is linear and in its linearity characterizes
whole cultures as uncivilized, undeveloped, unprogressive. Progress is the
universal measuring stick of modernity, underlying which is a substratum
of intolerance and violence. It reduces the cultures of the Third World to
a single monoculture, a uniformity. The concept of progress in its linear
movement is intrinsic to the typology of the evolutionary scientists who
describe society in stages: a hunting culture is more primitive and therefore
less civilized than an agrarian one, and that in turn more primitive than
one committed to the industrial mode. The industrialized society is the
peak of progress that the 'other' civilizations must aspire to. The dominant
mode must become the universal.

   This linear mode of thought determines not only civilizations but also
consciousness: it becomes the norm by which 'other' consciousness is
measured. Other, meaning Third World; other, meaning women. Consciousness in this paradigm is stratified into higher and lower states, where
higher is the rational, objective, scientific, the masculine: and the lower
strata of 'false consciousness' is populated by the women, the daliths, the
indigenous and other oppressed people. And it is this 'false consciousness'
of the masses which must be inculcated with a 'scientific temper', so that
the ultimate goal is attained – 'people becoming rational and objective ...
favouring a universalist outlook'. This 'scientific establishment' goes on

to describe the 'scientific temper' that must permeate our society as 'neither a collection of knowledge or facts, although it promotes such knowledge; nor is it rationalism although it promotes rational thinking. It is something more. It is an attitude of mind which calls for a particular outlook and pattern of behavior. It is of "universal" applicability and has to permeate through our society as the dominant value system, powerfully influencing the way we think.' Ashis Nandy in the M.N. Roy Memorial address, entitled *Science, Authoritarianism, Culture*, analyses how modern science is deeply structured isolation: 'our future, as we all know in this society, is being conceptualized and shaped by the modern witchcraft called the science of economics. If we do not love such a future, scientific child-rearing and scientific psychology are waiting to cure us of such false values and the various schools of psychotherapy are ready to certify us as dangerous neurotics. Another set of modern witch doctors have taken over the responsibility of making even the revolutionaries among us scientific.'

And all this can be justified in the pursuit for scientific knowledge, in the development of a scientific temper, in the inculcation of the scientific world view – the one, monolithic cosmology that must subsume all; legitimizing itself in the name of 'universalism'.

But what if this world view which has depended on a logic of time lines is erroneous? What if the most fundamental error is the search for a single cause? What if the world is really a field of interconnecting events arranged in patterns of multiple meaning? What if the scientific world view is only one of the world views? What would happen to science and social science which have become mega-industries? Scientists and social scientists who need their power and privileges are part of an ideological status quo which in turn needs the universality of the social sciences, in all their alleged value-neutrality, their rationality and their objectivity, to legitimize and reproduce a violent social order, nationally and internationally. Science explains the world by drawing a clear line between who is subject and what is object. The object is the Third World, machines, drugs, weapons, women – objects which can be measured, managed, manipulated. It then proceeds to collect and collate data, to fragment, to arrange, to analyse, to fit the objects into categories and concepts and explain its arrangements in a language so confusing that it has nothing to do with reality. It separates the subject from the object distancing the observer from the observed. And it does more. It fractures the human being, separating the human self from human knowledge, the professional from the personal, and the personal from the political. It not only rends the 'subjective social world from the objective one, idealism from materialism', but also 'involvement and emotion from reason and analysis.' (Stanley and Wise, 1983)

As in the Eurocentric knowledge construct, the West came to be the norm and the 'universal', excluding other civilizations, other cultures. In its androcentric dimension, the male became the norm, and in its masculine mind set excluded the feminine. This knowledge generated a patriarchal scholarship in which the lives and experiences of women were invisible; 'the codification of knowledge is a cumulative process with silence built on silence ... for generations women have been silenced in patriarchal discourse unable to have their meanings encoded and accepted in the social repositories of knowledges.' (Spender, 1980) Their meanings of power for instance: what is enshrined in the different disciplines and social order is a concept of power that patriarchy uses – the power to control, the power to manipulate, the power of the winner. This concept of patriarchal power pervades all cultures. In cultures where concepts of woman power (*stree shakti*) exist, it has been pushed to the periphery: woman's power remains on the margins of knowledge, of life. Moving out of the patriarchal mind set would mean refusing the monodimensional definition of power, seeking to redefine power, to relocate power, to discover an alternative concept of power, to find new patterns of power. It means finding the power to name the world differently from world views that are non-modern. Because the modern world view fragments things and also isolates. It divides ideas from feelings. It develops the capacity to take ideas to their objective, rational conclusion without being burdened by feelings. Real science requires the suppression of emotions. It must, for there are no categories which can contain personal experience, no mathematical formulae to measure emotions, no place in the traditional sciences obsessed with objectivity to explain the subjective.

Modern science and its world view brought new meanings of violence to the world.

In the dominant paradigm there is no concept of sacredness. There is no place for a Black Elk who sees 'in the sacred manner of the world'. Nature, the Earth, is 'resource', forests are resources, diverse species are resources. All the answers to the world's problems will come, we are told, from science, technology and development, which are all part of a global terrorism that has not only destroyed cultures and civilizations, but has denigrated women and desacralized nature.

The dominance of a unifying world view is frightening. Environment has become the new universalism. Many of the deliberations and visions of UNCED were based on the Report of the World Commission on Environment and Development entitled *Our Common Future*. The Report outlined what it considered the 'global commons' – the oceans, space, Antarctica. Suddenly it seemed that this was a unanimous Report drawn on a common analysis and perspective for the world community. The Report appeared to identify common goals, to agree on common action towards a vision of a common future. What it never spelt out was that all this would be through a common market place. Many, many years ago, Chief Seattle spoke wisely of the commons: 'How can you buy or sell the sky? We do not own the air or the water. How do you buy them from us? How do you now want to control the commons?' In the vision for a common future, there can be no place for a multiplicity of futures; no place for differences; no place for a plurality of cultures.

References

Capra, Frithjof (1982) *The Turning Point*. Simon and Schuster, New York.

Easlea, Brian (1983) *Fathering the Unthinkable: Masculinity, Science and the Nuclear Arms Race*. Pluto Press, London.

Hales, Mike (1982) *Science or Society: The Politics of the Work of Scientists*. Pan Books Ltd., London.

Keller, Evelyn Fox (1989) *Gender and Science*. Yale University Press, New Haven.

Rifkin, Jeremy (1984) *Algeny*. Penguin Books, Harmondsworth.

Spender, Dale (1980) *Man Made Language*. Routledge and Kegan Paul, London and New York.

Stanley, Lis and Sue Wise (1983) 'Back into the Personal: or Our Attempt to Construct Feminist Research', in Gloria Bowles and Renate Duelli Klein (eds) *Theories of Women's Studies*. Routledge and Kegan Paul, Inc, London and New York.

7

Woman/Body/Knowledge: From Production to Regeneration

Marja-Liisa Swantz

Introduction

This chapter examines an encounter between traditional and modern systems of knowledge experienced by some Tanzanian communities. The account is based on a close village level experience with these communities over 30 years. The experience of the Zaramo around Tanzania's largest city, Dar es Salaam, along the Indian Ocean, forms the base for the discussion, while comparative cases are drawn from other ethnic Tanzanian communities.

Participatory development planning in 1992 and 1993 in some originally matrilineal communities in southern Tanzania helped formulate the basic argument presented here: that people experience an existential clash of systems which has historical continuity. It enters into their lives today in terms of 'development', but it is a continuation from earlier interventions since colonial times. Using the framework originated by Stephen Marglin (Apffel-Marglin and Marglin 1990), two different systems of knowledge which split people's lives into incompatible spheres are examined. (Apffel-Marglin and Marglin 1990, 1993)[1] Various attempts have been made to bridge the gap, but basic differences are still evident in the way life is conceived and lived out.

This clash of systems becomes apparent when development planners try to make people in coastal societies invest in what they define as 'development'. Development agencies, whether national or international, centre attention on modernizing means of production, on improved marketing and making money in order to build more modern structures, houses, schools and health systems. In general, people recognize that in themselves, these are good things, yet in practice their implementation often brings about a clash of values and creates contradictions in people's lives; contradictions which they are often unable to overcome.

One way of framing this conflict is in terms of women's bodily experience and how it is embedded in present development discourse: the attempts to retrain traditional birth attendants and to place them as mediating agents of development of modern health services. Training village health workers on a voluntary basis is another example. These women are part of the village community, yet to train them, even minimally in the context of 'development', transfers them from the sphere of 'life' to the sphere of 'development'.[2] At the same time, this means transfer from the sphere and categories of 'regeneration' to 'production' and concomitantly, 'regeneration' becomes 're-production.' This transfer has profound effects on the culture of the village.

Another practice which has been changed due to development is the way in which maturing girls are introduced to womanhood in the coastal Tanzanian societies, and the internal conflicts these girls and whole communities face between two systems of knowledge and meaning.

The case studies are from the Makua and Makonde communities in South Tanzania, but I have more intimate knowledge of the ways the Zaramo frame their social and bodily experience and have so far resisted full incorporation into a way of life which would endanger the regenerative base and continuity of their community.

At the heart of the issue looms an existential threat: people fear they will lose their capacity to regenerate their communities. The basic element in life is continuity through generations; central to life is to be part of that regenerative process, symbolically and physically. Symbolically it means not defying the forces which control the regenerative powers in human beings; physically it means securing the knowledge of human sexuality and its relationship to all organic life. At the same time, people also desire to have a share in 'modern' life, *maisha ya kisasa*.

Conceptual clarity is needed to understand what lies at the heart of the development issue, not only in developing countries but also in industrial societies. Continuity of life is threatened globally, and women especially experience these threats organically as well as intellectually.

Engaging human productive life in 'the market', and making them targets of ever more effective technological devices, alienates them from 'life' and from their bodies; it threatens regeneration and continuity of life in general. Such a loss of continuity will eventually destroy people's capacity to live meaningful lives. 'Development', quantified solely in terms of marketed and consumed produce, cannot 'succeed'; it narrows life and threatens people's existential base. This chapter suggests that the concept of development needs to broaden its focus to enable regeneration to regain its centrality and production to be subjected to regeneration as but one essential component.

The clash of values

Development agencies, as we have noted, whether national or international, constantly urge people to bring about development. Development turns around two things, money and education. People are asked to produce in order to provide money for themselves and for the country. They are supposed to build schools so that their children can go to school and thereby have access to higher learning. In Tanzania, the Standard 7 school leavers are continually classified in terms of 'failures' and 'successes', according to whether or not they received a place to continue in secondary schools. Yet in some South Tanzanian villages not a single child had ever continued beyond Standard 7; nevertheless, the school succeeded in alienating the youth from the village needs.

As to finance, development planners are frustrated by villagers who show no signs of wanting to 'develop' their villages after receiving cash. A village in Mtwara Region had sold cashew nuts for 50 million Tanzanian shillings, but according to developers, no evidence of this was to be seen anywhere in village improvements, in house building, or in quality of life. Where did the money go? Why did people spend it on celebrations, in social events, in family obligations?

In another example of a clash of cultures, a family, asked what they would do with the money they received from the bumper crop of maize just harvested, said that they would live in town for the remainder of the year and rest from their toil until the next cultivating season. They had family events to take care of, no ambition to 'develop'. And a further example is that of a carver, who sold two carvings and, when asked what he would do with the money, said that he would use it to eat a good meal and rest. When it was spent he would then make and sell another carving.

Officers coming from more ambitious parts of the country despair at such answers: are the people serious? Is this a conscious choice between 'good life' and 'development' or have they had so many disappointments that they do not wish to take risks any more, or are they just lazy, as so many tend to believe?

It is important to understand the categorizing which takes place in the minds of villagers. During recent visits of District Officers to the villages in Mtwara Region their main message was to point out all the development tasks neglected by the villagers. Self-reliance meant realizing that development was theirs and to be done by themselves; their school-going children were theirs, their village was theirs, the school was theirs, so they should take care of them, pay for them and work for them. But to the coastal people, who have little previous educational tradition, all these aspects are part of development defined from outside. The state takes their children out of their hands and determines what is to be done with them. In their minds there is no link between modern and traditional education or traditional sources of knowledge. Efforts to include children's existing knowledge of their environment or elders' songs about history of the village as part of the school context have seldom been successful.

Another example of development which has little meaning in traditional culture is the expectation of villages to build cement houses with iron roofs. Building neatly-constructed, well-proportioned traditional houses in order to create an artistically and practically functioning village has been outside the scope of development planning. Waiting to be given the means for 'development', because what people have is not good enough, is also typical of an interventionist rather than an enabling development. 'Waiting for the nails' was the phrase coined to describe the paralysing effect of donors who define what development is. In a goat project, a man with a fair number of goats did not build a goat house, because he had not yet received the nails which were distributed free to those who wanted to have an improved goat house. He was 'waiting for the nails' and lost the benefit of the goat house that, pre-development, he would have built himself with no nails. This mentality of 'waiting for the nails' indicates some of the damage externalized development efforts can bring. People's own building skills, traditional grain storage with slight improvements, hoes, traps and fishing gear made by artisans; knowledge of seas and shores, soils and trees, use of leaves, fruits, roots and animals are all skills and knowledge that have no place in 'modern' systems of knowledge and thus do not fit into the new knowledge system introduced through 'education'.

The whole development effort is caught between these two positions: only what is conceived to belong to the development sector passes as development, is of *kisasa*. What is people's own is also perpetuated, but kept in a different category.

The case of retrained traditional midwifes

The health sector seems to form an exception to the rule. Tanzania's Ministry of Health has launched a programme for retraining 'traditional midwifes', *wakunga*, or 'birth attendants', in a one-week course conducted by the District Nursing Officer and her team. Some of the trainees have been practising midwifes in the traditional family system; others have been chosen because they have had some education (Standard 7). They are taught how to work hygienically and when to send the mother to a clinic or hospital.[3]

Blandina was a woman in her late 30s, chosen on account of her suitability and education. Hadija and Gabriela had been selected to attend the one-week training course not only because they had been midwives for a long time but because they were also instructors for the maturing girls, *wali*. In Tanzania, if a delivery is anticipated to be normal, mothers are encouraged to give birth in their home villages, but to attend an ante-natal clinic for check-ups. If problems are anticipated – for example if the child seems to be very big, or is a first delivery, or the mother is very young, or the child is not lying well – the mother is advised to go to the clinic for the delivery.

She might walk there herself or be taken there on the back of a bicycle, or carried on a home-made wooden stretcher or an upturned matted bed. A motor vehicle might occasionally be available.

The mother's relatives are expected to provide hot water, a razor-blade for cutting the cord, a bed or mat and a plastic sheet for lying on. Traditionally the mother sits, leaning against a supporting woman who assists at the delivery, but after the midwives have been trained they prefer the mother to lie down as they see them do in hospitals and clinics; this is not always possible due to the lack of available space or bed. Whether better or not, the belief that the 'modern' way must be better, because it is taught by an 'expert', has been firmly inculcated.

These midwives are an interesting study of how development intervention disrupts traditional practices without necessarily benefiting all actors. Two of the retained midwives (*wakunga*) explained that although they were not paid for the deliveries, they felt they should be provided with the instruments they needed: a razor-blade or a knife for cutting the cord and a pincer for holding it, and possibly gloves, which so far they had not had. The medical personnel were not supportive of these requests, and saw no problem in procuring such simple tools. Either the village could provide them or the people who invited the midwife could have them ready, or she herself would come with them. The prevalent wisdom by the medical personnel was that the little training the birth attendants received should change traditional practice as little as possible. People should continue as before and not become accustomed to receiving outside assistance; they had to be self-reliant. Also they did not think that the midwives should be renumerated for their services from government sources.

One can question why the *wakunga*, who perform such an essential function, should not be paid at all or, at most, receive only *posho* (cereal to make a kind of porridge), one tenth of the government regulated minimum salary, yet they were even called for deliveries several times a week. A traditional *mkunga* would have received at least *pombe* (beer) to drink after the delivery was over and gifts later. Why should the retrained attendant receive nothing? This issue surfaces over and over again: why are traditional practices seldom transferred to new situations?

As soon as a development agent or government touches a matter, people categorize it differently; it becomes 'politicized'. Just one-week's training course separates a woman, who otherwise is fully part of the community, from the customary practice and recategorizes her as *kisasa*, 'modern', or of 'government', *kiserikali*.

It is interesting that Hadija, who as a retrained midwife receives nothing when performing that role, when performing in her other role – as instructress teaching the maturing girls – she is paid. For this ritual, which has retained its traditional context with no developmental interference, she receives anything from 2,000 to 6,000 Tanzanian shillings, depending on the ability of the family to pay and the extensiveness of the ritual. Among the Makua these instructions nowadays are performed in one day, from sunrise to sunset. The instructors sing as a pair, as also do the Zaramo instructors, responding to one another, harmonizing and interweaving their words to each other's singing. If the midwife and the instructor is the same person, she has a continuing role in the life of that child. She is honoured at every ritual occasion relating to that child: when the child is presented to the kin, when bringing the mother out from seclusion after the birth, at the name giving, and later when the girl or boy matures and is instructed and brought out of seclusion. On all these occasions, together with the mothers, grandmothers and the girl's personal attendants (her *kungwi* and *somo*), she is honoured and given her share when drink or food is served.

This custom is an example of how people hold on to reciprocal social ties which give them support in time of need. The total process is regenerative. But with a person who delivers a parturient woman as part of her 'job' there is no shared reciprocal responsibility, the woman has been removed to another category. She becomes part of a reproductive, not a regenerative act. In that capacity she is not associated with the child. She performs her work as a job. A minimal touch of officialdom marks the person and separates her from communal relationship and shared responsibility.

The same is the case with the village health workers who are selected from among the villagers for a few weeks' training to assist in primary health care. The traditional healers, *waganga*, are paid for their services (at least after the healing takes place), sometimes considerable sums. But no obligation towards the health assistant is recognized within the developing health system. The patient who is treated no longer feels any relationship to the healer and consequently no responsibility; it becomes the village government's duty to make the payment from the common fund, if there is one. The village funds are collected from the villagers and the whole act has become impersonal.

The Tanzanian socialist, *ujamaa*, policy emphasized self-help; it promised that the state would provide social services and defined suitable forms of co-operation for the people. People's 'ignorance' has been the main overt reason why development authorities of all kinds have removed people's powers to determine the course of their own lives in central areas of life. 'People cannot know what they should do if they are not first educated; only then they can make right choices,' is a quote from a planning officer's words in a recent seminar on people's participation in planning. The measures introduced from outside are nominally acceptable because they are 'modern', but the inherent conflict too often neutralizes them in practice. Time and effort alone is not sufficient for pursuing the old and new, own and alien goals of life.

Here then lies one basic reason why it was not possible to transform traditional colonialism into *ujamaa* socialism, as its architect Julius Nyerere had envisaged. The distance between two systems is further apart than one week's training course. People who have not entered into the 'modern' system have insight into the basic difference between the systems. It turns around two symptomatic matters: money and education. The way they are dealt with imply different systems of knowledge, different conceptions of life.

Is integration possible?

There are areas in the South where the Makonde and Yao people are largely Christians. The Anglican Church perpetuated the traditional initiation systems, *jando* with circumcision for the boys and the *mwali* puberty rites for the girls, with one to two weeks' seclusion, instruction, dressing up in new clothes and jubilation at the coming-out ceremony. At the time of introducing the rituals, there was resistance from the modern wing of the growing Christian community: the teachers. In their minds, tradition was not compatible with the 'modern.'

In general, historians have considered the missionaries' experiment a failure at the time, especially in trying to mix the girls' traditional rites with the Christian teachings, partly because the modernizers and the teachers, then as now, wanted to abandon tradition and be modern, partly because the missionaries had not understood the meanings of traditional symbolism and left out essential parts. (Ranger and Kimambo, 1972) The central sexual message of the initiation ritual sounded to them like abuse – as the Zaramo say – *ni matusi tupu*, 'it is all abuse'. But in time, when people were able to work it out themselves without external pressure, they have made the necessary adaptations. Now the people in Southern Tanzania maintain that their Christian ritual differs not at all from the traditional one, even the instructions are the same. The difference between the old and new is in the coming out (of seclusion). The girls and boys come from their different camps, the boys from their *kumbi* and the girls from their seclusion house or hut. The *kumbi* house is burnt down at the end of the ritual, the boys are bathed and dressed in their new clothes. In the same way the girls are bathed and dressed and brought in two lines to the Church where they are then blessed and declared adults. The clothes are given by the father, the mother's brother, *mjomba*, and other relatives, according to his or her responsibility and role toward the celebrant youth.

The appreciation of the traditional teachings on sexual behaviour has been brought into focus because of the increasing number of pregnancies of schoolgirls and mere children. The need for teaching about sexual behaviour has become especially important with the spread of HIV-AIDS. Teaching of the dangers of AIDS and ways to protect oneself are added to instructions about sexual behaviour. Men and women reporting on the rituals still perpetuated in southern Tanzania maintain that young people who have not experienced these ritual teachings on sexuality and symbols of life do not know how to behave in adult life; their conduct differs considerably from that of those who have undergone traditional teaching.

Possibly a similiar kind of integration as in the adapted initiation ritual might take place within development efforts that now seem like an effort to produce alienation rather than integration. But with the imposed changes, the values emphasizing continuity of life and regeneration, which have the potential to raise the quality of life out of its reductionist emphasis on productive forces, might deteriorate too quickly for integration to take place. Integration of systems takes time, and the danger is that the old disappears before it has a chance to become an integral part of change, unless there is change in the dominating system of knowledge. Before it is too late, it must be realized that continuity of life itself is threatened if its regenerative forces are not given precedence over productive and market forces.

Adaptations to new modes of socialization

Attitudes toward girls' education have changed in the Zaramo country as they have elsewhere during independence, perhaps more of necessity than free will. The independent government decreed that any parents who withdrew children from schools would be fined or arrested, as in fact did happen. A new practice began that allowed a girl to stay at home for a few weeks when she 'broke the limb' (as the onset of menstruation was called and publicized). In 1970, prompted by the rapid change that was taking place, it seemed that the prevailing ritual mode of life would disappear and girls would soon reject the custom of seclusion. For the Zaramo, after 20 years, however, there is little evidence of this. (Grohs, 1980: 174-6)[4]

Initially, parents feared that if girls stayed in school after they had reached maturity they would become prostitutes. At the same time that traditional practices were changing, however, it was becoming common, for example, that a Zaramo girl could not go directly to a husband when she was 'danced out' from her seclusion. In spite of its drawbacks, parents became more lenient as it became evident that school gave girls a better chance to find some form of income and perhaps also brought a better bridewealth. At present in many of the coastal schools there are more girls than boys because of the economic situation which attracts boys to go into trade early.

I argue that the stronger initial position of women in matrilineal societies contributed to the survival of women's rites in these societies. In spite of many changes in everyday life, the practices of seclusion and subsequent ritual celebration have continued unabated among the Zaramo as well as among the neighbouring and southern ethnic groups. It could be argued with some justification that it was because women become so firmly established in their female role of procreation that they were able to adapt themselves to external influences without losing their distinct identity.

From 1986 to 1992, in the villages surveyed, girls or young women continued to undergo a period of seclusion, usually for a year. The year in terms of duration might have been as flexible as other specifications of time (in so far as it might not be twelve calendar months) but it is an indication of how the girls themselves perceive it. When asked who was in or had been secluded, how they liked it and whether they would prefer not to have the experience, the girls and women stated that they did not mind the leisure it gave them and considered it necessary for establishing their image as a woman.

Persistent social symbols[5]

The persistent social symbols are drawn from the body, the human organism. The universality of body symbolism facilitates a shared symbolic interpretation. The basic weave of life is continually affirmed in the many ritual gatherings through which social relations are perpetuated in interaction between the city and village people. (Swantz, 1986)

Women play a central role in maintaining this continuity. They themselves first experience the significance of symbolism existentially in regenerating puberty seclusion and in childbirth; then they transfer the symbols to new generations through instruction and symbolic action. The strong emphasis on the basic universal symbolism of life through to death, expressed in colours of the vital elements of life, white (purity), red (fertility) and black (death), makes it possible for the girls to identify with the symbols and not to rebel even if they find the ritual itself is of little interest.

In order to maintain their own identity and self-esteem the Zaramo have created a symbolic way of self-identification, easily maintained, because it is based on the human body. The basis of their social sharing is both universal and specific. The meanings of common symbols have common sense connotations and are thus congenial even to the educated since they refer to universal human experience. At the same time, the interpretation is specifically Zaramo and thus preserves their particular identity.

The persistence of women's rites can be related to the perpetuation of social custom in general. The care with which the male kin members attend to many of the details of the women's rites and support them financially and in the form of goods, is an indication that the issue is not only of a special women's sphere of life. Although men tend to be more evasive when answering questions about tradition, there is little indication that they would support the abolition of the rituals. The general interpretation has been that men's interest expresses a concealed male dominance over women, as they control and regulate their regenerative powers. (Vuorela, 1987) The question is how historically shared social experiences are embedded in the total social system. The basic experience is the same for men and women. The central importance of women in the symbolic interpretation has the potential to shield them from change. We need to have more information about how the girls actually feel today about the whole system of instruction and seclusion. This information is not easy to come by because of the girls' passivity while they are secluded. Only if women in concert begin to ask for changes will changes take place.

The Zaramo girls' long seclusion – up to seven years in the old system – could be seen as degrading in many ways and as a limitation of young women's opportunities in life. But the custom is a statement which needs to be heard. Its persistence tells us that the people who maintain it thereby make a statement about the threats to the continuity of life that hides in modern forms of life. They will also have the capacity to create something meaningful in its place.

Notes

1. This chapter also draws ideas from ch. 5 in Apffel-Marglin and Marglin (1993).

2. Apffel-Marglin quotes E.P. Thompson who calls 'life' the private sphere, which was created by making work an abstract, quantifiable and homogeneous commodity, the public sphere. The body and generation and eventually most women became confined to the private sphere of 'life'. Similarly, 'development', itself a Cartesian construction, also creates its own categories which leave no room for categories of 'life'. (Apffel-Marglin and Marglin, 1993: 7, quoting Thompson, 1967: 56-97)

3. The information reported here is based on discussions with three retrained, practising midwives, interviews with some trainers and leaders of the programme and listening to village people and leaders talking about their experience in the midst of intense development thrust and conflicting values.

4. Elizabeth Grohs reports from the Christian parts of Handeni District among the Zigua that girls there reject the custom of seclusion and the rituals and laugh at those who go through them. This has caused a backlash among Christian leaders and parents who, perhaps too late, are trying to introduce more teaching on sexual matters into the Church's teaching. The same tendency is observable in the whole country, especially being driven by the rapid spreading of AIDS.

5. This theme will be further elaborated in a forthcoming publication. The results here are tentative.

References

Apffel-Marglin, Frédérique and Stephen A. Marglin (eds) (1990) *Dominating Knowledge: Development Culture and Resistance*. Clarendon Press, Oxford.

—— (1993) *Decolonizing Knowledge: From Development to Dialogue*. Clarendon Press, Oxford.

Ranger, T.O. and Isaria Kimambo (1972) *The Historical Study of African Religion with Special Reference to East and Central Africa*. Heinemann, London, Nairobi and Ibadan.

Swantz, Lloyd (1969) *Inter-Communication between the Urban and Rural Zaramo in Dar es Salaam Area*. University College of Dar es Salaam, Dept. of Sociology.

—— (1990) *The Medicine Man among the Zaramo of Dar es Salaam*. The Scandinavian Institute of African Studies in cooperation with the Dar es Salaam University Press

Swantz, Marja-Liisa (1970, 2nd ed. 1986) *Ritual and Symbol in Transitional Zaramo Society with Special Reference to Women*. Gleerup, Lund.

—— (1987) 'Concept of Space in Grassroots Dynamics'. Seminar paper in WIDER, June.

Thompson, E.P. (1967) 'Time, work discipline, and industrial capitalism', in *Past and Present*, vol. 38, Dec.

Vuorela, Ulla (1987) *The Women's Question and the Modes of Human Reproduction: An Analysis of a Tanzanian Village*. Monographs of the Finnish Society for Development Studies, no. 3, Transactions of the Finnish Anthropology Society, no. 20.

8

Between Terraforming and Fortune-Telling

Space flight and astrology: ambivalences of a post-modern world

Nina Lykke and Mette Bryld

'Terraforming' is a concept closely connected to modern space flight. The purpose of terraforming is to transform uninhabitable celestial bodies to fit human needs, so that the 'barren' planets, asteroids and so on become 'green' and inhabitable, turning whole planets into cybearths (cybernetic 'earths'). Today terraforming is science fiction, but in the discourses of space flight it is presented as a true future-perspective.

Assessed in retrospect, Earth's history during the last 300-400 years may also be considered as a kind of huge terraforming project. Unlike earlier cultures, the scientific revolution, with its mechanistic worldview, has not only transformed local and isolated ecosystems. On the contrary, what has been going on for better or for worse is terraforming, that is: a forming, transforming, deforming of global dimensions, involving the whole body of Earth, Terra. Today, we are not only worried about a local crisis, as in earlier times; rather it is the global, the planetary perspective, the terra-deformation and terra-healing, that heads official as well as alternative agendas. Such slogans as, 'Women for a Healthy Planet', used by the global ecological women's movement, are a clear sign of this planetarization.

While the terraforming project of the mechanistic worldview today appears all-encompassing, its limits, too, are becoming visible. The deepening ecological crisis, with all its consequences from holes in the ozone layer to the feminization of poverty, now confront us as a global problem. If we define post-modernity as the condition in which the limits of the modern project become visible (Turner, 1990), we are no doubt in a post-modern or post-mechanistic phase.

The purpose of this chapter[1] is to discuss, from a feminist perspective, what the emerging planetary visibility of these limits means. How is the crisis of the modern, scientific project displacing all that which this project defined as its Others: Nature, Matter, Body, Mother, and the whole body of Earth and Cosmos, our most basic and existential conditions of life? How does a feminist perspective contribute to the rethinking of the Other, which is necessary in order to build an ecologically, socially and feminist sustainable cohabitation with Earth and Cosmos?

Our discussion takes its point of departure from two highly different reactions to the crisis, which typify the deep ambivalence of our time. On the one hand, attempts are being made to ward off the global crisis with science and technology, the remedies of the scientific project itself. On the other hand, we find tendencies that, while radically rejecting technology and traditional science, try to overcome the crisis by re-evaluating anti- or pre-modern systems of thought. This is manifested, for example, in the revivals of old pagan religions and rituals (such as the feminist Goddess-movement), in the conspicuously rising interest in old occult sciences such as astrology, and in many other phenomena in the culture of post-industrial societies.

As representatives of these two reactions – the scientific and the spiritual – we have chosen the discourses of space flight and astrology. In spite of their extreme differences they have at least one important thing in common: the focus on Cosmos, and consequently inherent to both is the inclusion of a planetary perspective.

Furthermore, the discourses of space flight, as opposed to those of astrology, thematize exactly the binary oppositions we wish to deconstruct: between the modern, scientific project and its Other. For even if astrology has gained more ground in post-industrial culture, it is still the Other of Science. A spokesman of the New Age movements has recently described the dichotomy between the so-called 'Big Science' and what he considers to be New Age science, including astrology, as follows:

> The world of Big Science tends to be male, corpuscular, and organized in centers of domination, while New Age science tends to be soft, feminine, intuitive, and dispersed to the margins or edges of the culture. New Age science is the landscape of the repressed – a twilight zone of witchcraft, palmistry, dowsing, geomancy, astrology, fairies, extraterrestrials, Kirlian auras, and morphogenetic fields. (Spangler and Thompson, 1991: 83)

As might be expected, the Cosmos of the two sciences, the big one of space flight and the small, marginal one of astrology differs crucially. In the first, Cosmos appears as the true region for expansion, development, and renewal of the modern project. An example of this is the idea mentioned earlier, of terraforming celestial bodies. Cosmos is described as the vast Unknown, the Void, which tempts with unlimited resources only waiting to be terraformed or otherwise fertilized and cultivated by enterprising agents for 'civilization and progress'. As allegedly the future of humanity, Cosmos offers the next bold, yet inevitable step up the ladder of evolution. Seen from another critical point of view, this Cosmos represents the ultimate escape fantasy of the modern evolutionary project and its inherent concept of linear development: the last resort for the endeavours of the modern subject to transform the world, the Other, in his[2] own image. Due to the ecological crisis, however, there are significant changes in the relationship to what were traditionally the Others of the scientific project, that is, Nature, Mother and Earth.

Speaking from the margins, astrology views Cosmos in quite another way. Here, Cosmos is not a passively waiting objectified Void, but a subject permeated by substance, Fate, which determines our origin and destiny, life and death. Cosmos is Fate, the inescapable past, which is often personified as a female essence, for example Greek Moira and Roman Fortuna (Greene, 1984), who weaves herself into our bodies, feelings, thoughts, and denies a basic prerequisite for the modern project: the free and thinking subject's detachment from and control over matter, over the Other. Astrology does not adhere to mechanistic science's basic principle of mind over matter. Instead, it claims synchronicity[3] between mind and matter, which means that the movements of the inner psychic and outer physical world are synchronized so that 'one does not move without the other'.[4]

Finally, the deconstruction of the binary opposition between the discourses of space flight and astrology puts gender difference at stake on two levels; the first concerns the texture of Cosmos itself. As we shall see later, space flight discourses tend to identify the universe with the Father, while those of astrology seem to be in quest of the Mother. Furthermore, the Father, as in many other systems of thought, signifies Mind, and the Mother Body. The second level concerns the senders and receivers of the two discourses. In both the USA and the Soviet Union/Russia, the two superpowers within space flight, space is overwhelmingly dominated by men; and almost exclusively attracts the interest of a male public. Conversely, the discursive system of astrology is voiced by, and attracts, both women and men, although it seems to have a particularly wide female audience today.

Macrophysics of power and the Other

Our conception of the mechanistic terraforming-project is based on Michel Foucault's concepts of bio-power which, for instance, signify the construction of human sexuality, that is, the forming of the bodily Other (Foucault, 1980), and which on the basis of its specific and local mode of operation may be aptly described as a 'microphysics' of power. (Braidotti, 1991: 88) In the context of the Foucauldian discussion of sexuality, the concepts of bio-power and microphysics of power interpret the way in which institutionalized, scientific discourses of sexuality in the 19th century took over the previous body-forming functions of religion; becoming bodily truth, science began to govern sexuality and to determine the sexual and bodily norm as opposed to deviation.

We have transferred the Foucauldian analysis of the relationship be-

tween institutionalized, scientific discourse and the Other from the area of
sexuality (scientific discourse of sexuality/human body) to the relationship
between natural science/body of nature. Analogous to the interpretation
of the former relationship as a microphysics of power, we characterize the
latter relationship (between natural science and nature) as a *macrophysics
of power*. We suggest that the scientific constructions of the Other (Nature
as the Body of Earth and the Body of Cosmos) may be interpreted as a
macrophysics of power. As in the discourses of sexuality, the scientific
revolution (classical physics, chemistry, mathematics, astronomy, and so
on) constructed and institutionalized powerful discourses about the Other.
Different ways of talking about this Otherness were defined as deviation.
For instance, astrology was split off from astronomy, alchemy from
chemistry, and almacabala (an old tradition for mystical interpretation of
numbers) from mathematics. Cosmology was demythologized. The body
of nature was constructed as passive, dead, inert matter, and defined by
lack of what positively characterized the subject of science: intelligence;
reason; free will; self-determination. Furthermore, the 'truths' of mechanistic science were able to permeate the body of nature, just as the 'truths'
of the scientific discourses of sexuality could pervade human bodies.
Through its close relationship to technology and industry, mechanistic
science has unquestionably produced 'truths' about nature, which have
been very effectively able to transform – terraform – Earth's nature on a
gigantic scale. It is, of course, this 'truth' (which can be evidenced), which
produces the current escape fantasy of the mechanistic project: the partly
scientific, partly fantastic visions of still more gigantomaniac transformations in outer space, of terraforming in galactic dimensions, which can be
found in space flight discourse.

Our second inspiration for an analysis of the scientific project and its
Others, stems from what have become known as theories of '*écriture
féminine*'.[5] A common denominator for this heterogeneous theoretical
body is the deconstruction of phallologocentric logic's ascription of lack
to its feminine Other. The critical aim is to break the destructive logic
which separates the Other as lacking, that is, to find traces of another Other
in discourse, traces of an Other that is not constructed on the basis of lack.

The theories of *écriture féminine* are, however, first of all concerned
with the displacements of the *micro*physics of power, its othering of
femininity: of the female sexual body, the mother body. Our deconstruction has another aim: the *macro*physics of power and its othering of
non-human nature, of the bodies of Earth and Cosmos. Nevertheless, we
have found the theories of *écriture féminine* and their tracing of discursive
spaces for another Other, inspiring and useful. We have therefore recycled
them in accordance with our deconstructive project. We interpret the
scientific construction of a dead, machine-like Earth and Cosmos as
expressions of an inscription of the Other in the reductive logic of lack. In

the displacements of the mechanistic worldview and its macrophysics of power we may, consequently, look for traces of another Other, that is, for discursive spaces, in which Nature, Earth, Cosmos are not constructed as machines without subjectivity, as instruments for the free, rational subject in the mythic figure of the entrepreneur.

While the macrophysics of power belongs to 'Big Science' and space flight, the small, marginal and othered 'science' of astrology may be seen as a discursive echo from the void. Each of these two sciences has its own outlooks on nature and its own answers to the crisis of modernity. Let us, therefore, examine them more closely.

The masculine birth of cybearths

As the limits to the modern project – the establishment of a macrophysics of power – eventually became visible, a new delineation of a frontier emerged, the high, or even final, frontier. The very last frontier to be crossed in order to eliminate the limits of the modern mechanistic project, its 'projectism'.[6] This new frontier, which ever since President Kennedy's 1961 speech on landing a man on the moon became the fixed point of US space travel, often conjures up two related series of images.

In one series, the boundaries of Earth are being moved out, virtually into infinity, so that all problems connected to lack of space or resources are abolished; after having been small and thin, almost emptied of resources, Earth suddenly becomes a macrocosmos – enormous, pregnant with promising abundance; as if it were a voyage we had almost completed, the space journey appears domestic and the way is prepared for coming colonizations. Through comparisons with Columbus, Magellan, or, more rarely, Lewis and Clark who headed up the Missouri 'to reconnoiter the lands of our "manifest destiny" ' (Wilford, 1969: 49), through emphasizing the riches and resources 'out there', the map from the epoch of the great discoveries, which are at the same time well-known and in safe, non-threatening formation, is reproduced.

In the other imaginary series, however, the new dark continent behind the high frontier stands clearly marked as Other in relation to Earth. While our own planet is delineated as an oasis or a pearl in space, everything on the other side of the frontier is depicted as alien, barren, sterile – as the void. As something which is, similarly to America or Africa before the coming of the white man or to pre-revolutionary Russia in the Soviet discourse, only waiting to become part of our world, to be conquered, colonized and subjugated to project terraforming.

To both series of images the reference to the renaissance is contained in the master picture of space age: the blue planet. A double picture which simultaneously maintains and repeats the symbols of the past and raises the references onto a 'higher' level – the level of the universe. The former period's well-known representations of man-with-the-globe slide in behind the even more famous space-man-with-the-blue-planet of our time.

Humanity has undergone an evolution from sea to land creatures and is now on its way to becoming space creatures, proclaims the evolutionary slogan of space discourse. And true enough, we are already becoming the space-man-with-the-blue-planet ourselves. As space creatures we are looking from outside at the bluish Earth which looks back at us from the advertising columns of the newspapers, from TV-logos, or from weather forecasts, communicated by satellites thousands of miles over our heads, or from t-shirts which promote space museums all over the world (an analogy would be an Earth museum on Mars, promoting Mars seen from the outside).

In a certain way we stand on a border – between the Earth, which the macrophysics of power have been so persistently terraforming during the past centuries, and the new terraforming projects beyond the atmosphere into which space discourse lures us to participate, and which, in view of the otherwordliness of the beyond, presupposes gigantic scientific and technological achievements. As promised in both East and West, the huge profits will, in return, be to 'the benefit of all mankind'.

It seems obvious that space research and space flight, on the theoretical, practical and organizational levels, traditionally belong to a male domain. First, these sectors are products of the 'hard' sciences, of Big Science, still strongly male-dominated. Statistics showing the composition of the academic staff at the John F. Kennedy Space Center, for instance, provide evidence that men make up the great majority, about 90 per cent in 1987. (Morgan, 1987) Although we did not succeed in obtaining the same kind of information during our visit to the Institute for Cosmic Research (IKI) in Moscow two years ago, the interviews we were granted left us in no doubt as to the firm links between the masculine gender and space flight in the mind of most Russians. Secondly, there are strong connections between the military and space flight as seen, for example, in the figures of the supermasculine astro- and cosmonauts of the 1960s, 'men of the right stuff', who in both the US and the Soviet Union were often recruited from the ranks of test and fighter pilots. In fact, there are few female astronauts – so far only two in the former Soviet Union, where the old proverb is still valid: 'a hen is not a bird, a woman not a (hu)man (*tjelovek*)' (women cannot fly). Finally, on the basis of the monoglot space discourse which has developed over the years, we can distinguish a heroic narrative, written by men and specifically appealing to a male public. The members of the large, private American interest organization, the Planetary Society, are similarly predominantly male.[7] (Murray, 1989: 348)

The master narrative of space is built on a theme with only a few variations, the main devices of which have been repeated countless times. They were already coined by the 'father of aeronautics', the Russian

Konstantin Tsiolkovsky, in his science-fiction novel, *Beyond the Planet Earth* (1960). In the shapes of the immortal fathers of science, such as Newton, Big Science/Big Mind constructs a space ship which pioneers the exodus of humanity to totally self-supporting and self-constructed, artificial worlds, huge space habitats in 'the deserts of space' outside the atmosphere (what today one might call suburbs of the Earth or cybearths). Out there, all lack is eliminated; there is an abundance of energy, materials, riches and freedom; diseases, distress, hunger, and poverty have gone; the happiest of all these 'glad tidings' is, however, the escape from gravity – from the body and the Earth. But just as the emigrants create their own world (from the deserts of the void, *ex nihilo*) the body may, through artificial gravity, be 'taken on or off', put into or taken out of existence at will. In a scene, for instance, where for a brief moment gravity is made equal to that on Earth, the coming into and out of the body is described as follows: 'How pleasant to feel the involuntary tensions of muscles when one stood up or raised one's arms! But their faces paled for want of the habit ... When it was over, they sighed with relief'. (Tsiolkovsky, 1960: 133-4) The body is no longer a must, but a choice, a possibility, a virtual reality, a cyberspace which humanity may enter or leave.

The most famous, most widely quoted sentence regarding space flight also originates from Tsiolkovsky. It puts into gendered language this ultimate escape fantasy of an exit from Earth and also places it into a phylo- and ontogenetic perspective: 'The planet is the cradle of mankind, but you cannot live in the cradle forever.'[8] Although the words were written in 1911, their continuous popularity proves the vitality and power of this metaphor.

Let us look a little closer at this image of an evolving mankind and in particular at its picturesque ramifications which could suggest why space life is so distinctly male. We have lived, the sentence implies, long enough with an infantile dependency on Earth; it is time for us to leave the womb of Mother Earth, to come of age and live as mature, independent and self-sufficient adults.

Today we seem to have left the womb. For whereas we were once dependent on Mother Earth, space discourse has, since the end of the 1970s, shown Earth to be dependent on us. Earth is now an old, 'fragile' mother towards whom we have obligations.

In the words of Soviet cosmonaut Pavel Popovich, Earth is 'an aged mother, totally dependent on us, her children'. (Koval, 1987: 8) And several times almost identical action plans for her transition to a peaceful existence as retired pensioner have been introduced. Plans, which in keeping with our social and cultural heritage, are based on the idea that we, her grown-up children, now must respectfully provide her with the loving care to which an ageing parent has the right. It could be by relieving the fragile and exhausted mother-body of the burdens which large-scale mining, polluting industry and the demographic explosion have brought about and undeniably will continue to bring. Relegation to space of everything that might wear out the wasted organism would heal the Earth and transform it into a peaceful nature reserve.

'Earth may be treasured and preserved as residential parkland, or as a wilderness area, while large-scale mining and manufacturing operations are banished to the moon and the asteroids', the well-known phycisist and NASA-consultant, Freeman Dyson, states in his book with the, in this context, remarkable title, *Disturbing the Universe* (1979). And in the East, an influential Soviet Moldovian, the philosopher and Academy member, A.D. Ursul, has recently advocated (Ursul, 1990: 154-5) a similar division of the Cosmos into a celestial industrial sphere and a terrestrial recreational zone.[9] Work and free time, man as cyborg and 'natural', unblemished humanity, each thus receive their place in an ordered hierarchy.

As a refuge from work, as an enormous natural park in an otherwise pulsating cosmos of industry, as a reminder of our innocent childhood, Mother Earth is transformed into the 'sacred home', where in future, when our cosmic duties allow, we may be on holiday and recuperate, and which, when the time has come, also may provide our last resting place. Thus the wheel has come full circle between cradle and grave, between our mythical genesis and utopian ending in a paradisiac garden. With the pictures of Earth as a flowering and, in relation to the rest of the Cosmos, (temporarily) enclosed garden and of humanity as a cosmic gardener, our culture's traditional metaphors for both immaculate femininity, the Virgin, and caring fatherliness, God, who after all created paradise, are set in play.

The Earth is not only an ageing mother. Her femininity seems so distinct, so explicit, that in the 1970s and 1980s a number of scientists with connections to space discourse seriously speculated upon how on earth (!) it happened that she became a mother. In other words, how the Earth generated life.

Scientific take-off for these speculations, which are neither science fiction nor 'science fact', but rather science 'freaktion', date back to the beginning of the 20th century (1908), when a Swedish chemist, Svante Arrhenius, developed a theory about a 'natural' impregnation of the Earth through semen – a so-called panspermia – from the universe. During the 1970s and 1980s this theory of cosmic sperm that allegedly 'gave life' to Earth, was revived, perhaps inspired by the successful theory about the birth of the universe in a great cosmic orgasm, the Big Bang, and/or by the experiments on artificial insemination with frozen semen.

The most extreme and imaginative version of the idea of panspermia was produced by the Nobel laureate, Frances Crick, in direct relation to the notion of interplanetary travel. Together with his colleague, L. Orgel, he suggested the concept of a 'directed panspermia' (Crick and Orgel, 1973) as original procreator of life. (The term, panspermia, he translates as 'seeds everywhere'.) Billions of years ago, an ancient, highly developed civilization on a faraway planet, the scientists claim, launched the sperm, frozen bacteria, in an unmanned rocket, aiming at the virginal Earth. 'Life started here when these organisms were dropped into the primitive ocean and began to multiply', Crick speculates. (Crick, 1981: 16)[10] Whether the Earth thus turned mother through a cosmic rape or through a peculiar form of immaculate conception is open to debate. (A point of resemblance between the two kinds of impregnation is that the feminine body is not asked, only 'chosen'. As in Aristotle's theory of conception, with which the notion of panspermia has a striking similarity, she provides only the passive receptacle for life.)

In the circle of gendered thinking which we have met here, there may be a continuity between the images of a future mankind as a cosmic gardener and the universal sperm ('seeds everywhere' indeed!) which some believe impregnated Earth. In fact, the two pictures may be one. For not only are we (in a new terraforming?) to remake the Earth into a rich nature garden, we shall also, as the Russians put it, be 'cosmocreative' by, for example, transforming the universe and undertaking the greening of other celestial bodies in keeping with our own planet. A chapter in Dyson's book (1979), in which he suggests planting trees on the asteroids by means of 'green technology', the technology of genetic manipulation, is called 'The Greening of the Galaxy'. And James Lovelock, well-known for his holistic theory of Earth as Gaia, has co-authored a book, *The Greening of Mars* (1985), the title of which speaks for itself. In conclusion, it may be said that the heroic astro– or cosmonaut appears to be one and the same with the panspermia which will impregnate the universe and make the barren stars flower. Space man has come out of the cradle, has become adult and potent, and is now ready to repeat the hypothetical genesis created by Crick's panspermia.

But what about Earth? On a synchronic level we have been introduced to an Earth in a patriarchal version of the mythical, threefold shape of the Goddess as the virgin, the mother and the old woman. Diachronically another story emerges. In her book, *The Death of Nature* (1980), Carolyn Merchant has argued that modern science during its formation in the 17th century formulated its thoughts in sadistic language, demanding the torture and rape of nature. Within space science, from Tsiolkovsky to Dyson and Ursul, a discourse has evolved which, in keeping with our newly gained 'independence' and present theories of management, now demands a healing of the wounds and of the violently broken vagina of the mother. For Earth, 'the pearl in space', project rape has been substituted by project nursing. But project rape is far from dead; it is very much alive, on its way out into the galaxy, to 'the barren Moon' and her 'sterile' celestial brothers and sisters – to the new deserts in the void.

Moira's cosmic writings

Space flight represents the reaction to the crisis of the mechanistic terra-forming project, which holds on to solutions originating in the technological-scientific project itself. The ambivalence in post-industrial and post-modern culture, however, is revealed in that opposing reactions are also gaining ground. These are reactions which radically try to turn away from technological-scientific 'projectism' in favour of revivals of pre-modern and pre-scientific solutions.

Modern astrology represents such an alternative. Nevertheless, it shares with space flight discourse the desire to turn our attention towards Cosmos. While to space flight, Cosmos first of all appears as object, resource and the scene of seemingly free rein for projectistic imagination, for the devotees of astrology it is, on the contrary, a living subject, in whose hands lies our destiny, for better or for worse. In the universe of astrology, Cosmos principally defines us; we are playing Cosmos' game, and not vice versa. Like the projectist utopian visions of space flight discourse, astrology seeks to make us visible to ourselves as cosmic beings, but on very different conditions. Our cosmic goal is not the heroic quest and the colonizing of Cosmos, but rather acceptance of our cosmically outlined destiny – recognition of the synchronicity: that the rhythms and movements of Cosmos are also ours.

Seen from the perspective of the linear and patriarchal master narrative found in space flight, astrology seems regressive. If space flight represents the bright future, symbolized by the hero's emancipation from Mother, Womb and Cradle, astrology seems fixed in the past, to a regressive return to the original symbiosis with the omnipotent mother. We may, however, also reverse the argument and ask why astrology should not make a claim for those who, like us, want to find other ways out of the crisis than the quest of the patriarchal hero – for those who are trying to trace another Other.

Astrology speaks from the margins. Originally closely linked with astronomy, astrology has been split off from science since the scientific revolution of the 17th century. It has been positioned as the irrational, undeveloped, simple, childish and womanish Other of Science. In the very first phase of the scientific revolution astrology was indeed still a natural preoccupation of the founding fathers of the new sciences. Famous astronomers, such as Kepler, Tycho Brahe and Galileo juxtaposed engagement in astrology with their more 'serious' scientific activities: the construction of a modern, demythologized cosmology, that is, a cosmology in which Earth and the other planets moved around the Sun with the precision of a clock, the ideal prototype of the mechanical machine. But astrology – together with the whole of the occult tradition of the magician and the witch – was soon split off from science and, furthermore, condemned, stigmatized, demonized and criminalized. In England astrological predictions were forbidden by law. The Witchcraft Act of 1735 and the Vagrancy Act of 1829 include astrologers and imply a prohibition of fortune-telling. The prohibition was in force until the middle of the 20th century (but tacitly disregarded). In the rational, scientific world view of modernity there was no room for the mythic cosmology of astrology – and especially not for its belief in Fate and synchronicity between macro- and microcosmos, Cosmos and human body. It was banished as a belief which contradicted humanist ideals of modernity: the idea of the rational subject's free-will and the idea of mind over matter. As part of popular culture, astrology nevertheless has continued to exert an attraction throughout the history of modernity. It has continuously attracted attention as one of the demonic Others of the scientific world view. Together with other occult sciences it has kept alive the question whether or not there are more things in heaven and earth than the phenomena which may be watched through the telescope and described in accordance with mathematical and physical laws. The present crisis of the modern world view has in many ways given astrology more space. Its influence has increased concurrently with the wave of spiritual revival, which in the West has manifested itself as New Age movements, and which in the Eastern and Central European countries grew explosively after the fall of communism. But even if astrology has thus gained more ground in post-industrial and post-modern culture, nevertheless, it still appears as the Other of 'Big Science', as we noted earlier. (Spangler and Thompson, 1991)

Astrology definitely represents something very different from the 'Big Science' in which space flight discourse is inscribed. Let us, furthermore, call attention to the different gender profile which this other approach seems to attract. While the discourse of space flight is heavily or almost exclusively male-dominated, the entry of the other occult sciences in post-industrial culture has attracted the attention of many women. The spiritual wave has gained ground in Western feminism: as (re)constructions of the link between a powerful femininity and the Sacred (the Goddess movement), but at the same time also in the shape of a feminist occultism, a cultivation of feminist healing, tarot, astrology and so on. Furthermore, many offshoots of the broader New Age movements (astrological schools, courses and publications) have had a broad appeal to female audiences.[11]

Women's attraction to astrology, which represents an idea of Cosmos very different from that of 'Big Science' and space flight discourse, raises the question: what kind of Otherness, what kind of alternative cosmic fantasies does astrology represent?

Let us suggest that the reason why astrology is positioned as the Other of 'Big Science' is to be found in its demonic touching on fears and desires linked to fantasies about merging with the omnipotent Mother and to the notion of a cosmic Fate, which determines the basic, existential thresholds of birth, life and death. Let us suggest that the mixture of repulsion and attraction that is typical of attitudes to astrology today, is because it brings together all that represents the ultimate Other, that is, the Other which we cannot control – the Other that controls us. It is the Other which exerts an existential constraint; the Other, the control of which is the ultimate goal of projectism; the Other from which projectism seeks to emancipate humanity. It is, however, also the Other which seems able to represent the Sacred to those who reject the macrophysics of power of projectism in favour of the search for spiritual healing and reconciliation with outer and inner nature; the Other which seemingly may lead those who feel spiritual hunger to the authentic mystery – to that which is beyond rational explanations, designations and control, and which therefore may appear as a source of true guidance.

In order to describe how the themes of omnipotent Mother, cosmic Fate, birth and death, are linked in astrology, we turn for inspiration to the theories of *écriture féminine*.

The tracing of another Other in language, which these theories undertake, takes various pathways. One focuses on the way in which our early interactions with the mother body may leave tacit but speaking traces in language. One scholar who has inspired the theories of *écriture féminine* – the psycholinguist and cultural analyst Julia Kristeva – analyses these linguistic traces of the early interplay with the mother body through the concept of a semiotic dimension in language. The semiotic is to be distinguished from the so-called symbolic order, that is, the dimension of language which constitutes conceptually demarcated meaning, hiding and repressing the Otherness of the semiotic. We suggest that at least part of the attraction of astrology in post-industrial culture arises from its role as exegete or interpreter of a kind of cosmic *écriture féminine* – a 'writing' which like the semiotic dimension in language seems to utter a repressed Otherness. This Otherness has been repressed and hidden from modern human beings through the construction of a demythologized mechanistic Cosmos, but it is an Otherness for which the crisis of the modern and mechanistic world view now opens new discursive space.

Let us look more closely at this interpretation of astrology.

First, the object of astrology may principally be described as a sign system, a semiotic system, a language, a cosmic writing. The signs in the cosmic language, which astrology interprets or constructs (the zodiac signs, the planets and their mutual constellations) will, however, in a certain sense differ from our 'normal' language. For those who believe in the enunciative powers of the celestial signs, they appear as natural, non-human signs.

Analogous to the semiotic dimensions of language, to which the theories of *écriture féminine* are connected, the 'writings' of the zodiac and planets may – secondly – be considered as a kind of bodily writing. Astrology is firmly rooted in a pre-modern, organic world view, which saw a deep and ineradicable connection between human body and Cosmos. Cosmos was perceived as a living body, and the living, human body was perceived as Cosmos. Or, expressed through an old astrological formula, 'as above, so below', microcosmos, the human body, mirrors macrocosmos, the universe. This organic way of thinking is a basic point of departure in astrology, both in its original cultural historic context and today. In the inspiring analysis of mythic thought as a system of signification, undertaken by the German philosopher of language, Ernst Cassirer (1922 and 1964), it is thus the bodily way of conceptualizing the universe which explains why astrology believes in a deep connection between planets and stars on the one hand and the destiny of the individual on the other. To astrological thought everything – for example the particular star- and planet-constellation at the moment of birth and the particular newborn individual – is in continuity, connected by bodily, contiguous relations, by indiscernible transitions of a living cosmic body. Everything will therefore influence and be influenced by everything else. (Cassirer, 1922 and 1964)

Building from the Russian analyst of literature and culture, M. Bachtin (1984), we may futhermore describe astrology as dealing with a grotesque body writing. In the conception of the body which we, according to Bachtin, may ascribe to the organic world view, the focus is on the body's mirroring of the thresholds of life and its basic existential body themes: birth, death, copulation, food and defecation. At the same time the focus is on situations in which the singular body transgresses its boundaries in an interaction with other bodies, human as well as animal, earthly and heavenly – where every body-boundary is ambiguous and temporary, where two-bodies-in-one, androgynity, animal-humans, and merging of body and landscape, and of body and Cosmos into one another are cultivated. It is in this body image that astrological thought is embedded. It focuses on the basic and existential thresholds. For example, birth has a decisive influence on the destiny of the individual, on both her/his life and death. Futhermore, the astrological universe is in itself – as a cosmic body – a model example of the Bachtinian grotesque. The same goes for the separate 'organs' of this cosmic body. In astrology the zodiac and the planets are not dead matter in mechanical motion, but, on the contrary, gigantic living bodies: sexed, human or animal creatures, who constantly copulate with one another in ambiguously shifting constellations: Venus in Leo, Mars in Scorpio, Moon in Virgo, Sun in Gemini and so on. Similarly, in astrology the separate human body is never individually demarcated. The destiny and the existence of the individual are by virtue of the birth-moment bound to a specific constellation of living planetary and astral bodies which, so to speak, make up the individual's cosmic parenthood. Furthermore, the separate outer and inner parts and functions of the human body are also connected to specific zodiacal signs and planets which rule them for better or for worse. (This, for example, has played a big role in medical astrology.) A correspondence is for example set up between the intestines, the digestive system, the planet Mercury and the zodiacal sign of Virgo; furthermore, Virgo's heavenly form is interpreted as an expression of female genitals. Another correspondence is seen between sexual organs as such, the generative system, the planet Mars and the zodiacal sign of Scorpio, whose form is understood as the male genitals. (Hone, 1951)[12]

Through the description of astrology as grotesque body writing we may once more point to an analogy with psycholinguistics and to the theories of *écriture féminine*. For the basic body functions, which according to Bachtin characterize the grotesque body, are at the same time in psycho-analysis the functions which define the childs early experiences of the bodily interaction with the omnipotent Mother. In language they make themselves known in the semiotic: as everything which evades fixed conceptual outlines and semantic references to demarcated objects, speci-fied by names, in the world of reality. It is oral, anal and genital impulses, closely connected to the experience of a symbiotic unity with the almighty mother body which to the small and totally dependent child will appear as pleasure– and life-giving as well as threatening and potentially lethal. Or in other words, as something which may very well later in life function as associative background to the concept, Fate, in the sense of astrology.

In this context it seems obvious to mention the long and widespread tradition of constructing Fate as feminine, for example, Moira and the Eumenides in Greek mythology and the Norns in Nordic. (Greene, 1984) Within a Jungian conceptual framework, today very popular in astrology, this might lead to reflections on possible universal relations between Fate and the archetype of the mother.

But when we suggest a configuration of these two cultural fantasies, on the one hand the astrological image of cosmic Fate and on the other the pre-Oedipal mother of psychoanalysis,[13] we have another purpose in mind. We want to suggest that the two images may be related to a common tendency in post-industrial culture: the tendency to look for ways out of modernity and the mechanistic world view by constructing modes of tracing and voicing another Other. The theories of *écriture féminine* express this tendency on the level of the bodily microcosmos, but the same tendency seems also to emerge on both the micro- and macrocosmic level, on which astrology focuses.

The point of no return

We have now seen how the discourses of space flight and astrology respectively, represent opposite reactions to the crisis of the modern, mechanistic enterprise, of the modern macrophysics of power. As such they mirror an ambivalence in post-industrial culture, which, on the one hand, is fixed to solutions which create the need for a renewal of the old macrophysics of power and its othering of Nature (Earth, Cosmos) at least as escape fantasy, and on the other hand, seeks spiritual reconciliation with the othered body of Earth and Cosmos through a radical reversal of the hierarchy between the human subject and its ultimate Other.

Apart from being an overall characteristic of post-industrial culture, this ambivalence also to some extent mirrors our own position. So let us situate ourselves in this context of ambivalence, before we try to push the argument further. We are white, North European academic feminists, brought up in a modern, rationalist tradition and educated within a scientific world view. As feminists, however, we also became sensitive to the structures of domination and othering inherent in this world view; therefore we also understand why the spiritual search for another Other, for example, often is combined with radical rejections of the modern world view.

Although we are thus able to identify with the ambivalence, we realize that a mere statement of its existence does not solve any problems. But nor can we conclude simply by choosing sides with the radical reversal of hierarchies, with the astrological (re)construction of the voice of the Other. It is true that astrology transgresses the mechanistic macrophysics of power, radically repositioning the othered and objectified cosmic body as subject. But voicing the Other through a reversal of hierarchies, for example through a consequent choice of an astrological world view as a pathway out of the crisis, would presuppose a total repression of the scientific world view, which seems highly unrealistic, given the way its macrophysics of power, for better or for worse, has pervaded today's world. We are doubtless beyond the point of no return in the historic narrative of the mechanistic terra-, mind- and body-forming enterprise. Furthermore, a vision of a return to the world of the old organic world view is not only illusionary today, but would in many respects appear undesirable and constitute a kind of 'reverse' projectism.

Even more obvious, the reactions to the crisis, represented by space flight, are extremely problematic when seen from a feminist perspective. Contrary to its allegations, space projectism does not solve global ecological problems. Deeply embedded in the notion of a linear, progressive evolution, its monoglot discursive practice still puts mind over matter and consequently still perpetuates the binary hierarchy that splits off the Other, the chtonic, sensuous dimensions, connected to Mother and to the bodies of Earth and Cosmos. Neither grounded nor situated, space man seems unable to cope with the crisis. Instead, he will only exercise his macrophysics of power on a new, cosmic level.

So both reactions to the crisis have their obvious limits as regards the search for pathways leading to an ecologically, socially and feminist sustainable cohabitation with our existential conditions of life, the body of Earth and Cosmos. Nevertheless, both reactions also bear witness to significant displacements of the classical macrophysics of power and its otherings.

As for space flight, three displacing movements may be mentioned. First, its contribution to our understanding Earth not in a fragmented, but in a truly global and holistic way. Without the pictures of our planet, seen from the outside, from the panopticon of the sky, the planetary perspective, so important also to both feminism and ecology, would not have evolved. Secondly, its new, protective attitude towards Earth has led to the transformation of project rape to project nursing. From having been embraced by Jack the Ripper, Earth now seems in the hands of a Florence Nightingale, dressed up as space man. As caring, however, is better than killing, this is indeed an improvement. Finally, the old globe, itself an expression of pure mathematics, has been replaced by the blue planet with its remythologized and remythologizing connotations. In the discursive system of space flight the planet no longer appears as the fragmented, dead and passive, yet captive mother womb of yesterday, but rather as a living, though fragile, organism in her own right.

As for the voice from the void, astrology, we cannot speak of displacing movements in the astrological system as such; being the voice of a repressed tradition, this occult science bears witness to the displacements in the modern project simply by its rapidly increasing popularity. Undermining projectism and re-valuating the force of mythic thought, it teaches the wholeness of the World and an unbreakable interconnectedness between human mind and body, Earth and a bodily living Cosmos.

As mentioned earlier, the growing interest in astrology may not least be due to its special appeal to women. Identifying, perhaps, with the voices of the void, women engaged in the spiritual wave thus play an important role in post-industrial culture, tracing the knowledge which was and is so vehemently othered by 'real' science.

Although in very different ways, and despite different fixations in either modern or anti-modern conceptualizations of the relationship between subject and Other, mind and body/matter, fathering and mothering, both space flight and astrology discourses thus call attention to displacements of important thought-figures of the classical scientific world view. They do so separately. But in joining the two, through opening a discursive space for dialogue between them, the outlook is broadened. In a complex sense, this conversational space makes us aware of ourselves as the planetary and cosmic creatures that we are, according to both space flight and astrology.

Seen from the othered perspective of astrology, it becomes on the one hand very clear, how the projectism of space flight discourse is based on a denial of our ineradicable bodily connections with Earth and Cosmos. We are chtonic and cosmic beings in the very concrete bodily sense that our bodies are connected with basic existential ties to both Earth and Cosmos. We are Earth and Comos, and Earth and Cosmos are us. Separation is possible only in the illusory conditions of escape fantasies and virtual reality. Seen from the perspective of space flight, it is on the other hand obvious that astrology is rooted in a basic denial of the possibility of a subject-position towards Earth and Cosmos – a denial which seems somewhat outdated, given the history of the terraforming project of the mechanistic world view. The dialogue we set up between space flight and astrology discourse will therefore not position us dichotomously as subjects and masters of Earth and Universe or as their destined objects and innocent victims, but instead open a discursive space for a deepened understanding of our conditions as planetary and cosmically embodied subjects and objects.

Notes

1. This chapter is based on a larger research on 'Gender, Cosmos and New World Views'. The empirical part consists of interviews with female and male academic staff at the John F. Kennedy Space Center in the US and at the Institute for Cosmic Research in Moscow and with Russian and Danish astrologers.

2. Space flight discourse being so vehemently dominated by male voices makes 'his' the proper possessive pronoun.

3. The use of the concept of synchronicity in astrology is inspired by C.G. Jung.

4. The quote refers to the title of a book by Luce Irigaray (1979), the French philosopher and psychoanalyst whose theories on sexual difference and femininity have played a significant role for feminism. The theme of Irigaray's book is the early mother-daughter relationship. Our point is to emphasize the appropriateness of Irigaray's title as metaphor for the astrological concept of the existence of a synchronic relationship between psyche and physical world.

5. The theories of *'écriture féminine'*, a feminine writing closely related to the body, were primarily inspired by the works of French theorists, such as Luce Irigaray, Hélène Cixous and Julia Kristeva.

6. The word 'projectism', which aptly describes the replacement of reality with the project, is often used in post-Soviet discourse as synonymous with the mechanistic world picture.

7. In 1989 the membership comprised 125,000 individuals. This society is very actively lobbying the US politicians to increase the space budget.

8. The original sentence reads: 'The planet is the cradle of reason, but ...'; 'reason' evidently being the equivalent of 'mankind', the words have become interchangeable.

9. Ursul presupposes the development of new, non-polluting space shuttles as the existing ones seriously damage the ozone-layer.

10. Crick's wife tried, in vain, to persuade him of the non-scientific and phallocentric character of his panspermia-hypothesis, cf. 1981: 148-9.

11. Some of our women interviewees in Russia and Denmark confirmed this impression very clearly.

12. As this example of an astrological interpretation of correspondences between zodiacal signs, planets and genitals shows, a phallocentric logic is also to be found in astrology: the male genitals are seen as correspondent with genitals as such. Today, the patriarchal bias of astrology is criticized by feminist astrologers who try to reclaim what they consider as an old, female tradition. (River and Gillespie, 1987; Farrant, 1989)

13. In psychoanalysis the pre-Oedipal mother is defined as the omnipotent mother image of the earliest childhood.

References

Arrhenius, S. (1908) *Worlds in the Making*. Harper and Bros, New York.

Bachtin, M.M. (1984) *Rabelais and his World*. Indiana University Press, Bloomington.

Braidotti, R. (1991) *Patterns of Dissonance*. Polity Press, Cambridge.

Cassirer, E. (1922) *Die Begriffsform im Mythischen Denken*. Teubner, Leipzig and Berlin.

—— (1964) *Philosophie der symbolischen Formen, Zweiter Teil: Das mythische Denken*. Wissenschaftliche Buchgesellschaft, Darmstadt.

Crick, F.H.C. and L.E. Orgel (1973) 'Directed panspermia', in *Icarus* 19, pp. 341-6.

Crick, F. (1981) *Life Itself: Its Origin and Nature*. Simon and Schuster, New York.

Dyson, F. (1979) *Disturbing the Universe*. Harper and Row, New York.

Farrant, S. (1989) *Symbols for Women: A Matrilineal Zodiac*. Unwin Paperbacks, London.

Foucault, M. (1980) *The History of Sexuality*, vol. 1: *An Introduction*. Vintage/Random House, New York.

Greene, L. (1984) *The Astrology of Fate*. Allen and Unwin, London.

Haraway, D. (1989) *Primate Visions: Gender, Race, and Nature in the World of Modern Science*. Routledge, New York and London.

—— (1991) *Simians, Cyborgs, and Women: The Reinvention of Nature*. Free Association Books, London.

Hone, M. (1951) *The Modern Textbook of Astrology*. L.W. Fowler, London.

Irigaray, L. (1979) *Et l'une ne bouge pas sans l'autre*. Les éditions minuit, Paris.

Koval, A. and L. Desinov (1987) *Space Flights Serve Life on Earth*. Progress Publishers, Moscow.

Merchant, C. (1980) *The Death of Nature: Women, Ecology and the Scientific Revolution*. Harper and Row, New York.

Morgan, J.H. and J.M. Ragusa (1987) *Women: A Key Work Force in Preparation for Space Flight*. Paper for The Third International Interdisciplinary Congress on Women, Dublin, June.

Murray, B. (1989) *Journey into Space*. W.W. Norton, New York and London.

River, L. and S. Gillespie (1987) *The Knot of Time*. Harper and Row, New York.

Sjöö, M. (1992) *New Age and Armageddon: The Goddess or the Gurus? Towards a Feminist Vision of the Future*. The Women's Press, London.

Spangler, D. and W.I. Thompson (1991) *Reimagination of the World: A Critique of the New Age Science, and Popular Culture*. Bear and Company, Santa Fe.

Tsiolkovsky, K. (1960) *Beyond the Planet Earth*. Pergamon Press, London.

Turner, B.S. (1990) 'Periodization and Politics in the Postmodern', in Turner (ed.) *Theories of Modernity and Postmodernity*. Sage, London.

Ursul, A.D. (ed.) (1990) *Osvoenie kosmosa i problemy ekologii*. Shtiintsa, Kishinev.

Wilford, J. Noble (1969) *We Reach The Moon*. Bantam Books, New York and London.

9

Sustainable Development Through Women's Groups: A Cultural Approach to Sustainable Development

Corinne Wacker

Sustainable development

In common with many other terms in development politics, the term 'sustainable development' has been defined controversially and its meaning has changed over time. With the report of the Brundtland Commission (World Commission on Environment and Development, 1987) the environmental discourse shifted from a focus on remedial means to environmental degradation, to a preventive and human centred approach to sustainable development, a policy echoed by the IUCN/WWF/UNDP policy 1991. Sustainable development has been linked with concepts of justice, both within and between generations as well as within and between nations. As a normative concept, sustainable development requires a political system that gives communities an effective say over the resources on which they depend. It requires promoting citizens' initiatives, empowering people's organizations and strengthening local democracy.

Women and sustainable development

The Brundtland report makes only a brief reference to women and the environment. Within the debate on sustainable development 'the wealth of women's traditional knowledge and sound resource management is ignored/forgotten'. (Rodda, 1991: 77) Dankelman and Davidson (1988: xii) highlight the necessity to reorient development towards sustainability by putting rural women in the South – the principal victims of environmental degradation and the most underprivileged people – at the centre of consideration. Their responsibility for daily survival tasks qualifies them to be 'among the most important and best experienced actors in bringing about that sustainability'. (Dankelman and Davidson, 1988: xiii) Other authors perceive Southern women rather as contributors to environmental degradation. Both perceptions are linked to concepts of 'feminization of poverty', a concept that implies that development combined with a male bias has caused a relatively greater impoverishment among women. But gender blindness leads both to the glorification and humiliation of the relation between women and their environment (van de Hombergh, 1993: 20). Feminist researchers have pointed out the need to develop solutions out of the experiences of grassroots women and their organizations with their environment.

Sustainable development and people's participation

There has been little research relating the environment to social aspects and to the role of local people and their initiatives in finding solutions to the problem, rather than as obstacles to environmental improvement. The controversial use of the term 'participation', either as a goal in itself or as an instrument for project implementation might be one reason, and the fact that rural people are unlikely to perceive and articulate the problems which they face in everyday life as 'environmental problems' another. (Redclift, 1990: 14) The term participation is used here as defined by UNRISD (Pearse and Stiefel, 1979): 'the organized efforts to increase control over resources and regulative institutions in given situations, on the part of groups and movements of those hitherto excluded from such control.' Empirically, lack of participation is often linked with poverty and cultural degradation. In situations of powerlessness, rural people lack the means to secure access and control over natural resources as well as to enforce rules and regulations to ensure that their environment is not damaged by others. As Vivian (1992: 93) points out, 'poverty is rather a symptom of one of the primary underlying causes of local-level environmental decline in the Third World today; the disempowerment of local communities'.

Breakdown and redevelopment of resource management systems

As a result of the integration of local economies in the world market and of changes in the political and economic environment, local resource management systems need to be transformed and maintained or they may collapse. Excessive exploitation of natural resources or uneven access of community members to market opportunities, income and other sources of power can lead to the breakdown of legitimized rules of access and use of natural resources, leading in turn to poverty and the marginalization of weaker population segments who might then be forced illegally to exploit resources to meet their basic needs. Local management systems rely on institutional arrangements, defined by Gibbs and Bromley (1989: 22) as 'rules and conventions which establish peoples' relationships to resources, translating interests into claims, and claims into property rights'. The current discussion on property rights and sustainable development (Bromley, 1984; Gibbs and Bromley, 1989) focuses on the relevance of various categories of ownership of natural resources (such as state property, private property, common property) in resource conservation, ecological sustainability and livelihood security. Among these ownership types 'common-property rights are a special case of property rights which assure individual access to resources over which they have collective claims. Common property regimes are forms of management granted in a set of accepted social norms and rules for the sustainable and independent use of collective goods such as forests, grazing grounds, fisheries and water resources.' (Gibbs and Bromley, 1989: 22) This discussion focuses on a crucial aspect of women's participation in sustainable development, but the authors mentioned above neither include a gender perspective in analysing property rights nor discuss the relationship between property rights and user rights in natural resources within household and local communities. A gender analysis of resource rights which includes a differentiation between ownership and user rights might contribute to define viable strategies to enhance women's access to natural resources and their means to foster sustainable development. As Oboler (1985: 292) points out, rights in most resources for most societies do not reside exclusively with members of one sex. One must examine the structure of various parties' rights to resources, taking into account, where one sex has greater rights than the other over a particular resource, the size of the differential as well as the fact that it exists.

This chapter focuses on the effects on women of the transformation of the resource management system among Kikuyu agriculturalists in Kenya and discusses women's groups as institutions which 'redevelop' common property resource management systems among their members under new terms in a fragile ecological environment in Kenya.

Kenya's fragile environment

Most African soils are fragile, soil fertility is low and requires careful management. In African history complex farming systems have evolved, relying on experience, skills and labour input by the land managers. Women are central to African food systems south of the Sahara, and valued for their labour as well as for their potential to create it through childbearing, and customary rule dealt primarily with control over labour and with people in terms of membership in a group, lineage or clan. Complex, interlocking systems of reciprocal responsibilities were designed to spread risks and give a measure of insurance against calamity. These systems usually defined a balance between women's responsibility for agriculture and human capital production, and secured their access to such resources as land, labour and capital, necessary to fulfil their tasks. (Cloud and Knowles, 1988: 256)

The major agricultural zone of Kenya is located around Mt. Kenya; this is the home area of the Kikuyu people. In the 15 per cent of the country suitable for agriculture (Link, 1973: 5), 'female farming systems' (as defined by Boserup, 1970) have developed, involving the use of the hand-hoe in conjunction with patterns of shifting cultivation.

The Kikuyu resource management system

Around Mt. Kenya the Kikuyu, a lineage society, has developed a prosperous system of hoe and shifting agriculture based on intercropping up to 16 different crops and periods of fallow. The initial land clearing was men's responsibility, subsequent preparation of the soil, planting, cultivating and harvesting was women's work. Through clearing or purchase patrilineages acquired land rights. Under the trusteeship of the eldest, male, head of the patrilineage, sons at marriage were given a portion of their mother's garden for their wives to cultivate. (Sorrenson, 1967: 214) Within the polygamous household each wife was head of a matricentric unit composed of a house ('*nyumba*') and the garden ('*migunda*'). In pre-colonial Kikuyu society, land rights relied on two complementary principles: the management of common property (acquired by clearing and purchase) under the patrilineages; and individual land-user rights for each woman cultivator. Thus women's access to land was mediated through lineage and marriage, and women controlled the allocation of labour skills on the land.

Gender is a central concept in the traditional resource management system of Kikuyu culture. Gender conception is defined here as a functioning aspect of a cultural system through which actors manipulate, interpret, legitimate and reproduce the patterns of co-operation and conflict that order their social world. (Collier and Rosaldo, 1981: 311) Within the Kikuyu lineage mode of production, the gender roles were sharply differentiated, complementary and mutually dependent, rather than hierarchical. The status ascribed to women was dependent on their position in the age-grade system. The term '*nyakanua*' used in many women's groups today refers to the highest age-grade status of Kikuyu women, which they achieved after the circumcision of their first child. In traditional Kikuyu belief women are 'life givers' like the earth, and perpetuate the continuity between past and future generations. Men are 'life itself', as long as they relate through their women to the earth. Land is sacred and profane in one. According to their tribal legend, the divider of the universe, N'gai, dwelling temporarily on Mt. Kenya, founded the Kikuyu tribe as a matrilineal society of agriculturalists. But men overwhelmed the system in a *coup d'état* and installed patrilinearity with age-grades as the basis of kinship and tribal politics. (Kenyatta, 1938) Historians record this event to have occurred pre-17th century (Muriuki, 1974) when the Kikuyu, migrating originally from the interlacustrine area (Morgan, 1972) settled around

Mt. Kenya. Before the Kikuyu's southward expansion was halted by the British in the early 20th century, land was unlimited and the labour force and agricultural skills of prime value. Women monopolized agricultural skills, controlled the allocation of labour and the process of production of surplus, and decided what crops and how much to plant. Men had their own gardens where they produced only goods of social and ritual value, and also tended cattle grazed on communal land. Power, as defined by Weber, is 'the probability that one actor within a social relationship will be in the position to carry out his own will despite resistance, regardless of the basis on which this probability rests'. (Weber, 1947: 152) Authority is legitimized power. A person recognized by others as having the right to do so, can control resources and other persons by convincing them that a particular course of action is best. As the allocation of land following the patrilineage principle was based solely on use, women had a measure of real power in the economic organization of pre-colonial Kikuyu society. (Mackenzie, 1986: 386) Through marriage and childbirth women's authority increased and their structural position in the lineage was reinforced.

Environmental degradation, poverty and changes in gender relations

During Kenya's colonial period various factors affected Kikuyu women's access to land and other productive resources: the division of Kenya's fertile land into 'White Highlands' and 'African Reserves'; new cash crops; and land reform, as well as population growth led to land scarcity and ecological degradation in the Kikuyu Reserve. As women remained the main agricultural producers, their situation deteriorated. The colonial government's non-recognition of women's roles and organizations in Kikuyu culture affected the gender relationship among Kikuyu agriculturalists in a complex way, leading to a deterioration of women's control over resources, and a lowering of their status, wealth and authority.

After completion of the East African Railway, when the country was opened for European and South African settlement, colonial laws restricted Kikuyu agriculture within demarcated reserves. Taxes and wage labour regulations brought about a system of migrant labour economy (Stichter, 1982) in which some of the social costs of labour were subsidized by agricultural production in the Kikuyu Reserve. Until 1945, very few women were employed in wage labour. Gender roles among the Kikuyu varied, depending on families' type of involvement in the colonial economy. (Stichter, 1975/76) Men's temporary migration as wage labour on European farms increased women's workload and responsibility for agricultural production. (Kitching, 1980) A minority of Kikuyu men were able to invest their wage income and benefits from trade in cash crop production and in larger cattle herds, which brought pressure on communal grazing grounds and a realignment of land-user rights in which tenants' and women's user rights were reduced; this led to marginalization of poorer women's cultivations on steep slopes. Reduced fallow, new crops (maize, wattle), labour shortage and population increase resulted in land degradation and poverty. The process of class differentiation within Kikuyu culture resulted in social tensions, manifested in conflicts over customary rights and resource management systems, and were mainly responsible for driving Kikuyu families to seek employment as resident labourers (squatters) on European farms. Indeed, the Kikuyu were the main tribe involved in resident labour on European farms.

On European and South African settlers' large land holdings, squatters had land-use rights and a wage in exchange for labour days. The extent of squatters' land-user rights was the key factor in the labour struggles during the colonial period. While initially the system enabled Kikuyu squatters to achieve wealth and prosperity, labour arrangements later deteriorated. Between the first Resident Native Ordinance (1918) and that of 1937 (reinforced after World War II) squatters experienced a gradual proletarianization, loss of wealth and increased demands on their labour. Zwanenberg (1975), Kanogo (1987) and Furedi (1989) provide evidence that squatters' land-user rights were subject to price fluctuations on the world market. Increased income brought land owners to a position of power, which enabled them to invest in their agricultural enterprises and reduce the squatters' land-use rights. Furedi and Kanogo also note how squatters reproduced the Kikuyu cultural framework, including resource management institutions, in the White Highlands. But none of these authors analysed the consequences for women of the fluctuations in squatters' land-use rights. During my fieldwork in Laikipia District, Kikuyu squatter women explained how they gained and then lost their user rights to land, forests and swamps on European farms. In Laikipia, squatter women had rights to between one and three acres of land to cultivate, but they lost their land-user rights when their husbands were dismissed.

Breakdown of the traditional resource management system

Social tensions in the squatter community as well as in the Kikuyu Reserve culminated in the breakdown of the traditional resource management system, and led to a peasant revolt: 'Mau Mau'. Landlessness was a major factor in the Land and Freedom Army's armed struggle against colonialism and land alienation by the whites. Independence from colonial rule led to the removal of restrictions on African families buying land in the

European scheduled areas. In 1961, the opening of the White Highlands for African settlement on a basis of 'willing buyer, willing seller' meant that poor people – women, squatters and landless Kikuyu from the 'Reserve' – were rarely in a position to buy land. Kanogo (1987: 6) defines this land reform as 'ultimate disinheritance of the squatters'. Okoth-Ogendo (1981: 337) recorded two million landless people and estimated that their number increased by 1.5 per cent annually. For women, who represent only 18 per cent of wage labour (1983 in ILO, 1986: 33) and remain in low paid jobs, landlessness means poverty.

Under the state of emergency during 'Mau Mau' (1952-56) a governmental agricultural plan to control soil erosion and promote agricultural productivity was implemented, consisting mainly of land reform, involving the introduction of individual property ownership – the Swynnerton Plan; a process that continues in Kenya today. During the implementation of the plan, women's usufructual land rights under customary tenure were overlooked, with the result that the majority of Kenya's rural women are landless. (Byamukama, 1985: 17)

Kikuyu women today

In Kenya nine out of ten women live in rural areas, produce 80 per cent of the food and, substantially, cash crops and provide three-quarters of the labour used on smallholdings (World Bank, 1989: xv), but own title to only only five per cent of the land. (Davison, 1988: 157) As individualization of tenure progressed and pressure on land increased, women's usufructuary rights to land were no longer guaranteed. Although Kenya's post-independent Constitution acknowledges gender equity (Marina *et al.*, 1977), the law of succession relating to land and its products remained under the customary right of the different ethnic groups until 1984. The new law of succession accords women equal property-sharing rights upon their husbands' death, but lack of financial means and awareness prevent women from seeking the protection of their rights granted by the Constitution; without the support of parallel processes, the law has little practical effect. (May, 1985: 171) Thus, Kenyan women's legal position is still very insecure. Furthermore, in the present ethnic and political struggle in Kenya under deteriorating economic conditions, tribal land and inheritance rules are reinterpreted, reinforced and reframed by ethnic pressure groups in such a way, that women (for example, widows) lose their customary rights to access and use of resources such as land. (Stamp, 1991) Squeezed between these social forces, Kenyan rural women are losing their rights under both legal systems. As these women are the main farm managers, and responsible for the care of their families, this process leads to poverty and ecological degradation.

Kikuyu women maintained their responsibility over the livelihood of

their families and also retained a large measure of control over their labour.
(Stamp, 1975/76) But women's insecurity in the rural areas has increased
as a result of the individualization of land tenure, which leads to an
increasingly uneven distribution of land and also to incongruence between
different tenure systems. (Stamp, 1985: 29) Kikuyu women have a key
role in seed selection, planting, weeding and harvesting their plots. (Barnes, 1983: 59) In the process of social stratification in Kikuyu society,
decision-making on the farm shifted from men to women. (Kershaw,
1975/76: 179) Women still perceive themselves as having the prime
responsibility for the economy and well-being of their families but remain
dependent upon traditional tasks, as they lack access to the skills necessary
to participate equally in the changing economy. (Kariuki, 1984: 229)

Laikipia District

Today, one-third of Laikipia District's large scale-farms have been sold
and sub-divided into smallholdings ranging between 0.5 to 20 hectares.
Land transactions meant thousands of squatters lost their employment and
became illegal squatters on unsettled private land or in the forests. Population pressure, shortage of land and social tensions related to processes
of stratification among the Kikuyu in the former 'Reserves' – centring
around the issue of customary and modern land tenure – are major reasons
cited for Kikuyu families buying land in Laikipia District, despite its
unfavourable ecological conditions for farming. The resulting population
increase of 8 per cent per year leads to severe pressure on the ecological
carrying capacity of the area. Squatter and peasant women in Laikipia
produce crops in fragile ecological conditions, the soil erodes fast, rains
are unreliable, two out of four maize harvests fail, drawing water takes
between three and six hours daily, collecting firewood means facing the
risk of attacks by wildlife. In the dryer and poorer areas of the District, up
to 60 per cent of the smallholdings are headed by women.

Control over resources through women's groups

Women in Laikipia are not represented within the formal decision-making
institutions which make decisions about the resources on which the
women depend for their livelihood, but they participate indirectly by
influencing decision makers through their women's groups. Women's
groups formed by neighbouring farmers are the only formal organization
of rural women recognized by government ministries, donors and political
parties. Registered within the Ministry of Cultural and Social Affairs and
under the national KANU-Maendeleo Organization, women's groups
sometimes receive financial support from government and donor pro-

grammes. The groups, as we shall see, serve a crucial function in enabling rural women to gain access and control over resources. They generate resources mainly by their own efforts and involve themselves in legalizing their resource control by acquiring licences and land title deeds, and by gaining public recognition of the groups' resource control.

Women in Laikipia are joined into 354 women's groups, usually formed by 20-100 neighbours. The basis for affiliation is gender, neighbourhood and regular payment of monthly contributions in the form of cash and sometimes labour to the group. Resources controlled by the group are distributed equally among the members, and groups have clearly defined rules of operation and sanctions to maintain their control over common achievements and property. These groups cut across class barriers, involving squatter as well as peasant women. When large-scale farms are sold, these groups often collapse, to be redeveloped, often under a new name.

In pre-colonial Kikuyu society, woman were affiliated in kinship, clan, age-set and neighbourhood work groups (*ngwatio*) in which members cultivated each other's land. (Lambert, 1956: 67; Stamp, 1975/76) These groups also assumed wider political and social functions. Most of these forms of organization became informal and vanished under colonial control and post-colonial changes. While in traditional society women automatically became members of particular groups because of birth, age, sex, kinship and marriage, membership in today's groups is largely voluntary. In Mitero, Stamp (1975/76) observed continuity between past and present forms of Kikuyu women's organization, in Laikipia District too (see below). Reciprocity and sanctions are the crucial elements through which women's groups foster co-operation. Women's groups in Laikipia gain access over resources by involving members in rotating credit associations and negotiating legitimacy over the resources the group controls. Analytically this process consists mainly in transforming money and labour into gifts. In their rotating credit and labour associations the women bring money – which the members earned individually – and labour into the group. It passes through the chairperson in a ritualized procedure in which money and labour are equally distributed as a group gift to one member at a time; one by one all members get involved in a system of reciprocal gift exchange. The group tries to mobilize donations, licences and other contributions by outsiders. The group involves itself in a process of negotiation, which often includes substantial contributions in kind, labour, cash and time to build alliances with powerful outsiders: today, this is usually in the form of 'Harambee fund raisings' (under Kenyatta it was as dancing events) during which the groups address prominent persons whom they have previously contacted. In this public ritual the women's group receives recognition for their achievements and thus legitimacy for the resource control the group has achieved. After the event, everybody knows that the resource concerned is the legitimate property of the women's group, which then collects the title deeds and necessary licences from the government authorities. In Laikipia District 51 per cent of the women's groups gained access and control over, for example, natural resources, other means of production such as commercial plots and shops, as well as new skills, and maintained the group structure and control over the common property; 29 women's groups in Laikipia are involved in buying land for their members. The example presented below is one of the most successful group achievements in the District. It allows us to analyse the process of empowerment through which the group gained access and control over resources.

Mwenda-Niire women's group

This group was formed in 1963 by landless squatters on a large-scale European farm in Laikipia District. Within 20 years of saving funds, working together, politics and negotiating with authorities the women's group brought the farm (567 ha) into its possession, enabling 130 landless families to gain access to land. The group history was narrated by the group leader and was later translated and summarized.

The group leader Virginia was one of the wives of squatter employees on the farm. Only men were employed. Squatter women had user-rights to cultivate a one-acre plot and organized themselves to cultivate the gardens in common (*ngwatio*), following Kikuyu tradition. They also visited squatter women on other large-scale farms. The leader's mother, living in the Kikuyu Reserve in Nyeri, was a member of a Nyakenua Mabati Group, involved in a credit circle buying iron sheets for its members.

While visiting her mother and her group, Virginia decided to form a group among squatter women in the White Highlands and also to buy iron sheets. She travelled to other large-scale farms and 40 women became members of the group, some of whom were previously involved in knitting and sewing activities in Maendeleo ya Wanawake Clubs. Every month the group collected 20 cents from its members to buy iron sheets for roofing.

The Community Development Assistant would not authorize them to register as group as they had no land on which to build iron-sheet covered houses and no right to improve their squatter houses on the farm. Consequently, they realized that they must buy land. They therefore organized casual labour arrangements and earned two (Kenyan) shillings/day (by cultivating), which they kept in a group bank account.

In 1970 the group met a person who was willing to sell land. Their leader went to Nairobi to seek assistance on the procedures and information on land buying from the area's Member of Parliament. Various trips and invitations followed; the group was often misled but sometimes assisted in its project by outsiders.

During this period the group was also involved (as were many others at that time) in performing traditional dances for President Kenyatta. Each Chief brought 'his' women's group to Nakuru, where they danced and praised the President. The group members met other women's groups and learned that they could present their claims and needs through their songs directly to the President. The traditional *Dumo* and *Gichuka* Kikuyu dances include singers and the groups sang about their landlessness and about their children who had no school on the farm.

Back home the group began to cultivate maize and potatoes among the owner's crops. When this was discovered, the owner threatened to beat them, but the women raised their 'pangas' (big knives for cultivating) shouting: 'With these knives we fought for independence but we never had land, now we have found our land, it is here'. Subsequently, the group was involved in various clashes with the farm owner, for example, by illegally erecting a school on his farm and employing a teacher. And every month the group reported the events in new songs to the President.

That the farm owner destroyed the illegal school was decisive for what followed. President Kenyatta, hearing about it in the group's song, sent them a message asking if they had 60,000 Ksh in their account. They had only 3,000 Ksh, but the chairperson replied, 'Yes'. From then on the group increased its monthly contributions and involved new members, while continuing to struggle against the farm owner. Once it was known that the farm owner would sell his land, land speculators increased its price. Finally, however, the group acquired the title deeds.

At a public group meeting each member decided in whose name the land should be registered. Women without children said their own name, the others their husband's and son's (according to Kikuyu custom). The land was divided according to each member's contribution. Each received part of the swamp and part of the dry land.

Once settled the group started new projects, for example, digging drainage canals in common, and the members continued cultivating for each other. Some women formed new groups for other projects such as buying home utensils, constructing water tanks and knitting sweaters. When the leader became old, she gave her group shares to her daughter, but remained a member of honour in all women's groups in New Mutaro and continues to advise newer groups. She said that many women have shares in several groups for themselves as well as for born and unborn daughters for when they are adult and able to benefit from the group projects.

Many elements from traditional Kikuyu culture were reproduced in this group: organization in a gender distinct group; authority and leadership by an elder woman (*nyakenua*); farming shared among members (*ngwatio*);

the rules of allocating land and resources between the genders; land titles to men. Control of labour, infrastructure and produce of the land were kept by the women's group and inherited by women of the next generation.

After an initial phase as an informal institution conforming to traditional custom, the group changed, through its contacts with formal authorities, into a social movement, through which the women realized, first, increase in control of resources, then legitimacy over them. The group then consolidated into an institution which mediates between customary resource management rules and modern laws. Its success relies on its skills in mediating between both systems, deriving power from the one to achieve authority in the other.

To maintain the autonomy to mediate between customary and modern institutions seems thus to be a crucial factor allowing women's groups to redevelop resource management systems through which they regain access to resources which they had been deprived of during the colonial and post-colonial transformations in Kenya. Some groups maintain collective control over resources (of the type of 'common property'); others transform the resources acquired through the groups into a private property resource of each member.

Conclusion

Empowerment is about self-organization. 'Self-organization and democratization may do nothing for sustainable development in itself, but provide a type of enabling environment which makes progress along the path of sustainable development a real possibility.' (Utting, 1993: 171)

Through empowerment, groups become social movements and as such, they can obtain or regain access to their environment's resources to meet their livelihood needs; but only if the movement consolidates into an institution with legitimized control over the management of natural resources can an important precondition for sustainable development be met. Only then can the members adapt their production to the ecological conditions of their environment. To achieve long-term rights over resources is a crucial precondition for women to enhance their involvement in sustainable development.

In the example presented above, the members would probably have faced destitution and been forced to resort to short-term, illegal resource-use in Laikipia (as illegal squatters), had they not succeeded in organizing themselves and thereby achieved long-term rights over the land. Their success stems from the group itself as well as from a political environment, on a national level, which supports women's aims to regain access over resources.

Kenya's colonial and post-colonial history of land rights can be seen as a process of 'enclosure' of natural resources, which led to the exclusion of women's rights of access and use of natural resources. Major elements of the process of 'enclosure' were the colonial division of Kenya's fertile land into White Highlands and African Reserves, land reform, and the erosion of squatter land-use rights on large-scale estates.

The current discussion on property rights and sustainable development focuses on the relevance of various types of ownership of natural resources (such as state, private, or common property) in resource conservation and sustainable development as defined by the Brundtland Commission. In a historical situation which led to a collapse of Kikuyu women's access and control over natural resources, the achievements of Kikuyu women's groups in Laikipia can be defined as a grassroots 'redevelopment' of resource-management systems which 'encloses' resources for the poor. Within the nation-wide conflict between customary and modern land and inheritance rights in Kenya, small, local women's groups resolve this conflict by finding creative means to redevelop an institution rooted in customary law and legitimized under modern law. This institution is of crucial importance for sustainable resource-management in a fragile ecological environment such as Laikipia District.

References

Barnes, Carolyn (1983) 'Women in Kenya's Rural Economy', in A. Pala *et al.* (eds) *The Participation of Women in Kenya Society*. Nairobi Literature Bureau, Nairobi.

Boserup, Esther (1970) *Women's Role in Economic Development*. St. Martin's Press, New York.

Bromley, Daniel W. and Devenda P. Chapagain (1984) 'The Village Against the Center: Resource Depletion in South Asia', in J. Amer (ed.) *Resource Management in Developing Agriculture*. American Agricultural Economics Association.

Byamukama, James (1985) *Land Law Reform and Women's Property Rights in Land in Kenya*. Osgoode Hall Law School, Working Paper No. 14. African Human Rights Research Association, Ontario.

Cloud, Kathleen and Jane B. Knowles (1988) 'Where Can We Go From Here? Recommendations for Action', in Jane Davison (ed.) *Agriculture, Women and Land: The African Experience*. Westview Special Studies on Africa, USA.

Collier, Jane F. and Michelle F. Rosaldo (1981) 'Politics and Gender in Simple Societies', in Sherry B. Ortner and Harriet Whitehead (eds) *Sexual Meaning: The Cultural Construction of Gender and Sexuality*. Cambridge University Press, Cambridge.

Dankelmann, Irene and Joan Davidson (1988) *Women and Environment in the Third World: Alliance for the Future*. Earthscan Publications, London.

Davison, Jane (1988) 'Who owns What? Land Registration and Tension in Gender Relations in Kenya', in Jane Davison (ed.) *Agriculture, Women and Land: The African Experience*. Westview Special Studies on Africa, USA.

Furedi, Frank (1989) *The Mau Mau War in Perspective*. James Currey, London, Heinemann (Kenya), Nairobi, and Ohio University Press, Athens, USA.

Gibbs, Christopher J.N. and Daniel W. Bromley (1989) 'Institutional Arrangements for Management of Natural Resources: Common-Property Regimes', in Fikert Berkes (ed.) *Common-Property Resources: Ecology and Community Based Sustainable Development*. Belhaven Press, London.

International Labour Organization (ILO) (1986) *Women's Employment Patterns, Discrimination and Promotion of Equity in Africa: The Case of Kenya*. Jobs and Skills Programme for Africa, Addis Ababa.

IUCN/WWF/UNDP. The World Conservation Union (1991) *Caring for the Earth: A Strategy for Sustainable Living*. Gland, Switzerland.

Kanogo, Tabithia (1987) *Squatters and the Roots of Mau Mau*. James Currey, London and Heinemann (Kenya), Nairobi.

Kariuki, P. (1984) 'Women's Aspiration and Perception of their own Situation in Society', in Gideon S. Were (ed.) *Women and Development in Africa*. Gideon S. Were Press, Nairobi.

Kenyatta, Jomo (1938) *Facing Mount Kenya*. Secker and Warburg, London.

Kershaw, Greet (1975/76) 'The Changing Roles of Men and Women in the Kikuyu Family by Socioeconomic Strata', in *Rural Africana*, no. 29, Winter.

Lambert, H.E. (1956) *Kikuyu Social and Political Institutions*. Oxford University Press, London.

Link, Heinrich (1973) *Die Besitzreform von Grossfarmen im Hochland von Kenya. Analyse und Erfolgsbeurteilung. Forschungsberichte der Afrika-Studienstelle ifo 43*. Institut für Wirtschaftsforschung. Weltforum Verlag, Munich.

Mackenzie, Fiona (1986) 'Local Initiatives and National Policy: Gender and Agricultural Change in Murang'a District, Kenya', in *Canadian Journal of African Studies*.

May, Joan and Joyce Kazembe (1985) 'Beyond Legislation' in Gideon S. Were (ed) *Women and Development in Africa*. Gideon S. Were Press, Nairobi.

Marina M. *et al.* (1977) 'Law and the Status of Women in Kenya', in Columbia Human Rights Review, *Law and the Status of Women*, New York.

Morgan, W.T.W. (ed.) (1972) *East Africa: Its Peoples and Resources*. Oxford University Press, Nairobi, London and New York.

Oboler, Regina Smith (1985) *Women, Power, and Economic Change: The Nandi in Kenya*. Stanford University Press, California.

Okoth-Ogendo, H.W.O. (1981) 'Land Ownership and Land Distribution in Kenya's Large-Scale Areas', in P. Killick (ed.) *Papers on the Kenyan Economy: Performance. Problems and Policies*. Heinemann Educational Books Ltd, Nairobi.

Redclift, Michael (1990) 'Sustainable Development and Popular Participation: A Framework for Analysis', in D. Ghai and J.M. Vivian (eds) *Grassroots Environmental Action: People's Participation in Sustainable Development*. Routledge, London and New York.

Rodda, Annabel (1991) *Women and the Environment*. Zed Books, London.

Sorrenson M.P.K. (1967) *Land Reform in the Kikuyu Country: A Study of Government Policy*. Makerere Institute of Social Research, Makerere University. Oxford University Press, Nairobi.

Stamp, Patricia (1975/76) 'Perceptions of Change and Economic Strategy among Kikuyu Women in Mitero, Kenya', in *Rural Africana*, no. 29, Winter.

—— (1985) 'Kikuyu Women's Self Help Groups: Towards an Understanding of the Relations between Sex-Gender Systems and Mode of Production in Africa', in C. Robertson and I. Berger (eds) *Women and Class in Africa*. Holmes and Meier, New York.

—— (1991) 'Burying Otieno: The Politics of Gender and Ethnicity in Kenya', in *Signs: Journal of Women in Culture and Society*, vol. 16, no. 4, Summer. University of Chicago Press.

Stichter, Sharon (1975/76) 'Women and the Labor Force in Kenya 1895-1964', in *Rural Africana*, no. 29, Winter.

—— (1982) *Migrant Labour in Kenya: Capitalism and African Response 1895-1975*. Longman, Harlow, Essex.

The Swynnerton Plan (1956) R.J.M. Swynnerton, *Plan to Intensify the Development of African Agriculture in Kenya* and *The East African Royal Commission Report 1953-55*. Government Printers, London and Nairobi.

Utting, Peter (1993) *Trees, People and Power*. Earthscan Publications, London.

van de Hombergh, Heleen (1993) *Gender, Environment and Development: A Guide to Literature*. International Books, Utrecht.

Vivian, Jessica M. (1992) 'Foundations for Sustainable Development: Participation, Empowerment and Local Resource-Management', in D. Ghai and J.M. Vivian (eds) *Grassroots Environmental Action: Peoples' Participation in Sustainable Development*. Routledge, London and New York.

Weber, Max (1947) *The Theory of Social and Economic Organizations*, ed. Talcott Parsons. Oxford University Press, New York.

World Bank (1989) *A World Bank Country Study. Kenya: The Role of Women in Economic Development*. World Bank, Washington DC.

WCED (1987) *Our Common Future*. Oxford University Press, Oxford and New York.

van Zwanenberg, R. and A. King (1975) *An Economic History of Kenya and Uganda*. Humanities Press, New Jersey.

PART THREE

Politics and Resistance in the Sustainable Development Debate

10

Women and the Politics of Sustainable Development

Sabine Häusler

Introduction

Over a year after the United Nations Conference on Environment and Development, UNCED, it seems timely to reflect on the experience of the UNCED process in general and women's roles in it in particular. This chapter attempts to analyse the political process that is accompanying the new quest for sustainable development with particular reference to women's stakes in this process.

These are some of the questions I would like to raise: What did the women involved in UNCED achieve? What were the problems and shortcomings? What have we learned from the experience? What implications do the answers to these questions have for our strategies and actions now and in the future? And finally, what roles can researchers play in women's struggles around environmental issues in the future?

The experience of UNCED and the NGO Global Forum

In the 1970s and 1980s many non-governmental organizations (NGOs) and different social movements both in the South and the North started to be active on the margins of the dominant Western development model. They sought to formulate and implement alternatives to the mainstream export-led growth model of economic development that has led to an exploitation of both natural resources and human beings, in particular women. Over the years they became a force to be reckoned with and wielded considerable influence – both in practice and even more on the level of presenting powerful alternative discourses.

The development establishment in the North and its satellites in the South were engaged in gradually incorporating these valid criticisms. They co-opted ideas from the margins into their discourses and political agendas. A considerable proportion of Northern development funds was shifted from ineffective and slow Southern government bureaucracies to international and national NGOs, in the hope of making development more 'people'-oriented – the major point of criticism of mainstream development. Development projects thus became cheaper because NGOs do not require highly paid development experts and equipment. Meanwhile the pressure of criticism was reduced and large-scale development projects geared at industrializing the South continued.

In response to the accelerating global crisis of environment and development, in 1989 the United Nations passed a resolution to organize UNCED. The goal was to steer the world onto a path of 'sustainable development'. Within the preparatory process a new mode of 'partnership' and 'dialogue' between an increasing number of actors came into being. For the first time the UN opened the way for a large group of non-governmental actors to participate in the preparatory process for a UN conference.

These new actors on the global scene were different citizens' movements from the North and the South, women, indigenous people, environment and development NGOs, as well as business and industry. Even the most radical critics of the development model felt the need to use this opportunity to influence mainstream agendas directly. The different groups with very different agendas were lumped together as the 'independent sector' by the architects of the NGO Global Forum held parallel to UNCED. The fact that the term NGO was only vaguely defined, namely as any group which is not a governmental organization, led to the paradoxical situation of transnational corporations fighting for their interests rubbing shoulders with the Amazonian Indians, women's groups and so on – all in the same forum. The different groups organized in the independent sector engaged in several separate preparatory processes for UNCED and as a result reached a new level of co-operation and exchange.

The different groups used a two-fold strategy: on the one hand they lobbied their governments in the preparatory process for UNCED to incorporate their respective demands into governmental negotiations about global environmental regimes; on the other hand they prepared for their independent input into the NGO Global Forum.

The citizens' movements drafted treaties reflecting their visions for a sustainable world, alternative and additional to those proposed by the mainstream actors of UNCED. The Business Council for Sustainable Development, representing some of the environmentally most destructive industries and businesses, organized themselves and proposed reformative self-regulation of their own activities. Other non-governmental organizations, including the development and environment organizations, religious groups, youth organizations, scientists, the World Bank, UNEP, FAO and other UN agencies, prepared their own proposals for a sustainable future. All of these and more were given a space within the NGO Global Forum.

The net result of UNCED as a whole is a failure of global proportions. The UNCED Agenda 21 and the treaties are non-binding. One of the major winners of UNCED is the World Bank which is now managing the major financial mechanism for sustainable development projects to the South, the Global Environmental Facility (GEF). Northern governments got away with continuing business as usual – with minor improvements. One concession from Northern political leaders was commitments to transfer funds into the GEF; Northern aid agencies will reshape their aid policies so as to scale up environmental development projects in the South. Southern political leaders asserted their right to more Western-style development and hence a continued flow of aid funds.

Through their effective lobbying and advocacy of governments, transnational corporations escaped stringent control mechanisms to regulate their activities in the future. Citizens' movements had next to no influence on fundamentally changing mainstream agendas. They were invited to 'co-operate', but in effect it was only their language that was incorporated into the documents, while the nature of these documents remained largely conservative in respect of the present economic and political order. A large-scale co-option process of critical citizens' groups was in full swing during the UNCED process. However, the main success of citizens' movements was an increase in exchange with like-minded groups globally and a new level of – in particular electronic – communication. What will happen with the citizens' movements' alternative treaties, including the Women's Action Agenda 21, which were meant to be guidelines for future actions, remains unclear at this point. A great number of groups continue to monitor their governments' implementation of changes proposed in the UNCED Agenda 21, the new Commission on Sustainable Development and future international conferences, in the hope of influencing their agendas.

In short, 'sustainable' development has become the latest stage in the development discourse which has shown once again its incredible capacity to survive against all odds. We live in a global economic and political order in which mainstream actors will go on doing business as usual – touched up in 'green'. A new eco-cratic rationality is forcefully asserting itself.

Looking back on the experience, the most important lesson of UNCED is to understand the new and more sophisticated strategies of power that have developed within the process. Within the 'partnership' and 'dialogue' model of consultation with the independent sector, it has become obvious that marginal actors such as women, indigenous people and other citizens' groups have been not been able to change the parameters of discussion. The lobbying activities of citizens' groups and NGOs at the UNCED preparatory committee meetings were based on pre-set agendas – which, in effect, critics could only help to 'improve' in formulation – within the set parameters. Hence, elements of alternative development discourse were early on incorporated into mainstream discourse. The same holds true for gendered language in the documents.

By taking part in the whole process, including the NGO Global Forum, many of the radical critics indirectly legitimized it. Poor media coverage of the dissenters from the environmentally destructive mainstream development model assembled far away from the main venue of UNCED in Rio de Janeiro, effectively silenced their criticism. In the few press reports transmitted from the Global Forum, the emphasis was on portraying hopeless idealists, exotic Indians and groups of emotional women. During the UNCED process many NGOs promoting ideas suited to the interests of powerful funders and mainstream actors gained access to funding and now increasingly resemble the mainstream in their language and practice.

The great willingness of the different citizens' movements and groups to act as a united force against the mainstream may have been counter-productive in the end. They made it all the more easy for the architects of UNCED, and in particular the NGO Global Forum, effectively to manage and contain their discontent. So successful was this process that UN conferences in the future will operate after the same model of consultation with the 'independent sector'.

Within the political climate of the early 1990s, the results of UNCED seriously put into question the feasibility of changing dominant institutions from within. One of the main concerns today is whether 'dialogue' between radical critics and mainstream institutions is still possible without the former being co-opted into dominant political and economic frameworks and pre-set agendas. In the final analysis critics may end up being changed by them, instead of the other way around.

As Donna Haraway (1988) has pointed out, the powers of today no longer work by simple domination and normalization (into the Western mode of development); power today works through networking, communications redesign and stress management. I think the UNCED process has been a formidable illustration of Haraway's point.

These reflections raise serious questions about what the alternatives of today and the futures chosen by those who do not want to be 'normalized' and 'networked' into the global economic and political order could look like. Can there still be alternatives outside this all-pervasive global economic and political system? Are we not all part of it already? Do the alternatives have to be lived and fought for in spaces within it? or within ourselves? Realistically speaking, the visions of citizens' movements, including the Women's Action Agenda 21, will not become reality in any foreseeable future. We will have to live with this recognition. The challenge is to keep up critical positions to the dominant model of development while continuing to resist becoming co-opted into the very framework of thinking on which it rests. One of the most important tasks is to continue to make visible the ways in which the strategies of power operate and their increasing sophistication, and to analyse how they work in practice. Strategies for change have to start from a realistic assessment of the situation as it is, follow the full complexity and the constantly shifting grounds on which the issues are fought, and still allow room for action on all levels.

The new and ever more sophisticated methods developed by communication specialists who are in the business of managing and engineering consent – the technical term for this is issues management – need to be watched carefully. The new communication strategies aim at shaping public discourse by setting agendas rather than directly reacting to dissent. Some of the techniques used by the engineers of consent are: the silencing of critics by depicting them as 'confrontational' or 'irresponsible', by depoliticizing the issues and casting them in technocratic terminology, by diverting attention through pushing issues of secondary importance, or by fudging crucial issues brought up by critical actors. (Keysers and Richter, 1993)

The need to involve women on all levels and in all aspects of decision-making and action has been recognized by all mainstream actors in the UNCED process. However, their mention of women, indigenous people, children and other marginalized groups in the UNCED documents may have been just the promotion of an issue of secondary importance in order to make their documents more acceptable to a gullible public and thus divert attention from their reluctance to accept fundamental changes within the present economic and political world order. The UNCED formula for the independent sectors' 'participation' was so successful that it will be used for the upcoming UN conferences.

Women as actors in the UNCED process

Women as a group gained their official mandate to take part in the UNCED process in the middle of 1991, at a relatively late stage when preparations were already in full swing. Through the activities of a handful of internationally known women, in particular the International Policy Action Committee (IPAC), mobilization of a sizeable number of women to take part in the process was assured. In this mode of mobilizing wider support for women to be heard within the UNCED and Global Forum proceedings and women's roles in environmental management, their 'natural' closeness to nature and hence their special knowledge about environmental processes were stressed. The prevailing image of women as agents fighting the effects of the global ecological crisis cast them as *the* answer to the crisis: women as privileged knowers of natural processes, resourceful and 'naturally' suited to provide the 'alternative'.

A large number of case studies of women active and successful in environmental struggles was compiled for the Women's Tribunal, held in Miami in 1991. The Women's Action Agenda 21, containing a vision for alternative development from women's perspectives globally was the outcome of the Miami Conference. This document is unique in many ways: for the first time women across the divides of North/South, race, class and from a variety of professional and social backgrounds agreed on a common position which refuted the Western model of development as such.

A number of women were very actively lobbying country delegates at the preparatory committee meetings for the inclusion of women in the UNCED documents. The whole UNCED Agenda 21 was screened for gendered language, and chapter 24 on women as a major group to be strengthened in bringing about sustainable development was included. The proceedings at Planeta Femea within the NGO Global Forum in Rio made clear that the prevailing ecofeminist position had been a powerful way to mobilize and unite women across all divides. It has allowed women forcefully to voice their criticisms within UNCED.

Looking back on the experience of women organizing within the UNCED process a year after the Earth Summit, what were the problems? The mobilization phase before UNCED was too short effectively to work out alternative visions of a larger group of women than the few thousand that were actively involved in the process. The ecofeminist position that came to prominence in the process may have been a powerful move to unite women, but the differences between women were set aside when they saw the need to present a united position. But a sometimes too simple reversal of hierarchies of men over women and the reproduction of old patterns of domination among different groups of women were the result. I think here in particular of the passionate speech given by a black Brazilian woman at the end of the proceedings at *Planeta Femea*, who brought up the question of racism between women in the Brazilian women's movement.

Yet, during the UNCED process the longstanding stalemate of opposition between women from the North and the South has been softened and women across these divides have learned that they can fruitfully work together. It has been my personal experience in many different meetings and fora that women involved in WED issues show a great openness to work together with women from other cultural and political backgrounds.

Analysing the experience of UNCED we need to ask ourselves: Who participated in the UNCED process? What political frameworks do the different women participating think in? Whom did these women represent? Broad-based coalition-building with other groups and movements, clarification of their political positions and mobilization of grassroots women within national settings remain a major challenge after UNCED for women active in the struggles for sustainable livelihoods for all people.

A question mark must hover over the many success stories presented in Miami. Do they still continue to be successful or have they already faltered by now? When everything in society works to marginalize women, how good are the chances for their successful actions to be sustainable in the long run?

Another phenomenon should make us suspicious: Virtually all actors within the UNCED process – NGOs, citizens' movements, the Business Council for Sustainable Development, governments, the World Bank, UN and aid agencies – agreed that women need to be involved in sustainable development. Hence women's aims were also accepted by those actors who have a distinct interest in preserving the dominant mode of development. In fact, in many cases, inclusion of women seems to have been one way of making their texts more widely acceptable.

Considering the net results of UNCED, it is likely that women in the South in particular will become further targets of development policies for sustainable development. The past experience of such development projects has shown that they put more strain on already overworked rural women without necessarily leading to much-needed wider legal and political changes for these women. Also, a stepping-up of population programmes geared mainly at women in the South and women of colour in the North and South alike is underway.

The women's vision presented in the Women's Action Agenda 21 and the other NGO treaties drafted at the NGO Forum in Rio are beautiful and powerful, but how realistic is their implementation? The activities of different women and women's groups after UNCED seem to be heading in two directions: either geared towards the integration of women into the mainstream of sustainable development as expressed in the UNCED Agenda 21, or to a criticism of the Western development model as such as expressed in the Women's Action Agenda 21. Much of the lobbying after UNCED of, for example, the Commission on Sustainable Development is geared at integration of women: equal gender representation within the board, and so on.

The struggles within the women's movement on the question of reproductive rights vs. feminist population control programmes within the preparatory process for the 1994 UN Conference on Population and Development illustrates the problem of differences between women. Much can be learned from the recent struggles and extrapolated to other struggles over environmental issues. A deep split is currently running through the women's movement on the not-so-new question of integration vs. autonomy, or – to borrow from the Greens – realism ('realos') vs. fundamentalism ('fundies'). Further studies of the sophisticated processes of co-option of feminist women into the project of the powerful population control lobby are much needed.

Within the present political climate, can we still hope to change the dominant institutions from within without being trapped by having to argue with them within their frameworks – and without being changed by them in the process? How do the alternative visions of development as proposed in the Women's Action Agenda 21 and the integrative position proposed in chapter 24 on women in the UNCED Agenda 21 relate to each other if we agree that the most effective road to sustainable development must be to change the parameters of the framework itself? These are old questions within the women's movement, but we are not much closer to answering them now than we were a decade ago. The answers to these questions and strategies for the future need to take into account the experiences of women organizing within UNCED and the newly emerging methods of co-option and manipulation.

The question arises whether all or most of our efforts should concentrate on the 1994 Population Conference, the 1995 Conference on Women and Development, or the many UN conferences that will come up in the next few years, or whether we should spend a large part of our energies in building up some more lasting organizational structures that can have a long-term impact and survive such mega-events. We need time and space to experiment further with alternative ways of being, thinking, acting and relating to one another. Also, more analytical clarity on conceptual issues regarding women's alternatives to development is needed.

Future research on women and environment-related issues

I do not mean to imply that research can in any way assume a privileged role in the struggle for sustainable livelihood of all people globally. We need a clearer idea of who is doing what, in terms of action, research and policy formulation, and where are the crucial gaps that need to be filled.

What role can research play in the struggles ahead? Starting out from women's lives, the epistemological sensibility of feminist researchers should further help and strengthen grassroots women North and South to determine their own agendas for change. Recent developments within feminist research methodologies need to be considered. The emphasis should be on situated knowledges. In this sense, research could take a strategic role in support of alternatives proposed by people at the grassroots. A lot of work on the theoretical level needs to be done in order to provide the conceptual basis for alternative visions of development and help grassroots people's experience to influence the theoretical discussions of the architects of 'sustainable' development. Many of the newly emerging alternative discourses and proposals for change lack women's and feminist perspectives. Further criticism of Western science and technology as the solution to the crisis from feminist positions is much needed.

Research on women and environment-related issues within the last two decades has been mainly about women in the South in the context of development work. The vast majority of earlier studies focused on either proving or disproving women's inherently closer connection to nature and their 'natural' interest in safeguarding their environment. Today this question no longer seems relevant; we know that women suffer disproportionately from the many different manifestations of the global ecological crisis. In any event, the question of women's relation to nature/the environment has to remain open-ended. Women's own perception of their relation to nature and their motives for getting involved in ecological action may vary according to cultural, religious or ideological backgrounds, across the division of North and South. The question is no longer what is the 'correct' position on the woman/nature relation, but rather how we situate ourselves as women and agents committed to fundamental change of the Western development model within the present crisis and how our actions and struggles can be most effective. Within the politics of rainbow coalitions, what are effective strategies to preserve people's, and in particular women's, interests?

There is now widespread recognition that development is not just a problem of the South, but a global problem. Frameworks of analysis have to be grounded in the perspective of a global crisis that manifests in different forms in the different regions of the world. At issue for sustainability are relationships of power at all levels, the bargaining power of different groups of people and their different knowledges (see Chapter 16 below). Sustainability implies a questioning of what kinds of lives we wish to lead and what kind of development we want.

Research challenges

One of the major challenges remains to provide inroads into dismantling the Western framework of thinking itself. Women researchers in mainstream natural as well as social sciences have a crucial role in further challenging their disciplines' Western, white, male frameworks of thinking and, accordingly, the solutions and policies they propose for environmental reforms. The implicit values and ideologies behind environmental managerialism need to be further disclosed and challenged. Feminist philosophers, scholars within cultural studies and in particular non-Western feminists could provide further fundamental criticism of Western, patriarchal, Enlightenment thinking that is at the very root of the crisis of environment and development. On a theoretical level, the vantage point of women and environment has been a particularly useful perspective from which to criticize the Western development model. Non-Western feminists could make important contributions in challenging the almost all-pervasive Western framework of thinking, not from within its own parameters, but from genuinely non-Western modes of thinking. The development indicators applied at present to assess human well-being may thereby be dismantled as highly reductionist; the validation of local people's experiential knowledge about natural processes also falls into this category.

Western-type environmental education for sustainable development extended to Southern people must be questioned and challenged if the sustainability of existing non-Western lifestyles and modes of living is taken seriously. However, the tendency to romanticize such lifestyles must be avoided.

Further co-operation between Western, Eastern and Southern researchers will be crucial in the future. Networking of researchers, policy-makers and activists engaged around different environmental regimes, such as biodiversity, forests, climate change and so on, is necessary to monitor and keep up the analysis of these highly dynamic fields and constantly shifting terrains. Ever more complex amounts of information produced within international conferences and negotiations need to be processed, analysed and made available to action groups. Very often such analysis lacks a feminist perspective. Hence, this is an area of specialization for feminist researchers. Together, activists, policy-makers and researchers could think through the effects of international developments in these fields and devise effective strategies for action on different levels.

In order to bring women's issues into macro-frameworks of analysis, conceptual work is needed to link women's experience at the micro-level to macro-level theory. Some of these are issues regarding international trade agreements, the neo-classical economic framework, high-tech agriculture, commercially oriented forestry, industrial fishery, and so on. People's, and in particular women's, initiatives and self-determined ways of managing natural resources need to be strengthened where they exist by providing conceptual foundations for their validity and long-term sustainability in order to challenge the environmentally highly destructive practices in the fields mentioned above. Also, further sex-segregated data collection is necessary fully to reflect women's contribution to the economy. Work on alternative economic frameworks, for example, that will take into account the real costs of women's work and nature's destruction is needed to provide the basis for development alternatives. The challenge here is to strike a balance between accounting 'real' costs while keeping in mind intrinsic and non-accountable values.

Careful analysis and monitoring of the politics of sustainable development and how power relations unfold, shift and assert themselves are needed. It is necessary to keep an overview of the political process in general and women's stakes in it. We also have to grapple with the question of women's politics and politics between women. How can women from different backgrounds and from different cultures work together more closely without reproducing the old patriarchal structures of domination? Can we make each other accountable as we work on transformative projects? How can we avoid marginalization of women by women? Certainly, a mere redefinition of power by women which emphasizes women's values and culture may not be sufficient to tackle this issue.

Conclusion

These few reflections have made it clear that the UNCED process and the emerging politics of sustainable development present formidable challenges to everyone genuinely interested in sustainable livelihoods for all people. For women active in environmental struggles the real challenges still lie ahead; the small successes achieved so far need to be fought for continuously. Alliances and bridges built between women and other actors interested in fundamental transformations of development globally need to be nurtured carefully as a long-term project. Looking back to the early 1970s when the interest in women's role in the management of natural resources first emerged and reflecting on the last two decades since then, we have come a long way in the WED debate and practice. However, the phase of global mobilization of women around environmental issues which started in the early 1990s within the UNCED preparatory process will have to move into a new phase.

References

Alliance of Northern People for Environment and Development, (ANPED) (1992) *Agenda Ya Wananchi, Citizens' Action Plan for the 1990s*, Global Conference of NGOs, Paris, 17-20 December 1991.

Braidotti, Rosi, Ewa Charkiewicz-Pluta, Sabine Häusler and Saskia Wieringa (1993) *Women, the Environment and Sustainable Development: Towards a Theoretical Synthesis*. Zed Books/INSTRAW, London.

Haraway, Donna (1988) 'A Manifesto for Cyborgs: Science, Technology, and Socialist Feminism in the 1980s', in Linda Nicholson (ed.) *Feminism/Postmodernism*. Routledge, New York and London.

Keysers, Loes and Judith Richter (1993) 'Dialogue on Population: Power and Co-option Mechanisms in Women's International Networking around Reproductive Rights'. Paper presented at the SID/WUMEN Roundtable Women, the Environment and Development Alternatives. Institute of Social Studies, The Hague.

United Nations (1992) United Nations Conference on Environment and Development, Agenda 21.

Women's Environment and Development Organization (WEDO) (1992) World Women's Congress for a Healthy Planet, Official Report. Miami, Florida, 8-12 November 1991.

11

Interbeing and the 'I' Habit: An Experiment in Environmental Literacy

Julia Martin

We must try to think beyond our homes, beyond the fire burning in our fireplace, beyond sending our children to school or getting to work in the morning. We must try to think how we can help this world. If we don't help, nobody will. It is our turn to help the world. (Trungpa, 1973: 29)

Introduction

I began working on this chapter the Easter weekend that Chris Hani was killed. Since then, we've marched with students to the local police station, watched the funeral on TV, and seen the burning rage of young people from apartheid's ghettos calling 'War! War! War! Kill! Kill! Kill!' Since then, these questions have been speaking more urgently: How can those of us working in educational institutions contribute to progressive social change? How can training in literary analysis and contemporary theory inform responses to the local/global crisis of environment and development? Is it possible to challenge from within the power/knowledge economy that is the business of our universities? Is academic education as we know it a sustainable commodity?

I work at the University of the Western Cape (UWC), a historically 'coloured' institution which in recent years rejected the ideological basis on which it was founded, and came to be known as 'a Home of the Left'. My colleagues and I in the English Department were trained in the study of something called 'literature', but increasingly these days we find ourselves talking about 'cultural studies', and working with more and more interdisciplinary material. My own work in teaching and research has come to focus on defining what I am calling 'environmental literacy'. Our students are fairly familiar with race, class and gender reading lenses, but what about ecology? I have written elsewhere about some possible theoretical starting points, but here I would like to locate these in a specific teaching situation.[1] The cultural studies course I describe is experimental and imaginary: it gathers material I have taught and some that I plan to teach, but this gathering is provisional, incomplete and open. If nothing else, studies in 'women and environment' can surely teach us about how we are connected: research of this kind cannot be 'owned' by one person.

Let us call it 'Interbeing and the "I" Habit', an experiment in environmental literacy which is motivated by a variety of desires and aims. Here are the ones that speak most loudly:

- To extend postmodern critical theory to include responses to the South African impact of the global crisis of environment and development, with a particular emphasis on women's lives and feminist critique. At this strange, transitional time in our history, this project seems particularly urgent.
- To find alternatives to the theory/practice separation that characterizes so much academic work. After university, some students will be potentially influential teachers, lawyers, policy-makers, community leaders, and members of NGOs. The exploration of theory within the institution should equip them, as well as those who are less prominently placed, to make valuable contributions in these contexts once they leave. But for this to happen it seems necessary to set tasks specifically aimed at empowerment with respect to eco-political activism in the community.
- To develop students' analytic skills in reading cultural texts, as well as to explore alternatives to this kind of enquiry. So, in addition to the familiar procedures of textual analysis, we work to encourage students to be agents of situated knowledge through 'creative' writing and personal narratives or story-essays, and some of the material we discuss deals with spiritual practice as a way of knowing.

There are numerous ways of focusing such a programme. In this case, I am exploring the metaphor of interdependence, which seems to offer a powerful conceptual tool for postmodern-eco-political-feminist-activist-intellectuals. The Vietnamese Zen teacher, Thich Nhat Hanh, refers to interdependence in terms of the Buddhist concept of dependent co-arising (*pratitya samutpada*), which he calls 'interbeing'. In using this term in the title of this chapter, I mean to indicate that my interpretation of these issues is informed to a large extent by the philosophy and practice of engaged Buddhism. I refer to a variety of cultural texts, but give particular attention to the work of William Blake. Produced at the beginning of the modern period, his writing seems to offer warning signals that we, 200 years later, may now be able to hear.

In the description that follows I outline six major components of the course. These represent areas of focus which would be discussed in several seminars. Each module includes a summary of the main issues to be considered, an outline of how key resources are dealt with, and a description of written and/or oral projects arising from and contributing to this material. I have included more of these 'homework' assignments than I would expect any one student to complete, but this was in order to suggest a range of possible projects.[2] As I present it here, the course is planned for students in an Honours (fourth year) Cultural Studies programme at UWC, all of whom would have experience in detailed textual analysis. The focus is locally situated, but much of the material could be applied in other contexts, with different specifically local content. Although my description assumes a formal tertiary educational institution, it would be possible to raise many of the same issues at high-school level, and in grassroots community education programmes.

Several of the activities and resources referred to have been used in these contexts, and many of the others could be adapted. The main ideas about waste, development, consumption, mental apartheid, othering, interdependence and the need for engagement are not difficult to communicate. The References at the end of the chapter are divided into sections corresponding to the six modules.

Module one: what is the environment?

We begin with a brief analysis of the connotations of 'environment' and 'environmentalism' in South African discourse. Most people in this country have historical justification for seeing ecological issues as irrelevant, and even inimical, to the struggle for social and political justice. In its most recent form as green consciousness, the environmental lobby easily becomes the voice of bourgeois comfort that denies the delights of consumer capitalism to the oppressed majority. In its older, and still dominant form, environmentalism as conservation ethics has been a significant element in colonial and apartheid policy. If 'the environment' is to be taken seriously in progressive critical theory and political activism, we need to understand the history of the term's use, and articulate a different interpretation which recognizes that human society is grounded in natural ecosystems. In this section we focus on a definition of 'environment' that emerges from participants' descriptions of where they live, and contrast this with the discourse of conservative environmentalism.

- 'What is it like where you live?' This was the question posed at the beginning of a national conference on ecology and politics in 1991, and in answering it here, participants in the seminar introduce themselves to the group through a description of their home environments.[3] Through a discussion of the quality of air, water and housing, as well as access to energy, transport, waste disposal, green spaces, community organization and so on, we begin to get to know one another as people whose daily living is situated in a particular eco-social network. This enables us to question dominant assumptions about the environment and human autonomy.
- We begin an analysis of what environmentalism has meant in conservationist discourse by watching *Fair Game*, a BBC video about wildlife

management in South Africa. It tells a story of dispossession in the name of conservation, involving the repeated forced removals of people from ancestral land in order to make way for game reserves. The historical segregation of environmental priorities from human ones is unambiguously established in the game reserve fences that separate ecological wealth from the starving township poverty on the other side, and by the presence of armed guards who are set to police the divide. It is not difficult to detect the ideological agendas of a minority government in the construction of these 'national' parks. The preservation of wildlife in South Africa has been a significant feature of both British colonialism and the apartheid state. It should not be surprising, then, if the conservationist discourse by which it is motivated promotes similar interests. In examining the history of this discourse we refer to my analysis in 'New with Added Ecology?' (Martin, 1992a) of the (racist, sexist, paternalistic) representation of a wandering hippopotamus in two colonial texts, and then go on to discuss the (similarly conservative) assumptions of mainstream environmentalism as described by Eddie Koch *et al.* (1991) and Ramphele (1991).

Homework

- What is 'the environment'? Where do 'I' begin and my 'environment' end? What are the borders of 'me'? Ask a variety of people how they respond to these questions, and then write a report on your findings.
- Read one of the popular Afrikaans children's novels by P.J. Schoeman (*Drie Jong Jagters, Fanie word Groot Wildjagter* or *Fanie se Veldskooldae*), the chapter on 'Die Voortrekkerswet en -Belofte' in *Eerste Handboekie vir die Voortrekkers* (Dalebout, 1932), and *The Soldier and Nature*, a pamphlet compiled jointly by the South African Defence Force and the Wildlife Society. Now write a critical essay in which you discuss the correspondences in this material between conservationism, hunting, Christianity, racist stereotyping, macho and patriarchal authority, and Afrikaner Nationalism.
- If alienating conservationist practices have been intrinsic to an ideological package that most South Africans reject, are alternative conservation models likely to succeed in the future? Are such projects likely to be sustainable? Plan a fact sheet for high schools and grassroots organizations in which you raise some of the problems associated with conservative models, and introduce recent examples of conservation initiatives in which local people are involved in managing reserves. (For case studies see the Dossier on the Richtersveld National Park, and articles by Boonzaier in Ramphele (1991) and Ngqobe (1993). For examples of fact sheets see Eco-Programme's Eco-Fact Sheets #1 and #2 in their appendix.)

- Review a month's material from the 'Green Pages' of a local newspaper. To whom is it addressed? Whose interests does it prioritize? Any significant silences or omissions? Write a letter to the newspaper in which you give an account of your response, and suggestions regarding changes if you have any.

Module two: what are we throwing away?

Our industrial culture has traditionally depended on an 'ethic of disposability' for which natural resources, other people's ecosystems, 'other' human beings in general, and the disposable beercan have had roughly the same (exchange) value. Having taught that all that it defines as environment is disposable, modern industrial society has only just begun to learn that 'the system which disposes of its environment disposes of itself'. (Wilden, 1984: 207)

This module uses a bag of kitchen garbage to introduce a discussion about waste, consumption and the epistemology of what Anthony Wilden calls biosocial imperialism. It is instructive to look closely at the things middle-class South Africans throw away as 'garbage': plastics, glass, paper ... . Each object can be used to tell a story of interconnections in which people, animals and the natural environment are treated as resources for another's profit. When we ask where the waste comes from, this question leads to a discussion of commodity fetishism, excessive consumption and an idea of modernity founded on the myth of insatiable growth and development. But if the lifestyle of middle-class South Africans imitates Northern models, it is similarly premised on the impoverishment of others. Where does the waste go? You do not have to travel far out of the apartheid city to find the refuse dumps, the townships and squatter camps. Examining the literal waste provokes an analysis of the ruling mental apartheid which relegates all the 'others' (women, the colonized, the poor, 'other' races, animals, natural resources ... we know the list too well) to silence and invisibility. Our exploration includes a garbage workshop, an excursion, discussion of theoretical material, and analysis of some literary texts.

- In the garbage workshop we assemble a collection of refuse from a middle-class kitchen and ask questions about, for example, a plastic bag: What is its purpose? Is it made from a finite resource? Does the manufacture of the plastic bag involve the exploitation of people? Can it be recycled? and so on. Our questions reveal structures of eco-social connection which are often obscured.
- Where does the waste come from? Studying what Arjun Appadurai calls 'the social life of things', reveals, in the case of kitchen garbage, extraordinary patterns of consumption and commodity fetishism. As

Frank Lentricchia describes it, capitalism in its consumer stage produces alienation, and then appropriates that alienation by projecting a utopia of commodity-gratification as the instrument for structuring desire. But if the goal of commodity utopia is an ever-receding one, this is not only because capital is always creating new objects of desire. We now understand that Northern models of modernity, premised on an idea of limitless growth and development, require the degradation of the environment, and the impoverishment of the majority in order to pay for the lifestyles of the rich. As many Southern participants in the recent UNCED process were at pains to point out, the present global crisis is linked to unsustainable patterns of consumption and production in the so-called developed countries. In discussing these issues, we begin with the Third World Network's description of the North-South debates that dominated the Earth Summit, and then go on to consider the evidence in the Southern African region of a similar dichotomy of interests.

• Where does the waste go? Perhaps the most disturbing feature of waste in our society is its invisibility once we have thrown it away. So at this point in the course we read the chapter on Waste in *Water, Waste and Wildlife* (Koch *et al.*, 1991) and then set off on an excursion.[4] Our journey begins in Cavendish Square, a shopping mall in Claremont, an affluent, historically 'white' suburb of Cape Town. We meet for tea, look at some shops, stop at a garage for petrol, and then begin driving on a good tarmac road through the leafy residential area, past floral verges and big gardens. We take a route through the Mowbray transport nexus, and on to Klipfontein Road which leads to the Cape Flats, a windy duneland where 'coloured' and 'black' people were resettled by the apartheid legislation's forced removals. The environment is becoming poorer, more garbage on the streets, smaller houses, fewer trees, more people. We pass through Athlone and the edge of Gugulethu. The tarmac is broken, patched, and now it gives way to a pot-holed dirt road which leads to houses upon houses made of plastic, iron and bits of wood. This is Crossroads, a squatter settlement: young men without jobs, hungry dogs and children in the street, women carrying firewood on their heads. From here we go on to the Municipal Refuse dump, not far away, where adults and children pick through the discarded rubbish. Then on to Khayalitsha, another township, where we have arranged to meet members of the Khayalitsha Environmental Action Group to discuss their work on a recycling project, a people's park and a play about waste.

• Looking closely at the waste which our culture produces, and the ways in which this waste is rendered invisible and forgotten, we recognize clearly some familiar structures. 'Resourcing', 'othering', 'orientalism', 'core and periphery' ... contemporary theory has many metaphors for describing binary epistemology and its imperialist implications. With reference to the work of Susan Griffin, Julia Kristeva, Edward Said, Anthony Wilden and our own experience, we construct a table of oppositional relations. Everything on one side signifies value, power and authority in the dominant discourse, while everything on the other side constitutes the silenced, the invisible, the disempowered, the waste.

Homework

- Baudrillard (1988: 25) argues that:

  the desire to 'moderate' consumption or establish a normalising network of needs is naive and absurd moralism. At the heart of the project from which emerges the systematic and indefinite process of consumption is a frustrated desire for totality. Object signs ... can proliferate indefinitely: and 'they must' do so in order continuously to full-fill the absence of reality. It is ultimately because consumption is founded on a 'lack' that it is irrepressible.

  Do you agree? If consumption is founded on a 'lack,' what is it a lack of?

- Write a story-essay in which you describe and reflect on our excursion from Cape Town to the townships.
- Research the waste disposal and recycling facilities available in your neighbourhood, and then write a letter to the City Council in which you suggest improvements on the present arrangements. You will find some useful ideas in *The WARMER Bulletin*, an international publication which deals exclusively with waste and recycling.
- To what extent is Anthony Wilden's description of an 'ethic of disposability' an accurate reflection of your experience of living in South Africa? Write an essay in which your argument is supported with local examples.
- Julia Voznesenskaya's *The Star Chernobyl*, Maggie Gee's *Grace* and Peter Carey's *Bliss* are all recent novels which deal with the issue of toxic waste. Write a short literary review of one of these texts.

Module three: women, nature and all the others

What do the others have to say? We begin with a role-play in which we experiment with assuming the voices of subjects who have historically found themselves on the wrong side of the epistemological divide. This leads to a discussion of whether liberation involves an inversion of oppositional relations, or whether it is possible to act from a non-binary, non-essentialist standpoint. The writing of Northern ecofeminists does offer a critique of binary epistemology and recognizes correspondences between different forms of oppression. But it often tends towards an idealist focus on individual transformation, universalizing a view of 'nature' and a rhetoric of reduced consumption which implies a degree of choice that has never been available to most people in the Two-Thirds World. Our reading of this material is followed by an assessment of the work of Southern writers such as Vandana Shiva and Bina Agarwal: critiques of post-colonial development, responses to the othering of 'woman' and 'nature', alternative models and strategies. In considering the applicability of existing theory about women, environment and sustainable development to the South African situation we discuss case studies of grassroots activism and cultural practice.

- Working from the table of oppositional relations we constructed in the previous module, we role-play the perspectives of some of the 'others' of industrial society. Is it possible to do this without essentializing 'woman', 'nature' and so on? Is it possible to resist oppressive mastery without replicating another dualistic epistemology? We experiment with metaphors of liberation.
- Ecofeminism is a heterogeneous discourse emanating largely from the developed North which recognizes correspondences between the exploitation of the environment and women's oppression, and is generally critical of binary, hierarchic epistemology. In some cases it promotes essentialist views of 'woman' and 'nature' which serve to retain a dualistic model, avoids global economic and political realities, and assumes a middle-class readership. But there are also a number of ecofeminist voices which would challenge each of these assumptions, and could usefully contribute to South African theory. In order to assess some of this material, participants present to the rest of the group short critical reviews of writing of their choice from two recent anthologies, Judith Plant's *Healing the Wounds: The Promise of Ecofeminism*, and Irene Diamond and Gloria Orenstein's *Reweaving the World: The Emergence of Ecofeminism*, as well as Ariel Salleh's debates with Deep Ecology, Carolyn Merchant's work on ecofeminist environmental history and Patrick Murphy's ecofeminist reinterpretation of Bakhtin.
- Our examples of Southern theory on women and environment are drawn from the work of Vandana Shiva and Bina Agarwal.[5] In Shiva's harsh critique of the models of modernity and development that have impoverished the South in the post-colonial era, Southern women emerge as both the victims of the crisis of environment and development and a source of its solution. In assessing the usefulness of this perspective with respect to our own situation, we consider Braidotti *et al.*'s criticism of Shiva's 'nature feminism', contrasting this with

Agarwal's emphasis on (an anti-essentialist) 'feminist environmental-ism'.

- In order to return to a sense of what Sandra Harding calls 'theorising from women's lives', participants report to the group on some case studies: information about UNIFEM projects in Africa and other parts of the world, documentation of the WorldWIDE Network's workshop on 'Women's Voices' at the Rio Global Forum, examples of the 'Success Stories of Women and the Environment' made available at the Miami Global Assembly, and publications by Dankelman, and Davidson and Sontheimer. This leads to a discussion of priorities for action in our region.

Homework

- Projects focused on women's activism and empowerment have been a significant element in environmental activism elsewhere in the world, but in South Africa there are as yet very few such initiatives. Conduct a survey of existing organizations and working groups in order to identify what projects are currently being run. Now write a report on your findings in which you suggest reasons for the relative absence of such projects at present, and assess the possibilities for future work in this area.
- Plan an illustrated fact sheet on women, environment and sustainable development for mass distribution in South Africa: emphasize the theoretical issues you consider most important, quote some case histories, and make suggestions for local activism.
- Read Patrick Murphy's critique of the tendency to 'sex-type the planet Earth as female' in the Northern ecology movement's popularization of Gaia imagery. Then write a critical essay in which you discuss the contemporary use of traditional Earth goddess imagery as it appears in (1) Mazizi Kunene's poetic reinterpretations of Zulu mythology in *The Ancestors and the Sacred Mountain*; and (2) the discourse of women's environmental activism in India.[6]

Module four: the 'I' habit

'I am,' and 'It is mine,'
These are false absolutes,
For neither stands existent
Under exact knowledge of reality.

The 'I' habit creates the heaps,
Which 'I' habit is false in fact.
How can what grows from a false seed

Itself be truly existent?
                    (Nagarjuna, in Thurman, 1988: 123)

A French advertisement for Jaguar cars consists of two words: *'Je, moi...'*
What else is there to say? Where would all the others be without him? The
modern construction of the 'self' as a skin-bound, consuming individual
is clearly illustrated in examples from the advertising media. In order to
explore alternatives to this powerful, oppressive, pervasive, invisible,
illusory dichotomy of self and other, we need to understand the history of
this mythical 'I' and criticize the assumptions by which it is sustained. We
begin with an analysis of the Enlightenment representation of the 'clear
and distinct' individual, and its socio-economic corollary in the rise of
capitalist industrialism. For William Blake, writing in the late 18th century, the atomizing, normalizing, alienating and imperialist character of
emerging modern society is embodied in the figure of Urizen ('your
reason'), a mythic patriarchal sky-god. But is the desire to solidify a
separate self peculiar to one ideological tendency? Lacan universalizes it,
arguing that the mirror-phase inaugurates both the subject's binary separation from the 'other' and an insatiable desire to establish a stable,
autonomous 'self'. Buddhism similarly identifies the root of our suffering
in the impossible desire to secure a stable point of origin, a separate 'I'.
But unlike post-structuralist theory it does propose a practical alternative.
Our discussion of these models of subjectivity is necessarily quite theoretical, but also includes some attention to our own experience.

- Participants bring to class examples of advertisements from the local
  media which use a particular construction of subjectivity to sell a
  commodity.
- Where does it all begin? We discuss Anthony Wilden's account of the
  emergence of 'the ideology of the self' in bourgeois individualism, in
  which Cartesian notions of 'clear and distinct ideas' have their socio-
  economic corollary in a notion of 'clear and distinct people', and the
  introduction of 'the technics of efficiency, substitutability, and organisation in the culture that was soon to dominate the world'. (Wilden,
  1984: 213) This leads to an analysis of Blake's representation of Urizen
  who locates himself in the transcendent vantage point 'above all
  heavens'. (Blake, 1972: 203) As such he embodies the 'single vision'
  which cannot tolerate diversity and difference, the 'selfhood' which
  sets itself apart from others, and writes a code of law by which to judge
  them. Our discussion of this harsh poetic critique of Enlightenment
  philosophy and science, 'State Religion', and the disastrous human and
  environmental cost of the emergent modern society refers to Foucault's
  account of the normalizing, disciplinary function of institutions in this
  period.

- In Jacques Lacan's influential description it all begins in the family. Emerging from the experience of syncretic unity with the mother, the child experiences in the mirror-phase a separation of 'self' and 'world', an image of itself that seems to confirm it as a separate, skin-bound totality. But for the child in all of us, the sense of autonomous selfhood is never complete. The subject is irremediably split, divided, decentred, and the insatiable dream of a return to completeness is only a dream. There are striking similarities between this model and the Buddhist story of the construction of the imaginary separate self. As Chogyam Trungpa (1973: 123) describes it, the process begins with open space: 'We are this space, we are one with it, with *vidya*, intelligence and openness.' Then it is as though a dancing begins in this space, and so the sense that 'I' am dancing, that 'self' and 'space' are separate entities. The *skandhas* (or heaps) which constitute subjectivity are accumulated progressively, until the 'self' is imprisoned in an illusion of separateness. Both Lacanian and Buddhist systems see our worlds being shaped by the painful, insatiable, impossible desire to secure a stable selfhood, a separate 'I.' But in Buddhist practice, the problem is not without remedy: the suffering that is intrinsic to the 'I' habit is identified in the Buddha's First Noble Truth, and what follows is proposed as a way out. Our discussion of these models is informed by Elizabeth Grosz's account of feminist critiques of Lacan. (Grosz, 1990)

Homework

- Write a poem entitled 'I am'.
- As feminists have shown, Lacan takes not only phallogocentric culture as a given, but also the alienation it produces. Write a review of Catherine Clement's *The Weary Sons of Freud*, an insider's critique of Lacanian psychoanalysis that argues for a moral imperative towards change and healing, as informed by the priorities of communism and feminism.
- In 'Self/Landscape/Grid', Terrence Des Pres describes the preoccupation in most contemporary North American poetry with 'nature' and an atomized, apolitical individualism. In its place he argues for 'poems that issue from the vantage of a self that accepts its larger landscape, a poetic diction testing itself against the magnitude of our present plight'. (Des Pres, 1983: 13) Read a selection of recent issues of the *American Poetry Review* in order to assess the accuracy of this judgement over ten years later.

Module five: interbeing

In one sheet of paper, we see everything else, the cloud, the forest, the logger. I am, therefore you are. You are, therefore I am. That is the meaning of the word 'interbeing'. We inter-are. (Nhat Hanh, 1987)

We now explore in some detail the idea of 'interdependence' in response to the crisis of modernity (as regards environment, development and the autonomous modern subject) which the previous ones have considered. We begin with a botanist-guided excursion to the University Nature Reserve, and a discussion of what professional ecologists, eco-political activists and systems theorists mean by interdependence. Philosophically, the recognition that the human subject, no longer at the centre, is inextricably connected with and constituted by her/his bio-social environment implies a basic epistemological shift. An awareness of our interconnectedness enables a different perspective on the post-modern deconstruction of the unitary subject, and all the other old stable points of origin. But if these ideas are new to Western metaphysics, they have ancient precedents in Mahayana Buddhism. The concept of *pratitya samutpada* (dependent co-arising or interbeing) is the traditional response to the idea of a separate self. In attempting to articulate a (post-modern eco-political feminist) interpretation of this material we discuss some contemporary views, and consider the treatment of interdependence in two literary texts, Blake's *The Book of Thel* and Ursula le Guin's *Always Coming Home*.

- We begin with a tour of the UWC Nature Reserve, where a member of the Botany Department explains to us what a Western Cape fynbos ecosystem is, pointing to some of the myriad ways in which organism and environment are interconnected. This leads to a discussion of Wilden's chapter on 'Epistemology and Ecology', in which he introduces ecological systems theory as an alternative to binary, oppositional thinking. In place of the Cartesian view of the biosocial universe which 'describes the unit of survival as the individual (the individual organism, species, family line, system and so on)', we need to recognize that 'the unit of survival is the message-in-circuit in the ecosystem'. (Wilden, 1984: 218) What are the implications of this perspective for ecological politics? Michael Cope's *Interconnectedness* uses examples from the Western Cape to illustrate the concept of interdependence in a popularly accessible form. In discussing its treatment of the politics of air, food, water, energy and information we consider how the issues which this material raises might be made available to the community.
- *Pratitya samutpada*, which Thich Nhat Hanh translates as 'interbeing,' corresponds to some extent with what ecologists and systems theorists

mean by interdependence. Like post-structuralism, it shows that all 'things', all mental and physical phenomena, take shape in interaction with one another. This means that all entities are empty, empty of a separate self, and there is no stable vantage point outside the pattern which connects them. Our introduction to this perspective begins with an audiotape in which Nhat Hanh discusses emptiness and interbeing. We then go on to read Nagarjuna's demonstration of the logical inconsistency of the idea of self-existence, and compare this with a post-structuralist as described by Jane Tompkins.

- What kinds of literary strategy may be used to illustrate interdependence? We read Blake's *The Book of Thel*, a long poem in which Thel's desire for selfhood – for identity, solidity and permanence – is greeted with a message of ecological interbeing. 'Everything that lives/Lives not alone nor for itself' she is told. (Blake, 1972: 129) The speaker is a Cloud, soon to dissolve as the rain that waters the Earth. Blake's simple story can be read as a response to Urizen's ideology of bourgeois individualism. Two hundred years later, Ursula le Guin's *Always Coming Home* (1988) uses postmodernist narrative strategies to tell the story of an ecofeminist utopia. Our discussion of this novel is introduced by participants reading aloud selected extracts.

Homework

- We can describe eco-social interdependence in a variety of metaphors: Chief Seattle in his (unauthenticated) speech to the American imperialists stated that 'we are connected ... like the blood which unites one family,' Buddhists may speak about the universe as a 'jewelled network' in which each jewel reflects all the others, and some people have referred to a 'web' or a 'weaving' of interconnections. Using the concept of interdependence, experiment with finding your own metaphors for articulating your situatedness in the eco-social environment.
- Dependent co-arising, or interbeing, has become a significant element in some of the discourse of Deep Ecology, where the idea of interdependence is related to the concept of an 'ecological self'. Joanna Macy describes the need to 'extend self interest to embrace the whole', quoting Arne Naess on a (supposedly desirable) situation where 'the self to be realised extends further and further beyond the separate ego and includes more and more of the phenomenal world'. (Badiner, 1990: 62) But is this really what we want? Read *Dharma Gaia*, a recent collection of essays on Buddhism and ecology, identifying the ideological assumptions which its interpretation of interdependence serves to promote.
- What evidence can you find in African traditional religion for a concept of subjectivity arising in interdependence?

- The mainstream (patriarchal/phallocentric) Judaeo-Christian tradition has frequently been criticized for propagating exploitative views of the natural environment as 'backdrop' and 'resource' for human progress and salvation. In response, certain theologians have been working to reinterpret Christian teaching from a different epistemological perspective which works from an understanding of ecological systems. Write a critical review of either Mathew Fox's 'creation spirituality', Jørgen Moltmann's description of the 'cosmic interrelations of the divine Spirit', Rosemary Ruether's idea of the 'God/ess who is primal Matrix' or Charlene Spretnak's account of 'green spirituality'. Your discussion should make comparisons with the Buddhist material we have discussed, and consider to what extent an ecological Judaeo-Christian theology of this kind might be appropriate to the South African context.

Module six: agency and compassion

Think of our life in nature ... daily to be shown matter, to come in contact with it – rocks, trees, wind on our cheeks! the solid earth! the actual world! the common sense! Contact! Contact! (Thoreau, quoted in Campbell, 1989: 205)

For feminist and ecological activists and others involved in left-wing politics, post-modern theory is sometimes perceived as an obstruction to engagement: if there are no longer any objective, absolute foundations of truth or value, and our subjectivity is all decentred, how can we begin to take action? How do we resist oppression, or assert the value of one system against another? In this final section we read a variety of essays which address such questions of subjectivity, knowledge and agency, without promoting a return to the old epistemology. If the concept of eco-political interdependence has much in common with post-modern theory, the crisis of environment and development can nevertheless teach this theory a sense of urgency, and situate it in the bio-physical reality which grounds all human activity. Buddhist deconstruction offers a model of compassionate engagement that is similarly situated. The idea of interbeing/emptiness arises precisely in response to a suffering world. In discussing these issues our purpose is to articulate a basis (a groundless ground?) for eco-political activism in South Africa. So we study theory in order to assess a variety of possible forms of engagement: grassroots organizing, work on environmental rights and policy formation, cultural practice and criticism, and so on.

- We begin with a discussion of several essays which attempt to define a political standpoint within post-modernism, an understanding of knowledge and subjectivity which can facilitate engagement. From a

feminist perspective, Susan Hekman (1991: 60), using Foucault, defines the problem as follows: 'the human conception of the subject as
a self-constituting entity is inadequate to deal with power relationships
in the modern world.' Kate Soper argues (1991: 128) for a 'post-post-
structuralist … re-engagement with value', while Sandra Harding
(1991) and Donna Haraway (1991) describe 'standpoint theory' and
'situated knowledge'. With specific reference to eco-feminism, Patrick
Murphy (1992) calls for an idea of 'volitional interdependence'.

- What does Buddhism have to say about taking action? An awareness
of interbeing includes a (remarkably post-modern) critique of totalizing
theory, of the hegemony of Reason, a taking-apart of all notions of
essence and selfhood: form is emptiness. But the purpose of such
deconstruction is to return us to the world in its thusness, to non-dual
awareness: emptiness is form. Engaged Buddhism, like ecology, is
grounded in Thoreau's 'solid earth'. As Sue-Ellen Campbell (1989:
211) puts it, 'we belong not only to networks of language and culture,
but also to networks of the land'. From such beginnings the *bodhisattva*
vows to respond to the suffering of all beings. This work is serious play
since its 'passionate detachment' derives from an awareness of the
emptiness of all slogans, theories and projects of liberation. In exploring the implications of this perspective we consider Gad Horowitz's
essay (1992: 163) which responds to Ernesto Laclau and Chantal
Mouffe's 'groundless' post-marxism from a Buddhist standpoint:
'Groundlessness as compassion is the no-ground of democracy'.

- The experience of women working in the field of environment and
sustainable development has led, at a global level, to prioritizing
specific rights, strategies and programmes of action. We study the
'Recommendations from the African Women's Assembly' and the
'Africa Region: Strategy and Action Plan' from the Miami 1991
Conference Proceedings, as well as the Women's Action Agenda 21.
In reading this material our aim is to note the priorities most relevant
to the Southern African region, to identify any others that have not been
given prominence, and to consider what local action might be taken to
give substance to the recommendations.

Homework

- Study Bill Devall's 'Exercise in Bioregional Studies' (Devall, 1990:
71) answering as many of the questions as you can. Now rewrite the
exercise, adapting it for a South African audience.
- Donna Haraway's 'Cyborg Manifesto' (1991: 181) argues that 'cyborg
imagery can suggest a way out of the maze of dualisms in which we
have explained our bodies and our tools to ourselves'. Write a critical

review of the essay in which you assess the view of subjectivity and agency which it proposes.

• Read Thurman's account of Nagarjuna's guidelines for social practice, and Macy's listing of the Sarvodaya movement's 'ten basic human needs'. To what extent are these texts of Buddhist social engagement adaptable to the South African situation?

• Choose one of the following examples of eco-political practice or engagement, summarize and analyse what is being done in this field in South Africa at present, and make suggestions regarding how insight into interdependence might inform further work in the future: grass-roots organizing (see back issues of *New Ground: The Journal of Development and Environment*); discussion of environmental rights and policy; eco-criticism (see the work of Cheryl Burgess and Stanley Frielick); and eco-political poetry.

In addition to the projects relevant to each module, students will be required to write an assignment at the end of the course:

• In order to articulate theory about eco-social interdependence in the context of engagement, the assignment takes the form of a detailed proposal for a project you would like to see carried out. You might want to start a resource centre, make a video, launch a campaign, start a recycling project, run a workshop … whatever.

Part 1 of the proposal will be a detailed theoretical motivation for the project which reflects your response to issues raised in the course.

Part 2 will describe the project in detail, indicating who is to benefit from it, how it is to be funded, what resources are needed, and so on. On completion of the assignment, make copies for everyone in the class, and we'll bind them together as a booklet.

Conclusion

This morning the newspaper was full of death and blood, talk of civil war, and the shouting voices of hatred and fear. One of my students told me how glad he was that I had asked them to work them together in pairs: 'We were able to get to know each other a bit, to talk to each other, maybe we'll then be able to talk to others.' He is a black African, she is a so-called coloured woman. Since Hani was killed our polarized society has seemed to be splitting further and further apart, or perhaps we are just seeing it all more clearly now. What is there to be done in times such as these? What can academics do? Driving to work these days we pass soldiers on the road, on guard against people who might throw stones or set a car alight. So what am I doing here talking about the environment when people are calling for war? Perhaps I sound more sure than I really feel. And yet, for Thich Nhat Hanh and others who cared for homeless people, buried the dead, and worked for peace in the war-zone of Vietnam, the awareness of our interbeing became the basis for engagement and compassion. Perhaps a course in environmental literacy might point to such awareness. Perhaps, for all of us who have grown up in the divided world of apartheid, it might suggest another way of seeing. Perhaps it could remind us that our separation is an illusion: I am, therefore you are. You are, therefore I am. We inter-are.

Notes

1. See Martin (1992a and 1992b).

2. This structure makes for some rather repetitive reading, I am afraid. I suggest you may want to read the summaries at the beginning of each module first, and then treat the rest of the chapter as a collection of resources. In trying to describe teaching process I have also found myself producing some rather curious sentences as regards tense and syntax. I am not sure how to avoid this.

3. The conference, organized by 'Eco-Programme', was held at the UWC in July 1991, under the slogan 'Ecologise Politics! Politicise Ecology!' It brought together participants from a variety of constituencies, and was generally recognized to have been something of a watershed in shifting debate on the relation between environmental issues and liberation politics.

4. At the time of writing, the journey I describe would be a dangerous one, due to civil violence.

5. I am referring in some detail here to the Indian example because at present I have more material on the theoretical and practical issues that have emerged from this region than elsewhere. I would particularly like to know the songs, stories, plays and poems which women are producing in the context of environmental activism, and the extent to which this material is informed by traditional and religious or spiritual practice.

6. Another query: where has the use of such imagery in India been documented (apart from Shiva's reference to *prakrti*). I am particularly interested in the cultural texts arising from this movement which refer to or reinterpret Hindu culture.

References

The following texts are relevant to the whole course, but for the rest, the list is divided into sections corresponding to each module.

Braidotti, R., E. Charkiewicz-Pluta, S. Häusler and S. Wieringa (eds) (1994) *Women, the Environment and Sustainable Development: Towards a Theoretical Synthesis.* Zed Books, London and New Jersey.

Cope, M (1993) *Interconnectedness.* Publication forthcoming by Eco-Programme.

Koch, E. *et al.* (1991) *Water, Waste and Wildlife: The Politics of Ecology in South Africa.* Penguin Forum Series, London.

Martin, J. (1992a) 'New with Added Ecology? Hippos, Forests and Environmental Literacy'. Paper delivered at the AUETSA conference, Zululand University, July. Forthcoming in *ISLE: Interdisciplinary Studies in Literature and the Environment*.

—— (1992b) 'The Snake Person Takes on the Cock-sure Boys'. Paper delivered at the Women's Studies Seminar, Utrecht University, October.

Ramphele, M. (1991) *Restoring the Land: Environment and Change in Post-Apartheid South Africa*. Panos, London.

Wilden, A. (1984) *System and Structure: Essays in Communication and Exchange*. Tavistock, London.

Module one: what is the environment?

BBC. *Save the Game* (video).

Dalebout, J.A. (1932) *Eerste Handboekie vir die Voortrekkers*. Nasionale Pers, Bloemfontein.

Ngqobe, Z. (1993) 'The Roots of Conservation', in *New Ground* 11, pp. 12-15.

SADF (nd, c. 1981) *The Soldier and Nature*.

Schoeman, P.J. (1935) *Drie Jong Jagters*. Nasionale Pers, Cape Town.

—— (1948; reprinted 1983) *Fanie se Veldskooldae*. Perskor, Cape Town.

—— (1950; reprinted 1983) *Fanie Word Groot Wildjagter*. Perskor, Cape Town.

Surplus People's Project (1990) *Richtersveld National Park*. SPP, Cape Town.

Module two: what are we throwing away?

Baudrillard, J. (1988) 'The System of Objects', in *Selected Writings*, Stanford University Press, Stanford, pp. 10-27.

Carey, P. (1982) *Bliss*. Picador, London.

Gee, M. (1989) *Grace*. Abacus, London.

Griffin, S. (1978) *Woman and Nature: The Roaring Inside Her*. The Women's Press, London.

Kristeva, J. (1986) 'About Chinese Women', in T. Moi (ed.) *The Kristeva Reader*. Blackwell, Oxford, pp. 138-59.

Lentricchia, F. (1985) *Criticism and Social Change*. University of Chicago Press, Chicago.

Said, E. (1978; reprinted 1991) 'The Latest Phase', in *Orientalism*. Penguin, London, pp. 284-387.

Voznesenskaya, J. (1987) *The Star Chernobyl*. Methuen, London.

Module three: women, nature and all the others

Practice, (1991) *Hypatia* 6:1, pp. 146-61.

Agarwal, B. (1991) 'Engendering the Environmental Debate: Lessons Learnt from the Indian Subcontinent'. CASID Distinguished Speaker's Series, Monograph No. 8, Michigan State University, Michigan.

Dankelman, I. and J. Davidson (1988) *Women and Environment in the Third World: Alliance for the Future*. Earthscan, London.

Diamond, I. and G. Orenstein (eds) (1990) *Reweaving the World: The Emergence of Ecofeminism*. Sierra Club, San Francisco.

Kunene, M. (1982) *The Ancestors and the Sacred Mountain*. Heinemann, London.

Merchant, C. (1989) *Ecological Revolutions*.

Murphy, P. (1988) 'Sex-typing the Planet: Gaia Imagery and the Problem of Subverting Patriarchy', in *Environmental Ethics* 10.2, pp. 155-68.

Ofosu-Amaah, W. and J. Martin-Brown (1992) *Proceedings of the Global Assembly of Women and the Environment*, vol. 1. UNEP, Washington.

Plant, J. (1989) *Healing the Wounds: The Promise of Ecofeminism*. Green Print, London.

Salleh, A.K. (1992) 'The Ecofeminism/Deep Ecology Debate: A Reply to Patriarchal Reason', in *Environmental Ethics*, 14, pp. 195-216.

Shiva, V. (1989) *Staying Alive: Women, Ecology and Development*. Zed Books, London and Kali for Women, London and New Delhi.

Sontheimer, S. (ed.) (1991) *Women and the Environment: A Reader*. Earthscan, London.

UNIFEM, *Action for Agenda 21: Women, Environment and Development* (dossier).

WorldWIDE Network, *Women in Development and Environment* (dossier).

Module four: the 'I' habit

Blake, W. (1972) *Complete Writings*. Oxford University Press, London.

Clement, C. (1978) *The Weary Sons of Freud*. Verso, London.

Des Pres, T. (1983) 'Self/Landscape/Grid', in J. Schley (ed.) *Writing in a Nuclear Age*. University Press of New England, Hanover, pp. 7-17.

Foucault, M. (1974) *Discipline and Punish* (trans). Vintage, New York.

Grosz, E. (1990) *Jacques Lacan: A Feminist Reader*. Routledge, London.

Thurman, R.A.F. (1988) 'Nagarjuna's Guidelines for Buddhist Social Action', in F. Eppsteiner (ed.) *The Path of Compassion: Writings on Socially Engaged Buddhism*. Parallax, Berkeley.

Trungpa, C. (1973) *Cutting through Spiritual Materialism*. Shambhala, Boulder.

Module five: interbeing

Badiner, A.H. (ed.) (1990) *Dharma Gaia: A Harvest of Essays in Buddhism and Ecology*. Parallax, Berkeley.

Blake, W. (1972) *Complete Writings*. Oxford University Press, London.

Fox, M. (1988) *Creation Spirituality: Liberating Gifts for the People of the Earth*. Harper, San Francisco.

Le Guin, U. (1988) *Always Coming Home*. Grafton, London.

Martin, J. (1990) 'On Reconstruction: A Conversation with Rosemary Ruether', in *Journal for the Study of Religion*, 3.2, pp. 75-90.

Moltman, J. (1988) 'The Ecological Crisis: Peace with Nature', in *Scottish Journal of Religious Studies*, 9:1, pp. 5-18.

Nagarjuna, (1967) 'Memorial Verses on the Middle Way', in F.J. Streng. *Emptiness: A Study in Religious Meaning*. Abingdon, New York.

Nhat Hanh, T. (1987) *Being Peace*. Parallax, Berkeley.
The Heart of Understanding: Commentaries on the Prajqaparamita Heart Sutra (audiotape). Parallax, Berkeley.
Spretnak, C. (1986) *The Spiritual Dimension of Green Politics*. Bear & Co., Santa Fe.
Tompkins, J. (1988) 'A Short Course in Post-Structuralism', in *College English*, 50:7, pp. 733-47.

Module six: agency and compassion

Burgess, C., (1991) 'Ecocriticism: The Greening of Literary Studies'. Unpublished conference paper, delivered at Third North American Interdisciplinary Wilderness Conference, Weber State University, Utah.
Campbell, S. (1989) 'The Land and Language of Desire: Where Deep Ecology and Post-Structuralism Meet', in *Western American Literature*, 24:3, pp. 199-211.
Devall, B. (1990) *Simple in Means, Rich in Ends: Practising Deep Ecology*. Green Print, London.
Frielick, S. (1992) 'Deep Ecology, the Environment and African Literature'. Unpublished conference paper delivered at AUETSA conference, Zululand University.
Haraway, D. (1991) *Simians, Cyborgs and Women: The Reinvention of Nature*. Free Association Books, London.
Harding, S. (1991) ' "Strong Objectivity" and Socially Situated Knowledge', in *Whose Science? Whose Knowledge? Thinking from Women's Lives*. Cornell University Press, Ithaca, pp. 138-63.
Hekman, S. (1991) 'Reconstituting the Subject: Feminism, Modernism and Postmodernism', in *Hypatia*, 6:2, pp. 44-63.
Horowitz, G. (1992) 'Groundless Democracy', in P. Berry and A. Wernick (eds) *Shadow of Spirit: Postmodernism and Religion*. Routledge, London.
Macy, J. (1991) 'Sarvodaya Means Everybody Wakes Up', in *World as Lover, World as Self*. Parallax, Berkeley, pp. 131-52.
Murphy, P. (1992) 'Rethinking the Relations of Nature, Culture and Agency', in *Environmental Values*, 1:4, pp. 311-20.
Ofosu-Amaah, W. and J. Martin-Brown (1992) *Proceedings of the Global Assembly of Women and the Environment*, vol. 1. UNEP, Washington.
Soper, K. (1991) 'Postmodernism, Subjectivity and the Question of Value', in *New Left Review*, pp. 120-8.
Thurman, R.A.F. (1988) 'Nagarjuna's Guidelines for Buddhist Social Action', in F. Eppsteiner (ed.) *The Path of Compassion: Writings on Socially Engaged Buddhism*. Parallax, Berkeley.
WEDO (1992) Women's Action Agenda 21, WEDO, New York.

12

The Politics of Research on Gender, Environment and Development

*Willy Douma, Heleen van den Hombergh
and Ange Wieberdink*[1]

The transformation of environmental research

Modern science has played an important role in the evolution of a mode of development that, more often than not, has been detrimental especially to the poor (in particular to women and children) and to the natural world. Academic research and contributions from scientific professionals can atone for this by stimulating processes that would reverse the spiral of impoverishment and environmental degradation. Starting from the knowledge and experiences of the marginalized people within their environment, scientific researchers can support those who resist mainstream development.

Besides the social sciences, the involvement of the economic, technical and natural sciences in this effort is indispensable. We cannot deny that the present environmental crisis has social as well as technical dimensions. In general, however, there is a technological bias in environmental science. Furthermore, the post-UNCED discussions on sustainable development are dominated by a strong belief in technological solutions, for example regarding biodiversity conservation. On the other hand, to dismiss technology as part of the solution to environmental problems, as do those scientists who emphasize the importance of social transformation, also has its dangers. To isolate oneself in a position does not serve 'the cause'. It seems that the scientific effort to contribute to social and technological transformation needs a marriage between the technological, economic, natural and social sciences.

This idea is not new, but there are many barriers facing intellectuals seeking conceptual and institutional change. Among these are resistance to gender as a relevant category; extreme specialization, which hinders effective communication between different disciplines; international scientific standards which reward a dissociation from social dimensions; political power-games concerning money for research; and the lack of know-how with respect to basic research and development. A multi-dimensional strategy is called for in which networking, education and exchange processes among scientists themselves and between scientists and NGOs are crucial. To acknowledge that research is a political process is the starting point.

The interconnections of gender, environmental degradation and unsustainable development models have received attention and to some extent gained recognition up to the highest levels of decision-making. Analytically, several factors seem interconnected: environmental degradation; gender inequity of status; access to and control over resources; the sexual division of labour in survival and management tasks directly related to the environment; and the feminization of poverty. Thus, gender and environment deserve interdisciplinary attention and approaches. (van den Hombergh, 1993) An interdisciplinary approach employing a 'bottom-up' approach with a gender perspective is needed. But what does this mean in practice? Let us focus on one particular issue: gender and biodiversity.

Gender and biodiversity

Loss of biological diversity (genetic, species and ecosystem diversity) is due to many causes. The most important one is the loss and fragmentation of natural habitats. Other causes are the over-exploitation of plant and animal species, the introduction of exotic species, pollution of soil, water and atmosphere and global climate change. (Global Biodiversity Strategy, 1992)

To stop this decline in biodiversity, a better understanding of the causes is urgently needed. Socio-economic and political causes should be examined, region by region. (Shiva, 1991) And, according to the Global Biodiversity Strategy (1992), further attention should be paid to the narrowing spectrum of trade from agriculture, forestry and fisheries; economic systems and policies which fail to value the environment and its resources; increasing human population; inequity in the ownership, management of, and flow of benefits from both the use and conservation of biological resources; deficiencies in knowledge and its application; and legal and institutional systems which promote unsustainable exploitation.

The importance of conserving biodiversity is beyond dispute. But what is disregarded is that a loss of biodiversity implies a loss of livelihood for those people who depend on its continued viability. How can we replace the current top-down approach of 'nature reserves with a fence around them' with a bottom-up approach to biodiversity?

Straightforward conservation in protected areas may be necessary to safeguard some of the world's most vulnerable ecosystems. But this process may increase the threat to people's livelihood if it means that they are deprived of control over their resources and forced to over-exploit others. Experience has shown that to establish national parks without incorporating the needs and ideas of local people simply does not work. They lose the essential sources for their needs, and, as a consequence, valuable traditional skills and knowledge of the conservation of biodiversity disappear.

Biodiversity loss threatens the livelihood of local people because it involves a decline in possibilities for sustenance, the provision of foods, fibres, medicines and other products for self-sufficiency and income; also, their autonomy is violated by the appropriation and monopolization of genetic material and information by foreign agrochemical companies. Sustainable agriculture is an important basis both for biodiversity conservation and for 'sustainable livelihood security'. (Chambers, 1988)

Women often play a significant role in managing the diversity of agro-ecosystems. The wide variety of their tasks provides for essential biomass flows from one part of the system to another (for example, from the forest to the home garden, the home garden to the animals, the animals to the fields). (Dankelman and Shiva, 1991) In addition, their understanding of the need to spread the risks of crop failure prompts them to practise intercropping and diversification of crops in their home gardens. These integrated agro-ecosystems also play a significant role in ecologically sustainable land use. It is women who carry out seed selection and storage and agricultural reproduction, and may also carry out experiments to improve species for agricultural use.

Almost everywhere can be found gendered differences in access to and control over different parts and products of the agro-ecosystem. Measures that reinforce women's lack of control over resources seriously threaten the diversity within and outside the agro-ecosystem; in turn, this decline in diversity affects women's own position. The suggested gender-aware planning and design of agroforestry systems (in which annual and perennial crops are grown on the same piece of land) to increase women's control while ensuring the necessary diversity of the agro-ecosystems (Rocheleau, 1987), should be based on existing practices, including the gendered knowledge of agroforestry, rather than scientific, outsiders' design.

Gender plays a role in the reductionist approach to science, biotechnology and agriculture and, too, in the conceptualization of (highly valued) 'production' and (less highly valued) 'reproduction' processes, 'valuable' and 'worthless' ecosystems and species. (Shiva, 1991) These are conceptual flaws which have serious ecological and social implications. It is essential to examine the gender bias on different levels of biodiversity/biotechnology discussions and decisions. As an area of study, this has been a 'central reality since the dawn of civilization', but the relationship between women, gender and biodiversity is fairly new. (Abramovitz and Nichols, 1992)

Different aspects can be distinguished in relation to gender and biodiversity conservation. First, straightforward conservation projects could damage the interests of women who need natural resources for their families' livelihood. Secondly, the conservation of biodiversity in agro-ecosystems can strengthen women's autonomy by enabling them to continue their productive and reproductive practices. Thirdly, achieving the empowerment of women should not be at the cost of damaging the conservation of biodiversity. Finally, women and men have different contributions to offer to biodiversity conservation on the basis of their experience and knowledge.

To analyse these interconnections in specific situations, and to find solutions to the problems, the attention of various professionals could be engaged: anthropologists, biologists, (agro-)forestry experts, political scientists, sociologists, economists, agricultural scientists and law experts, among others. It is important to consider the relevance of each of the disciplines (US National Research Council, 1992) and the methodologies involved from a political perspective. What additional knowledge and what methodologies are needed in order to integrate women's empowerment and biodiversity conservation and simultaneously to strengthen wise management of the environment and alleviate poverty, locally and internationally?

The need for an appropriate methodology

Awareness of problems related to gender and environment has grown since the NGO parallel forum in Nairobi, but it seems that women's empowerment and wise environmental management still need to be integrated. However, a number of serious political, socio-cultural and methodological barriers have first to be overcome.

Most environmental studies still lack a gender perspective, and fail to take an interdisciplinary approach seriously. But within gender studies too, greater attention to environmental issues and the technical aspects of environmental problems is necessary.

Questions such as: How can research benefit the more vulnerable categories of people and stimulate women's empowerment? How can we conserve biodiversity and at the same time alleviate poverty and gender inequality? are urgent.

The question of methodology also arises. How the research is carried out may be considered just as important as the subject under review. The selection and formulation of research questions, the choice of research methodologies, all involve political choices. We choose explicitly or implicitly which actors to involve, and which to exclude. If we are to empower women, their involvement in the environmental research process is crucial.

At the Global Assembly of Women and the Environment: Partners in Life (1991), organized by UNEP and WorldWIDE Network, several recommendations for academia were formulated, including the need to develop guidelines and implementation strategies based on experience and dialogue and to carry out interdisciplinary research leading to dialogue, policy formulation and action.

An actor-oriented approach

At the Institute for Development Research Amsterdam (InDRA), where we work, the central question is how a research programme, its content, questions and methods, can be steered towards the needs and necessities of 'those who live in poverty'; men, women and children of different socio-economic backgrounds, all having their own interests, needs and interpretations of their environment. We strongly support an actor-oriented approach to environmental research. According to Long and Long (1992), 'The essence of an actor-oriented approach is that its concepts are grounded in the everyday life experiences and understandings of men and women, be they poor peasants, entrepreneurs, government bureaucrats or researchers.' For environmental sciences, this may involve an understanding of the complex political economy of environment and development (Adams, 1990), which Piers and Blaikie (1987) called 'political ecology'. For the actors in the environmental scene, however, more than economic considerations are involved in decision-making; socio-cultural, emotional and other factors play a role. The researcher is an actor among all the others; he/she either explicitly or implicitly chooses for and with whom to work. (Schrijvers, 1993) As Daniel Janzen (1992) puts it: 'the tropical academic scientist studying biodiversity walks a fine line between being, on the one hand – unexpectedly and unconsciously – an industrial spy and on the other hand, being the source of lifegiving economic and social support for the conservation of tropical wildland biodiversity.'

In the research process researchers could be regarded as potential intermediaries between those who live in poverty and those who are in power. Sometimes researchers work together with social movements, taking up the struggles in the area collaboratively. NGO's views on the nature of the problem and the possible solutions may vary dramatically. A distinction should be made between different movements, in terms of their background, aims and 'beneficiaries', and their political, economic, social and cultural influence. Several studies regarding the role of NGOs in society have been undertaken. Research undertaken in collaboration with NGOs shows promising results. (Redclift, 1987) Furthermore, NGOs could, quite significantly be instrumental in facilitating the inclusion of bottom-up knowledge in the debate on sustainable development; knowledge which is too often absent from the debate. (Schrijvers, 1992)

Interdisciplinary approach

Most development problems, including that of biodiversity loss, have both social and bio-physical or 'technical' aspects. Therefore, within the scientific effort, an interdisciplinary approach is required, linking the social and technical. The problem with this particular interpretation of 'interdisciplinarity', however, is how it can be achieved. Social and technical sciences utilize different analytical references, concepts, objects, methods, time frames and so on. Moreover, they all have their own interpretation of a specific problem which is often implicitly supposed to be shared. In order to co-operate, all participants should be aware of the limitations and potentialities of their own (disciplinary) background; they should also be willing to exchange their knowledge with participants from other backgrounds. Only in this way can a new methodology emerge.

In practice, research on biodiversity is often dominated by natural scientists. Conversely, literature on gender, environment and development is usually presented from a feminist viewpoint which tends to perceive natural science practice as culturally and socio-politically inimical to feminist aims and thus to disregard technical environmental problems. But this attitude will prevent feminists from finding ways to break through the power bloc of science and business currently involved in the 'industry' of sustainable development.

It may be asked if it is worth the effort to invest a lot of energy in trying to marry a 'recombined pear' (social scientists) with a 'manipulated apple' (natural scientists). What is most important is that scientists approach their studies from a more problem-oriented perspective, based on social reality, considering theory development not as a goal in itself, but as a tool in social and technological transformation. If the diverse disciplines combine on the subject of biodiversity, they should find themselves united behind issues relevant to the everyday reality of the (poor) women and men living and/or working in the areas of study. This does not mean that researchers in either discipline cannot work relatively autonomously at times; but in every phase of research there should be a feedback to the central issues, ideally, for research on the local level, formulated and adapted together with women and men in the area.

An alternative methodology in development: Biodiversity, livelihood and gender in Rosas, Colombia[2]

The area in focus is situated at the foothills of a mountain massif of the Colombian Andes at an altitude of between 1,000 and 2,000 metres, close to the origin of four major Colombian rivers. The area is highly degraded, although it is supposed to have been mega-diverse a while ago. As some remnants of the forests are left, there is still a possibility of restoring at least part of this biological diversity.

The main source of income for most inhabitants is coffee cultivation. Several changes in national and international policies regarding the mode of production and marketing of the coffee severely jeopardize livelihood security of the inhabitants. Traditionally, coffee was grown under the forest canopy, which allowed for other functions of the forest such as water harvesting, soil conservation, and the provision of building materials, wood for fuel, wild fruits and medicinal plants. With the introduction of modern coffee varieties, forests have been cleared and even land on which subsistence crops were grown has been turned into coffee plantations. This has led to a reduction of biodiversity in the natural and agricultural system. As a consequence all basic needs from the area need to come from the people's own fields, leaving no room for landless people to survive in the area. They (and others) have left for urban areas. Another development, the cultivation of commercial tree crops for the pulp industry, drives people to abandon the agricultural crops previously grown in the area.

The central problem is how to ensure the quality of life of inhabitants of the region while conserving the biodiversity.

According to the inhabitants, the situation has caused the following problems:

- an impoverishment of diet due to removal of house gardens;
- a change in land-use and land-tenure system leading to further margin-alisation of the poorest inhabitants;
- increasing dependence on external inputs such as plant varieties and agrochemicals;
- alterations in the divisions of tasks between men, women and children leading to unequal distribution of power and access to economic means of production.

To proceed from the analysis of causes and consequences to possible action is a major step in the project. First, an action must be based on the needs, interests and priorities of the inhabitants of the region. Secondly, integration of the knowledge of inhabitants of the community, members of intermediary organisations, policymakers and scientists from both South and North, is one of the aims of the project. And thirdly, the research will be action-oriented and interdisciplinary. Differences in perceptions and interests of men, women and children will be taken into account at all stages of the project and these will determine the directions for change.

Barriers to change

Several barriers may face scholars striving for conceptual and institutional change in the effort to carry out relevant research on gender, environment and development.

There is still resistance to gender as integral to all research topics, even if at the same time the link between gender and the environment is increasingly recognized. In making this link, however, researchers and policy-makers tend to prioritize one element over the other, by either considering environment as more urgent than gender concerns, or the reverse. There are very few interdisciplinary, gender sensitive and participatory research projects. It is only through an integrated approach to gender and environment that we can help bring about the evolution of sustainable development.

There is a gap between what academics and what social movements consider to be important issues, methodologies and time-frames. Individual researchers who would like to bridge the gap and try to work from problems derived from the 'field' are often confronted with resistance from the universities against what are seen as unorthodox views and approaches. Because their research results might not fit into the scientific fields which dominate the scientific community, such research workers may not survive the increasingly competitive university climate. Consequently, scholars who are critical of current methods are forced to choose between the university or the social movement. These situations threaten entire departments and the work of those individual scientists who are, for instance, considered not 'productive' enough or 'too political'.

Another barrier is the apparently endless specialization within disciplines that makes interdisciplinary communication even more difficult. This is further aggravated by the value attached to specialization as such; some academics, either openly or secretly, often consider that their specialization is central, without regard to the framework into which the specialization fits. This attitude also masks an inability and/or unwillingness to assess the gendered social context of an environmental problem. As long as successful academic careers can be achieved without this assessment by the appropriate scholars, we are on the wrong path for sustainable development.

Several other reasons can be briefly mentioned: the lack of scientists' self-reflection on their own role in development and in their own society; the discouragement by present institutional frameworks (bilateral and multilateral agencies and increasingly the universities as well) of research critical of development (Hancock, in Schrijvers, 1993); and an overriding concern with the need to keep up with international scientific criteria. In much research on biodiversity the rule seems to be: the more remote from social reality, the higher the scientific reward. The new trend of donors to require the incorporation of social dimensions does not change this attitude; it simply alters the language of the research proposals.

Are the barriers too high to change? Can we influence the environmentalists to take gender seriously? Or ask social scientists to work from an environmental perspective? Will concerned gender-aware scientists (usually women) 'give up' and abandon their research when the struggle is too great?

The development of alternatives

An important dimension of a strategy to develop gender-responsible bottom-up environmental research is that initially alternative theories and concepts on gender, environment and development are further augmented and evolved. To arrive at such widely accepted, useful, well thought-out and reliable theories and concepts, networking among concerned individuals at universities and NGOs, in order to improve the dialogue, is an urgent need. It is probably easier to start creating small places in which these alternative ideas are worked out and improved, but this should be only a first step, or one of the parallel strategies to change academia from within. Based on our own experience we consider the following points to be important elements in designing alternative methodologies of environmental research:

- consciously choose the topics of research from a bottom-up perspective;
- carefully, tentatively introduce social factors (concerning poverty and gender) into environmental sciences; ensuring that researchers place and reformulate their problems in a social context;
- stress environmental and poverty issues in social sciences; (Schrader, 1990)
- invite NGOs with a gender perspective/women's groups to (re)formulate research questions to ensure the relevance of the research;
- involve NGOs with a gender perspective/women's groups in the research effort as translators and/or co-ordinators in the research programme;
- (further) develop problem-oriented research and education projects for students, including gender aspects and feminist approaches to science;
- introduce intensive training in 'listening' and participatory methodology for (student) researchers;
- be ready to deal with different interests, and to choose for whom and with whom to work, which is central to the bottom-up and interdisciplinary research effort.

We need to build coalitions between scientists and social movements, and between social and natural sciences in the process of problem-defining and problem-solving in relation to the conservation of biodiversity. These coalitions, in our view, have the potential to bridge the gap between nature conservation and poverty alleviation efforts.

Notes

1. The three authors are working in the environmental programme of the Institute for Development Research Amsterdam (InDRA), University of Amsterdam, The Netherlands. They are thankful to Philomena Essed and Kamla Peiris for their comments on an earlier draft.

2. In the South of Colombia, in the Cauca region, an action-oriented research project is being developed in order to design sustainable development strategies in a region of the coffee belt. The participating organizations are: a farming community; an NGO (FUNCOP); two local universities; and InDRA. Apart from the authors of this chapter, Sonia Salamanca at InDRA is involved in the elaboration of the methodology.

References

Abramovitz, Janet N. and Roberta Nichols (1992) 'Women and Biodiversity: Ancient Reality, Modern Imperative', in *Development*, Journal of SID 2: 85-90.

Adams, W.M. (1990) *Green Development: Environment and Sustainability in the Third World*. Routledge, London and New York.

Blaikie, Piers and Harold Brookfield (1987) *Land Degradation and Society.* Methuen, London.

Chambers, Robert (1988) Introduction in Czech Conroy and Miles Litvinov (eds) *The Greening of Aid: Sustainable Livelihoods in Practice.* IIED/Earthscan, London.

Chambers, Robert *et al.* (1989) *Farmer First: Farmer Innovation and Agricultural Research*. Intermediate Technology Publications, London.

Dankelman, Irene and Vandana Shiva (1991) 'Women and Girls Maintaining the Foodchain: A Case Study on Gender and Biodiversity in Garhwal' (North India)'. Draft report, unpublished.

Hombergh, Heleen van den (1993) *Gender, Environment and Development; a Guide to the Literature*. International Books, for InDRA (Institute for Development Research, Amsterdam), Utrecht.

Janzen, Daniel H. (1992) 'A South-North Perspective on Science in the Management, Use and Economic Development of Biodiversity', in O.T. Sandlund, K. Hindar and A.H.D. Brown (eds) *Conservation of Biodiversity for Sustainable Development*. Scandinavian University Press, Oslo.

Redclift, Michael (1987) *Sustainable Development: Exploring the Contradictions*. Methuen, London.

Rocheleau, Dianne (1987) 'Women, Trees and Tenure: Implications for Agroforestry Research and Development', in John B. Raintree, *Proceedings of an International Workshop on Tenure Issues in Agroforestry*, Nairobi, 27-31 May 1985. ICRAF/Land Tenure Center, Nairobi and Madison.

—— (1991) 'Gender, Ecology and the Science of Survival: Stories and Lessons from Kenya', in *Agriculture and Human Values*, vol. 8, no. 1, January.

Schrijvers, Joke (1992) 'Questions of Gender in Development Planning: Women's Experiences in a New Settlement of the Mahaweli Project'. Paper presented at the Symposium on Irrigation and Society, The Mahaweli Project, Sri Lanka, 23-27 August. Monte Verita, Switzerland.

—— (1993) *The Violence of 'Development': A Choice for Intellectuals*. International Books and Kali for Women, Utrecht and New Delhi.

Shiva, Vandana (1991) 'The Seed and the Earth; Technology and the Colonization of Regeneration'. Testimony for the World Women's Congress for a Healthy Planet, 8-12 November, Miami.

US National Research Council (1992) *Conserving Biodiversity. A Research Agenda for Development Agencies*. National Academy Press, Washington, DC.

Wieberdink, Ange (1992) 'The Actors behind the Scientific Scene: Research Agendas and Social Movements'. Paper for the Conference on Development-Related Research: A Second Look at the Role of the Netherlands, Groningen, December.

World Resources Institute (WRI), The World Conservation Union (IUCN), United Nations Environment Programme (UNEP) (1992) *Global Biodiversity Strategy: Guidelines for Action to Save, Study and Use Earth's Biotic Wealth Sustainably and Equitably*.

13

Feminism and Political Change: Women's Peace Movements[1]

Frances Connelly

Introduction

This chapter will look at the Women/Environment/Development (WED) debate in the context of other relevant international campaigning in an attempt to identify which strategies have worked and which were less successful, in order to help plan for the future. It mainly covers feminist peace and environmental campaigning in Britain in the 1980s. Some recent aspects of international feminist campaigning and of international law in relation to women, environment and sustainable development are also examined.

The 1980s feminist peace movement

There are similarities between experiences of the women's peace movement in the UK and several other West European countries, the US and Canada, Australia and New Zealand. The women's peace movement of the 1980s had enormous energy, albeit fuelled by fear and to some extent perhaps by nationalism and/or anti-American imperialism. It was organized along feminist principles, that is, it was decentralized, non-hierarchical and autonomous, not controlled by the state or state agencies, funders or a political party. It was international to some extent, although lacking a 'Southern' perspective. The first women's peace camp at Greenham Common inspired others throughout the world, such as at Seneca in the US, Pine Gap in Australia and La Ragnatela in Sicily.

These peace camps were a source of energy and ideas as well as protest and were inspired by visions which went far beyond the constraints of conventional political campaigning. Attempts were made to live in a new way, according each woman a respect that she may not have found elsewhere. The camps were visited by a wide variety of women, from all over the world, some of whom gave up jobs and careers in order to live there long-term. Some were already active feminists, others had never previously been involved in any kind of politics. Many of the less experienced women became politicized and extremely active. Participation was made easier by the fact that there also were many small groups meeting at a local level, and arrangements were made to subsidize those who could not afford to travel to meetings or actions which took place outside their home town.

These women linked 'peace issues' with other concerns: sexism; heterosexism; violence against women and against the environment; racism; the effect of the arms trade and liberation struggles; and so on. This was important as the mixed peace movement, at least initially, was much slower to see these connections, some of its members being interested only in the campaign against nuclear weapons. At the same time there were feminists outside the peace movement who thought that the women's peace movement concentrated too much on 'peace' issues at the expense of what they saw as the key feminist issues. There was, for example, disagreement over the portrayal of women as 'Earth mothers' and nurturers who were more able than men to tackle the problems of violence and militarism (a similar sentiment is still voiced by some environmentalists who appear to see women as providers of the main answer to environmental degradation). This is problematic as it consigns all women to a particular role, removes responsibility from men and blurs the fundamental inequalities between women and men.

At that time there was less interest in the UN and the role of international agreements than there is now. And many activists were deeply distrustful of the ability of conventional institutions to address their needs or to solve problems. Women did, however, use international law for propaganda purposes. The Genocide Act was regularly quoted in court cases and in 1983 a group of women were involved in taking President Reagan to court. They argued that the siting of Cruise missiles was illegal under international and US constitutional law. While it was not possible to win such a case, it did generate a great deal of publicity.[2]

The legal system was also used in other instances, not simply for propaganda purposes but where there was a chance of actually winning the case. Women from Greenham Common joined with others to work in solidarity with women in the Pacific region. They supported the people of Belau, in the Pacific, threatened by US plans to use their islands for military purposes.[3] Money was raised for them to challenge the US in the courts and at the UN. Women also raised money for several European speaking tours for women from the Nuclear Free and Independent Pacific movement. Two of them also spoke powerfully at the London Dumping Convention's meeting in favour of strengthening the Convention and so reducing the chance of nuclear waste being dumped at sea. This issue, together with the existence and power of the Convention, was publicized by a demonstration outside the International Maritime Organization where the meeting was held. This provided solidarity for the Pacific women, educated British women on the issues and demystified the legalistic and, to many, intimidating meeting.[4]

While it is impossible to measure the effect of the women's peace movement on the political process and on the momentum of the post-Cold War arms cuts, it undeniably drew attention to the links between militarism, the patriarchal system and racism. It also politicized and empowered large numbers of women. This strengthened many other campaigns, including environmental/development ones. Its international focus and use of international law with regard to weapons helped to prepare the way for greater NGO involvement in UN fora.

The strength of the peace movement declined from the mid-1980s and with the fall of the Berlin wall. It was hard to maintain the impetus of the movement in the face of the US and Eastern bloc arms cuts, prompted by the end of the Cold War and severe financial constraints. The fact that both sides still maintained formidable arsenals and that new and increasingly sophisticated weapons were still being manufactured, was largely overlooked by the media. As a result there was less public concern and this contributed to a decline in both the mixed and women's peace movements.

The decline of the women's peace movement has been linked to changes in the nature of the women's movement as a whole. The words 'women's liberation' disappeared, to be replaced by 'women's issues' and 'gender issues'. The amount of grassroots feminist political campaigning and consciousness-raising decreased. In the UK the situation was made more difficult by the fact that to some extent feminist organizations, once autonomous, had become dependent on financial grants from the state. When these were cut many groups weakened or collapsed altogether. Alongside these changes there was a worsening global economic and environmental situation and increase in poverty in many regions. The collapse of the Eastern bloc and of the Left led to a vacuum in ideology and a virtual abandonment of the concept of class.

At the same time there was an increase in internationalism, with more activity on the part of the transnationals and a greater mobility of labour. This, together with the increasing realization of global disasters and shortages led to more prominence for international and regional institutions and agreements, and there was greater expectations of the latter. During the 1980s NGOs became stronger and more sophisticated. People who had previously put their energy into campaigning from outside the system, became more interested in trying to effect change if not exactly from the inside, at least alongside the establishment institutions. And the international establishment started to allow NGOs greater access to conferences and meetings, although they are still largely excluded from the most important decision-making arenas. The UN Conference on Environment and Development (UNCED) and its preparatory committees involved NGOs partly because they lobbied hard for inclusion, but also because there seemed to be a growing recognition by some governments that it was in their interest to involve them. In the UK the British government and to some extent the business community, have become more prepared than before at least to meet with NGOs.

During this time of change the peace movement did not completely disappear. In July 1993 (the time of writing) the camp at Greenham Common was still in existence, mainly campaigning against the continued production of nuclear weapons and nuclear testing and also assisting the Shoshone people whose lands have been appropriated by the US government to enable it and the British government to carry out nuclear tests at Nevada.[5]

International environmental law

The role of international law in the protection of the environment and the fostering of sustainable development has been increasing steadily since the 1970s. The UN Environment Programme (UNEP) was established after the 1972 Stockholm Conference on the Human Environment which provided the first opportunity for the international community as a whole to address environmental problems. The Conference resulted in a Declaration which provided a basis for the negotiation of such international treaties as the 1973 Convention on International Trade in Endangered Species (CITES); the 1979 Convention on Long-Range Transboundary Air Pollution; and the 1985 Vienna Convention for the Protection of the Ozone Layer (followed by the 1987 Montreal Protocol). Specialized agencies, such as the International Whaling Commission and the International Maritime Organisation, also played a significant role in the formulation of legislation.

The UN Conference on Environment and Development (UNCED), held at Rio de Janeiro in 1992, was convened in part as a response to the Brundtland Report and to consolidate and develop further legislative achievements 20 years after the Stockholm Conference. Five documents were agreed: the United Nations Framework Convention on Climate Change; the Convention on Biological Diversity; a Non-Legally Binding Authoritative Statement on the Management, Conservation and Sustainable Development of All Types of Forest; the Rio Declaration on Environment and Development; and Agenda 21, which is a blueprint for action by national governments to achieve sustainable development. The first two are legally binding international agreements and contain financial commitments. The Climate Change Convention does not recognize or specifically address gender issues; the Preamble to the Biodiversity Convention, however, while it is not legally binding, does contain a clause:

> recognising also the vital role that women play in the conservation and sustainable use of biodiversity and affirming the need for the full partici-

pation of women at all levels of policy-making and implementation for biodiversity conservation.

However, this is not elaborated in the text of the Convention. (One relatively straightforward way in which a gender perspective could have been included in the Convention would have been a stipulation that there should be a quota of women involved in the bodies which controlled the funding and transfer of technology arrangements.) The other three documents, due to intensive lobbying by women, do contain clauses which relate to women and the importance of their role but none are legally binding at this stage.

While the extent of the financial commitments of the Climate Change Convention are unclear (due to the difficulties in obtaining consensus while the legislation was being drafted), the fact remains that the rich countries will be obliged to provide poor countries with financial resources in order to help prevent and mitigate the effects of climate change. Article 43 states:

> The developed country Parties and other developed Parties included in annex II shall provide new and additional financial resources to meet the agreed full costs incurred by developing country Parties in complying with their obligations under Article 12 paragraph 1. They shall also provide such financial resources including for the transfer of technology, needed by the developing country Parties to meet the agreed full incremental costs of implementing measures that are covered by paragraph 1 of this article.[6]

There were many conflicts between Northern and Southern countries in these negotiations. Some Southern country representatives were dissatisfied with the way in which the Climate Change Convention received more support from developed countries, arguably because climate change affects everyone, whereas drought and desertification, which primarily affect some of the poorest countries, are only beginning to be addressed by the international community.

There have also been problems with negotiations on forests as representatives of some countries with rainforests state that they should control their own resources. There appears to be greater effort on the part of some Northern countries to regulate the treatment of rainforests rather than temperate forests, when it is clear that the latter are also at risk. The rich countries have greater power in the negotiating process. The US blocked some of the more radical possibilities of the Climate Change Convention and by refusing to sign the Biodiversity Convention at Rio, damaged the momentum of the whole UNCED process. (The US did subsequently sign the Convention.) Small developing countries dependent on foreign aid have not always been able to withstand political pressure in international negotiations. For example, at the May 1993 International Whaling Com-

mission meeting in Kyoto, some small developing countries which had
previously been anti-whaling or had not recently attended the Commission
Meetings adopted a pro-whaling position, apparently as a result of pressure
from the Japanese. There is a clear power imbalance between rich and poor
countries at all levels of the international legal process, which has similarities with the way in which women's interests are largely excluded.
Hilary Charlesworth *et al.* (1991) argue further that:

> International organisations are functional extensions of states that allow
> them to act collectively to achieve their objectives. Not surprisingly, their
> structures replicate those of states, restricting women to insignificant and
> subordinate roles. Thus, in the United Nations itself, where the achieve-
> ment of nearly universal membership is regarded as a major success of the
> international community, this universality does not apply to women ... .
> The silence and invisibility of women also characterises those bodies with
> special functions regarding the creation and progressive development of
> international law. Only one woman has sat as a judge on the International
> Court of Justice and no woman has ever been a member of the International
> Law Commission ... the distribution of judges on the Court does not reflect
> the makeup of the international community.

They conclude that a feminist transformation of international law
would go beyond piecemeal reform and could lead to a revision of the
concept of state responsibility.

The Global Environment Facility

It looks as if gender and North/South inequalities will be perpetuated by
the fact that the funding arrangements for the UNCED conventions (and
perhaps for the potential Convention on the Prevention of Desertification)
will take place under the auspices of the new Global Environment Facility
(GEF). The GEF was set up by the World Bank, the United Nations
Environment Programme (UNEP) and the United Nations Development
Programme (UNDP) but appears to be heavily dominated by the Bank. It
has a very small staff based at the Bank's offices in New York and
dependent on the Bank's resources. Their current pilot budget is modest.
So far they have tried to fund small local projects with NGO involvement
in some cases, but the process by which projects are chosen is not public
and NGOs are not consulted at any stage. There is also concern that the
GEF will dominate decision-making which legally should be the province
of the Conference of the Parties of the Climate Change and Biodiversity
Conventions. In order to try and address these criticisms the GEF is
currently in the process of restructuring itself. A series of consultative
meetings have been arranged in which both representatives of governments and NGOs have participated.

How the GEF will decide between future conflicting demands on its funds is unclear. It is also unclear how much influence recipient countries and NGOs will be allowed to have on the GEF's policies. Feminists need to monitor and intervene in the GEF as much as possible in order to prevent it from repeating the disastrous policies of the World Bank. However, there is also the possibility, albeit a slim one, that as the GEF and the World Bank are so interconnected any improvements made to the GEF process could filter back to the Bank. It seems likely that the Commission on Sustainable Development (CSD) will be more open to lobbying from NGOs and hence women, but its role, power and future effectiveness is not yet clear, especially as it does not look as if it will have a budget to disburse. It seems that there is a greater willingness to allow genuine input from NGOs where the organization is weak, but more powerful organizations, such as the GEF and the World Bank, remain in practice inaccessible and resistant to pressure for change from outside.

Feminism and international law

There are good reasons for feminists to be cautious about expecting too much from international or domestic law. So far the areas of international law where women have succeeded in obtaining recognition of the roles and rights of women are those which are most disregarded by the international community. For example, the Convention on the Elimination of all Forms of Discrimination against Women (CEDAW), which came into force in 1981, is a binding and quite progressive instrument but is of low status and in practice has been largely ignored by governments.[7] In addition, lobbying is expensive and time-consuming and has to be limited to a small number of women, who do not necessarily relate back to a wider constituency of feminists.

Some academic feminist lawyers also have reservations on the value of the law to women. Carol Smart, in the following quotation, is mainly referring to domestic legislation, but what she says is also relevant to international law:

> Precisely because law is powerful and is, arguably, able to continue to extend its influence, it cannot go unchallenged. However, it is law's power to define and disqualify which should become the focus of feminist strategy rather than law reform as such ... . Law cannot be ignored precisely because of its power to define, but feminism's strategy should be focused on this power rather than on constructing legal policies which only legitimate the legal forum and the form of law. This strategy does not preclude other forms of direct action or policy formation ... it is important

to sustain an emphasis on non-legal strategies and local struggles [and] to resist the temptation the law offers, namely the promise of a solution. (Smart, 1989)

While such caution does seem justified, nevertheless the potential scope for the development and the implementation of international law with regard to environment/development is encouraging, as is the increase in power of the NGO movement, in which it is on the whole, easier for women to participate. It is crucial for women and especially feminists to increase their role in this arena. In addition, the propaganda value of women's participation in these international legal processes should not be underestimated. Agenda 21, for example, may not be binding but can be cited as an 'action plan' for governments, local governments and other institutions and can therefore be used, for example, to argue for quotas of women on decision-making bodies.

There are also intangible benefits to feminist participation in the UN. It is to be hoped that, informally, some of the women and men on government delegations and in the international agencies will be influenced by feminist arguments. And probably, in future, increasing numbers of feminist NGOs will move to the establishment – governmental and inter-governmental organizations and funding agencies. However, such a process is not unproblematic. In countries such as the UK the women with the education and skills to participate are a small group, who do not necessarily engage in any kind of dialogue with wider groupings of feminists. While inequality between rich and poor countries is a central issue in the WED debate, class inequalities within countries, or at least within the rich countries, are less acknowledged. It is extremely difficult for poor women to participate at any level. Moreover, there are few channels for the women who are participating to report back to larger groups of women interested in the issues but not directly involved. This raises issues of accountability and makes it more difficult to achieve implementation at national and local level.

Conclusion

In Europe in the 1980s it was possible to mobilize large numbers of women to campaign and take action on a number of interrelated issues. Methods of organizing were used which empowered women who had not before been politically active; and changes were made, such as the introduction of equal opportunities policies, from which women are still benefiting. In the 1990s it is impossible to organize large numbers of women, and this makes it difficult for the few women still attempting feminist political action. At present, international legislation with a gender perspective is relatively weak, there is little political will to implement it at a national level and there are not yet sufficiently large numbers of women campaigning for better implementation and enforcement. Lobbying is expensive and difficult to fund. It is difficult to organize along feminist lines in that only a small number and type of women are able to participate fully. However, even if the legislation such as CEDAW is not fully implemented or, like the Rio Declaration and Agenda 21, is only soft law, it is a helpful start and at least enables an increased number of women to become involved in international legal processes. International environmental legislation which, for the most part, is not 'gender literate', is nonetheless groundbreaking in other ways as it includes transfer of funding and technology from rich to poor countries, and feminists should become increasingly involved in this arena.

Notes

1. The ideas in this paper arise in part from numerous conversations with too many people to list here, but I would especially like to thank the following for their helpful comments: Pippa Adamson, Beatrice Chaytor, Derrick Purdue, Thobeka Mjolo Thamage, Jake Werksman, Farhana Yamin and the Current Affairs group.

2. Twelve Greenham women and several US congressmen took President Reagan, Caspar Weinberger and the Secretary of the US Air Force to court in New York. They supported their case with statements from expert witnesses such as Dr Alice Stewart on the long-term effects of exposure to radiation, Sean McBride on the illegality of nuclear weapons and Mary Kaldor and Professor Frank Barnaby on NATO policy. The case was given wider publicity by the creation of 102 peace camps at each of the 102 US military bases and facilities in the UK. Eventually Judge Edelstein ruled that the Court did in fact have jurisdiction over the case, but that 'the courts are simply incapable of determining the effect of the missiles' deployment on world peace'. While this refusal of responsibility by the US legal system was not surprising, what was interesting was the amount of publicity generated both in the US and in the UK. Many people were surprised to realize that ostensibly 'British' bases were in fact under US control, and that there were 27,000 US service personnel in the UK.

3. In July 1993, the situation in Belau was still unresolved, with the US continuing to try to gain access to the island for military purposes. The High Chief of Belau and a group of women elders are continuing to challenge this in the courts and by appeals to the international community.

4. Jacoba Seman of the Northern Marianas Committee against Nuclear Waste Dumping said at the London Dumping Convention: 'Nuclear superpowers are trying to remove nuclear waste from their own countries. Our Pacific Ocean has been chosen as the convenient dump site. Who will pay for the monitoring, retrieval and repacking of these wastes? We, the taxpayers of the world, will pay, not the Nuclear Industry Shareholders who have reaped and will continue to reap the profit, nor the military advocates of this life-threatening technology. Our future

generations will be burdened with the responsibility of clearing up nuclear garbage for millions of years to come. This is not justice.'

5. In July 1993 a group from Greenham, and other women, climbed over the wall and into the grounds of Buckingham Palace, to draw attention to the way in which the Queen was condoning the British government's nuclear testing programme on other people's – the Shoshone nation's – land. This single action got vastly more publicity than several years of more conventional campaigning on the issue.

6. Article 20, 2 of The Biodiversity Convention states: 'The developed country Parties shall provide new and additional financial resources to enable developing country Parties to meet the agreed full and incremental costs to them of implementing measures which fulfil the obligations of this Convention and to benefit from its provisions.'

7. It has been ratified by 103 countries.

References

Billis, David and Joy MacKeith (1993) *Organising NGOs: Challenges and Trends in the Management of Overseas Aid.* Centre for Voluntary Organisations, London School of Economics, London.

Charlesworth, Hilary, Christine Chinkin and Shelley Wright (1991) 'Feminist Approaches to International Law', in *American Journal of International Law*, vol. 85, p. 613.

Cook, Alice, and Kirk Gwynn (1983) *Greenham Women Everywhere: Dreams, Ideas and Actions from the Women's Peace Movement.* Pluto Press, London.

Dankelman, Irene and Joan Davidson (1988) *Women and Environment in the Third World.* Earthscan, London.

Dibblin, Jane (1988) *Day of Two Suns: US Nuclear Testing and the Pacific Islands.* Virago Press, London.

Enloe, Cynthia (1983) *Does Khaki Become You? The Militarisation of Women's Lives.* Pluto Press, London.

Feminism and Nonviolent Study Group (1983) *Piecing it Together: Feminism and Nonviolence.* War Resisters International, London.

Fineman, Martha Albertson and Nancy Sweet Thomadsen (eds) (1991) *At the Boundaries of Law: Feminism and Legal Theory.* Routledge, Chapman and Hall, New York and London.

Harford, Barbara and Sarah Hopkins (1984) *Greenham Common: Women at the Wire.* The Women's Press, London.

Jones, Lynne (1983) *Keeping the Peace.* The Women's Press, London.

Kennedy, Helena (1992) *Eve was Framed: Women and British Justice.* Chatto and Windus, London.

Public Sector International (1992) 'Paths to Power', *Report on the Public Sector International Trade Union.* 2nd World Women's Conference, Singapore.

Sands, Philippe (1992) *UNCED and International Law.* Unpublished working draft, London.

Sen, Gita and Caren Grown (1988) *Development Crises and Alternative Visions.* Earthscan, London.

Smart, Carol (1989) *Feminism and the Power of Law*. Routledge, London and New York.

Tinker, Catherine (1992) *Making UNCED Work: Building the Legal and Institutional Framework for Sustainable Development at the Earth Summit and Beyond*. United Nations Association, New York.

Werksman, Jacob (1993) *FIELD Working Papers on the Relationship between the Climate Change Convention and the GEF*. Updated for the GEF Participants Meeting, May 1993, London.

Women for a Nuclear Free and Independent Pacific Newsletter. July 1993, c/o 89 Great Russell Street, London, WCIB 3PS.

Women Working for a Nuclear Free and Independent Pacific (eds) (1987) *Pacific Women Speak*. Greenline, Oxford.

Women Working for a Nuclear Free and Independent Pacific (1987) *Pacific Paradise, Nuclear Nightmare*. CND Publications, London.

Women's Environment and Development Organisation (WEDO) (1992) *Official Report, World Women's Congress for a Healthy Planet*. New York.

14

Biodiversity and Gender Issues: Recognizing Common Ground

Janet N. Abramovitz

What is biodiversity?

Biological diversity – biodiversity – is the sum of genes, species and ecosystems coexisting on Earth at any point in time. As part of the evolving world, human beings are continually shaping their environment, for good or ill. The domestication of countless plants and animals, each bearing a wide genetic variation, is evidence of beneficial human interaction with other living things. Nature shapes humanity too. The struggle to survive in a particular setting has put nature's stamp on culture, giving rise to varied cultural forms – from social structure, diet and language, to land management practices such as nomadism, crop selection or shifting cultivation. One dimension of this continuing interaction which has been largely overlooked is the vital role women play in understanding and managing the living diversity of their surroundings, and the importance of that diversity to sustaining women and the families they support.

Biodiversity is usually divided into three realms: genes, species and ecosystems. Genetic diversity is the variation of genes within species, including distinct populations of the same species (for example, traditional varieties of rice in India) or genetic variation within a population. Species diversity refers to the variety of species within a region – not only the number of species (richness), but also how they vary taxonomically. Ecosystem diversity is more difficult to measure because the boundaries are less clear. Many other measures of biodiversity are also important (for example, relative abundance of species, pattern of communities within a region, changes in composition and structure over time, diversity in ecosystem structure and function). (WRI/IUCN/UNEP, 1992)

Biodiversity is not simply a shorthand way of referring to national parks, rainforests or endangered species (what conservationists sometimes call 'charismatic megavertebrates'). Neither is biodiversity another way to say 'biotechnology', although in many debates the terms have been used almost interchangeably. While some aspects of biotechnology deserve criticism and scepticism, I am concerned that in debates regarding biodiversity, biotechnology is too often viewed as a manifestation of all the evils of Northern capitalism, imperialism and patriarchy. The danger of this rallying cry approach is that it may divert attention from the much broader range of issues which I believe are fundamental to understanding and addressing the real connections between women (and other marginalized stakeholders) and the planet's resources – and the continued viability of both.

The evolution of biodiversity

The term biodiversity was coined as part of a broad effort to shift the understanding of and interest in the environment away from single-species perspectives. By using biodiversity as an organizing concept one could look at systems, how they function, what influences them, how they can be maintained, and where humans and their needs and interactions fit within these systems. As part of this evolution to a more holistic approach, biologists, anthropologists and others, including the general public, began to recognize that biodiversity – be it in the Amazon, a national park, or along a roadside – does not exist in isolation from the human domain. Biodiversity is part of people's daily lives and livelihoods and constitutes the resources upon which families, communities, nations and future generations depend. In essence, biodiversity conservation shifts from a defensive posture – that is, protecting nature from the impacts of development – to an offensive/proactive position seeking to meet people's needs from biological resources while ensuring the long-term sustainability of Earth's biotic wealth. (WRI/IUCN/UNEP, 1992)

Yet these resources are in jeopardy, and many of the reasons why biodiversity is in decline are also responsible for the decline in people's ability to achieve reasonable standards of living. While loss of habitats such as the tropical rainforest has gained widespread attention, other less glamorous areas are under much greater threat. For example, less than half of the temperate rainforests remain today, and they covered a very limited area to begin with – only 4 per cent of today's tropical forest area. (Weigand, 1991; Haisla Nation and Ecotrust, 1991) Mediterranean climate areas, coral reefs, coastal fisheries and freshwater lakes are also in serious decline. These areas are rich in plant and animal life upon which people heavily depend.

Loss of genetic diversity, especially apparent among crop varieties, has equally severe implications. Despite the fact that thousands of species (and innumerable subspecies) have been cultivated since the development of agriculture 12,000 years ago (Fowler and Mooney, 1990), today fewer than 100 species provide most of the world's food supply. (Prescott-Allen and Prescott-Allen, 1990) And within those 100 species, genetic diversity has been seriously reduced. For example, a recent survey of fruit and vegetable varieties in the United States revealed that up to 96 per cent of the commercial vegetable varieties listed by the US Department of Agriculture in 1903 are now extinct. Of the more than 7,000 apple varieties in use between 1804 and 1904 in the US, 86 per cent have been lost. (Fowler and Mooney, 1990) The more recent introduction of Green Revolution, high-yielding, high-input varieties has resulted in the loss of traditional crop varieties. In developing countries, these Green Revolution varieties are now used on over half of the agricultural land planted in wheat, rice and maize. (Dalrymple, 1986; Timothy *et al.*, 1989)

Besides the profound ethical and aesthetic implications, loss of biodiversity has severe social and economic costs. The genes, species, ecosystems and human knowledge which are being lost represent a living library of options for adapting to local and global change. A few examples may help to illustrate the value of diversity, the unique skills and knowledge women possess in managing and making use of this diversity, and the cost of its loss.

Narrowing genetic diversity, especially in crops, can be disastrous because diseases and pests can move swiftly through genetically uniform stands. For example, Brazil recently experienced its worst outbreak of citrus canker because of genetic uniformity. (Griffith, 1991) Large losses were also experienced in the Soviet wheat crop in 1972 and the Florida citrus crop in 1984. (Plucknett *et al.*, 1987) The potential for more devastating loss continues. In an impressive display of genetic uniformity, nearly all the coffee trees in South America are descended from a single tree growing in an Amsterdam botanical garden 200 years ago. The origin of that coffee tree was the forests of southwest Ethiopia, which have virtually disappeared. (Fowler and Mooney, 1990) In Bangladesh, 62 per cent of rice varieties come from a single maternal plant; in Indonesia and Sri Lanka the figures are even higher (74 and 75 per cent). (WRI/IUCN/UNEP, 1992) In Indonesia, 1,500 local rice varieties have become extinct in the last 15 years alone. (Government of Indonesia, 1989) Yet these local varieties and ancestors could aid plant breeders in their efforts to protect commercial agriculture and help the small farmer maintain diverse cropping systems.

Cash-crop and kitchen gardens are an important part of women's strategies for providing for their families and securing income. Such gardens are also important storehouses of plant genetic diversity; diversity that is maintained for specific desired traits and for the pride and status derived from this skill. For example, among the Aguaruna Jivaro in Peru, manioc provides over half the calories in the diet, and makes up over three-quarters of the garden plants grown by women. It has been reported that as a result of their strategy of planting many types of manioc, 100 varieties are cultivated by Aguaruna Jivaro women and shared within the community. (Norem *et al.*, 1989)

The importance of materials collected from off-farm, boundary and wastelands to women's coping strategies has been well documented, as have the forces restricting their legal access. (Falconer and Arnold, 1991;

FAO, 1987; FAO/SIDA, 1987; Fortmann and Rocheleau, 1985; Jiggins, 1986; Kaur, 1990; Lindstrom and Kingamkono, 1991; Rocheleau, 1991; Wachiira, 1987; Williams, 1992a,b) Because these resources usually require very little capital or external inputs, they are especially important to women and the poor for both home consumption and sale. Their knowledge about resources can literally be lifesaving information during lean periods or famine. Examples of women's unique skills and knowledge are available in every part of the world. In rural communities in Laos, Ireson (1991) reported that in the eight villages studied, 141 different forest products were collected for sale or home use, with most gathering done by women. Certainly the value of traditional medicines – the primary form of health care for most of the world's population – and their potential for the pharmaceutical industry is well-known (Farnsworth, 1988; Reid *et al.*, 1993), although this is another aspect of traditional knowledge in which women's roles are poorly understood. In Ghana, the majority of people depend on wildlife for most of their protein (Asibey, 1974), and women are the principal processors, distributors and marketers of bushmeat, including that consumed in urban areas. (Addo *et al.*, 1992)

It is clear that the goods that women collect, cultivate, harvest and process are vital to their families' health, nutrition and income. Almost invisible is the fact that the products and revenues are also important parts of national economies. It has been reported that non-timber forest products (NTFP) in India accounted for 'nearly two-fifths of total Forest Department revenues and around three-quarters of net export earnings from forest produce' – and that the majority of workers in the NTFP economy are women. (Kaur, 1990) Another study in India found that 6,000 women gained income through the collection and sale of a condiment of which local foresters were unaware. (Campbell, cited in Molnar, 1991) Among Indian tribal and forest communities, the collection, processing and sale of NTFP is the most important source of income. Households with little land are especially dependent on NTFP for this income, as well as for meeting household needs. (Kaur, 1990)

Contrary to the popular mythology of the male rubber-tapper, women in Amazonian extractive communities also play an important role in the NTFP economy. (Hecht, 1993) For example, in Acre, Brazil, not only do women cultivate the food, spices and medicines grown near the house, but they also carry the primary responsibility for processing forest products. Because processed goods fetch a higher price in the market, the skills and knowledge women maintain are of great economic importance. (Kainer and Duryea, 1992) Estimates on the percentage of income derived from forest products vary by community (Hecht, 1993; Jodha, 1986; Kainer and Duryea, 1992; Kaur, 1990), but it is clearly a critical element in the livelihoods of households with access to these resources.

Resources collected from the wild are also important in developed countries, and the loss of those resources has social and economic costs. The destruction of rich estuarine ecosystems in the US cost $200 million per year (1954-1978) in commercial and sport fisheries alone. (WRI/IUCN/UNEP, 1992) And these figures do not even include losses to subsistence fisherfolk or social costs related to the culture disintegration of these fishing communities.

The panoply of forces acting against the integrity of the environment imposes subtle pressures that may be even more difficult to measure than those described above. There has been – and continues to be – a severe erosion in the vast library of indigenous knowledge as both resources and those who are most knowledgeable about them disappear. With the passing of elders who recall useful plants and animals that no longer exist, irreplaceable storehouses of wisdom in what Rocheleau (1991) calls the 'science of survival' are lost. And it is the women who retain more of this knowledge who continue to be overlooked. Even if resources themselves survive there is no guarantee that women can continue to count on even the limited access they now enjoy if gender and class struggles over resources intensify. Furthermore, there is no guarantee that women's knowledge will be passed to a younger generation. Because of increased time spent on other activities, displacement of families, devaluation of traditional knowledge in favour of more 'modern' knowledge, or disruption of the rhythm or fabric of social structures, less time is spent transmitting the intimate knowledge women and men have of their environments. (Wachiira, 1987)

Nexus of the threats to biodiversity and women

A number of causes and mechanisms have been cited for the impoverishment of biological diversity. The direct mechanisms include habitat loss and fragmentation, invasion by introduced species, over-exploitation of living resources, pollution, global climate change, and industrial agriculture and forestry. The roots of these problems can be found in more fundamental issues. (WRI/IUCN/UNEP, 1992) I would suggest that the same phenomena which are diminishing biodiversity are impoverishing women as well. These underlying problems include:

- the unsustainably high rate of natural resource consumption;
- the narrowing of traded products from agriculture, forestry and fisheries, and the commercialization of many subsistence resources;
- the failure of economic systems to value the environment and its resources or the value of women's unpaid labour and the failure to account for intangibles such as social stability, inter- and intra-generational equity and self-sufficiency;

- the inequity in the ownership, management and flow of benefits from both the use and the conservation of natural resources;
- the deficiencies in knowledge and its applications;
- the promotion of unsustainable exploitation by legal and institutional systems.

The examples noted earlier help illustrate the connections between what is happening to natural resources and what is happening to women. People who care about women's lives should see the value in supporting efforts to sustain the Earth's biotic wealth. Those who are concerned about biodiversity should further be able to see that the world is on a collision course which presages environmental and social disaster unless women and the families receive an equitable share of resources.

Recent initiatives

Many efforts have been made – from the local to international level – which have the potential to improve the women's positions and the Earth's biotic wealth. A few examples will illustrate the range of initiatives. At the local level, in developing countries, as well as in the United States and Europe, there has been a groundswell of interest in maintaining or reintroducing diversity and indigenous species. For example, efforts are being made to find and reintroduce ancient or heirloom crop varieties or livestock, to propagate indigenous tree species, and to pass on elders' knowledge about crops and medicines to a younger generation. There has also been a resurgence of interest in natural products, and small-scale industries are being developed based on local needs and in response to global markets. Efforts to share the experiences of participatory research methods and the development of networks focused on indigenous knowledge have great relevance and potential for effecting change.

At the international level, UNCED and the Convention on Biological Diversity are probably the most well-known fora where biodiversity has been addressed. The Global Biodiversity Strategy (WRI/IUCN/UNEP, 1992) brought many groups together in a multi-year process in order to develop an outline of proposals and specific actions applicable from the local to the international level. The International Conference on Women and Biodiversity brought together a diverse range of theorists and practitioners to develop recommendations on those issues. (Borkenhagen and Abramovitz, 1993)

It should be noted that though recent global conferences have attempted to include other sectors (for example, environment and development, population and development) and other voices (such as participation of NGOs and the South), these types of conferences are very time- and resource-intensive, and the vast majority of the voiceless remain unheard.

Diversity as an organizing theme

Part of the basic dogma of ecology is that diverse systems are more stable and better able to adapt to change. The theme of diversity has expanded well beyond ecology and has become part of the language and approach of the broader environmental movement. Diversity has also been called for in the social and political arenas, in the United States as well as in international debates, and must continue to expand. If one accepts that in order to understand how nature functions one must examine its interconnections, and that nature is not isolated from the human domain, then it would seem logical to take this one step further and look at the political and social connections, including gender. Thus, in order for institutions to be able to adapt to change, they must become more diverse or risk irrelevance or extinction.

Living libraries

Biodiversity has been referred to as a library that enables adaptation to local and global change. That so much of this library is in danger of being lost, and the realization that the loss has implications for humankind, has caused profound concern. As Rocheleau has eloquently stated, 'while we are still making entries into the catalog of life forms on earth, we are increasingly aware that whole pages, some yet unrecorded, are being erased even as we write'. (Rocheleau, 1991)

Despite widespread concern, some portions of the library continue to be overlooked. The books – the knowledge – that women possess remain largely unread. These valuable books contain important information that has practical applications. And new books continue to be written as knowledge continues to evolve. Perhaps even more troubling is that the way women's body of knowledge is disregarded also speaks volumes about the way women themselves are treated.

I would concur with others who have cautioned against romanticizing indigenous knowledge or customs – including women's. (Agarwal, 1992; Charkiewicz-Pluta and Häusler, 1991; Hecht, 1993; Rocheleau, 1991; Sachs, 1992; Thrupp, 1991) Women are not closer to nature as a result of their biology. Many traditional cultures have practices that dominate women or use natural resources unsustainably. And the social and economic hierarchies that exist between North and South, and between countries also exist within countries, within communities, and even within genders (that is, women are not a monolithic group).

Yet the either/or view of noble or destructive native/woman persists in popular mythology. Rather than accept this polarized view I would suggest that traditional elements and modern elements can coexist and be blended.

Much as farmers select crops and technologies, blending old and new is as much a part of the human evolutionary process today as it has been since the dawn of civilization. Who makes the choices about saving, discarding and blending is one of the issues at hand. Ensuring that all stakeholders have a say in these choices is a struggle that we can all join in, each with our own paragraph, line or word.

Challenges and strategies

In looking towards the future, one can see that many fundamental questions can be raised such as: what structures and policies restrict and undervalue both women and the environment, and how can these be changed so that truly sustainable and equitable development can take place?

What is needed is sustainable and equitable development; development which takes a very different path from the one on which we now find ourselves. Such a development calls for transformation in economic, social and gender relations. Such a transformation would value women's roles as managers of their environment and providers for their families, communities and nations.

Realizing such a transformation would require changes in personal, professional, institutional and policy spheres. There are steps we can take while we are working towards a larger transformation. As we move along the path, there are a number of challenges which we will face and barriers which must be broken down.

Bringing women back from the margins

The evolution of early women-in-development (WID) programmes may be one reason why women are viewed as a special 'interest group', that is, a group outside of the mainstream seeking some special entitlement or handout. Thus, part of overcoming the marginalization of women and the environment is to examine barriers that may have been fostered by the way in which WID evolved. For example, it may be time to assess the value of maintaining separate women's bureaux and divisions versus total integration, or both.

But let us not ignore or underestimate the degree to which recognizing the knowledge and needs of women and the centrality of their contributions is a threat because it may require those in positions of power to give up something that they now have (for example, power, status, money, jobs, land, access to resources). In the difficult economic climate experienced by most countries and international agencies, we must be vigilant in ensuring that efforts on behalf of women and the environment do not continue to be eliminated or underfunded.

The examples of projects that failed adequately to address social and ecological realities abound. They underscore the need for good social and ecological analysis (not just gender analysis), interdisciplinary perspectives, and complementarity of roles, relations and disciplines.

Breaking institutional barriers

Women need more access to the resources of institutions. The niggardly financial resources currently allocated to women and the environment demonstrate that these areas are viewed as marginal. That women are far from being seen as central to the mission and interests of many funding institutions can be illustrated by examining the 'order of magnitude' estimates produced for various sections of Agenda 21. The estimate for implementing all of Agenda 21 was $600 billion, with $3.5 billion for biodiversity conservation. For implementing Agenda 21's recommendations on strengthening the role of women in all sectors, the estimated cost was only $40 million. In addition to financial resources, other resources – such as access to markets, education and training, health care, labour-saving technologies, political power and decision-making – are also lacking.

Another step on the path to broad transformation is to influence existing institutions. One way to rectify this blind spot when it comes to women would be to increase the number of women within decision-making ranks of institutions. Alliances with feminist men would help too. Some of the institutions in need of change are permanent (for example, UN programmes, bi- and multi-lateral development agencies and research institutions). There are other forums, structures and institutions that would also benefit from these changes. At the international level, these include the bodies charged with follow-up to aspects of Agenda 21 and the conventions (for example, Commission on Sustainable Development). But fundamentally, transforming institutions will require more than simply getting more women or more feminists into institutions.

In a transformation where technologies would be reoriented and resources reallocated to serve the many rather than profit the few, there are certainly many immediate and intermediate steps that can be taken. Steps include greater support for women-friendly and appropriate technologies, and the integration of women and participatory processes into existing institutions (for example, research, development). One concern about the promotion of biotechnology (or top-heavy big science solutions) as the next miracle cure for agricultural or environmental problems is that it will consume a disproportionate amount of already scarce resources to the detriment of smaller science and more appropriate technology with benefits that would be more widely disbursed, more likely to reach the poor, and more likely to be sustainable. Further, in the commercial-public partnerships that increasingly characterize academic and other research efforts, more research and more funding will be likely to support commercial interests.

Recognizing women's role

Women will not be valued at their actual worth without better information, and better dissemination of that information. Improved research and communication are both critical. Some of the areas where attention is needed include: improved documentation and understanding of what women do; how and why they do it; and what its value is to women, their families and their communities. The complementarity of gender-based roles and knowledge needs more study too, as does understanding the process of learning and transmitting knowledge. Teaching and learning are imbedded in a rich cultural web of social networks, reciprocal exchanges, social security and entrepreneurship. Knowledge divorced from this web loses much of its purpose, meaning and power.

That knowledge is recognized as a form of power in every culture is demonstrated by everything from the efforts to obtain a patent for a new invention to the secrecy surrounding the location of prime fishing grounds or the development of plants and seeds with desirable traits. The status or wealth that can arise from sharing – or withholding – this information is one form of power. Recognizing that women have knowledge is an admission that they possess a certain amount of power – an admission that has implications for the status quo.

Collecting information

Before launching into great new research programmes, one must first ask what is the real purpose, what methods will be used, and who will truly benefit? Critiques of the dominant scientific methods and even progressive participatory research methods have been the subject of much stimulating debate from diverse perspectives. (Chambers *et al.*, 1989; Charkiewicz-Pluta and Häusler, 1991; Pretty and Chambers, 1992; Sachs, 1992; Shiva *et al.*, 1991; Thrupp, 1989; Waters-Bayer, 1992) Rather than attempting to review all these critiques, we will discuss a few of the issues which will allow us better to understand women's knowledge of natural resource management, and how such knowledge could benefit others.

Waters-Bayer (1992) has noted that there are two types of research on indigenous knowledge: 'extractive research' conducted for the purposes of outsiders (for example, development planners or government agencies) and 'enriching research' conducted and used by local people to solve problems that they themselves have identified. The differences between extractive and enriching research are revealed in how information is collected, analysed and disseminated, what the purpose is, and who ultimately benefits and is empowered. Even when information is collected through ostensibly participatory methods at the community level, who decides what defines a community, and who decides who participates in such research can determine who benefits and who is empowered. (Schoonmaker Freudenberger, 1992) If, for example, outsiders learn how a seed was developed, where products are collected and what their properties are, or how they are processed and marketed, what happens to that information? Is it expropriated and used for the profit of others? In the case of milk processing in Nigeria (Waters-Bayer, 1992) or herbs in Sudan (Badri, 1993) is it used to take an efficient informal industry out of the control of women into the formal sector?

Simply providing better information and documentation is not enough. There are all too many examples of good information going unused and collecting dust on a shelf. Schoonmaker Freudenberger (1992) cited several types of constraints to explain why good information is not used, or is used for only symbolic purposes. These include conflicts in values, time frames, desired focus of activities, and local practices vs. official policies. Even truly enriching research (that is, designed and conducted by the community in response to its own problems) may be difficult to act upon when the solutions identified run counter to entrenched laws, customs or elites.

Transforming tools

Innovative work (for example, Participatory Rural Appraisal, Farmer First) provides valuable insight and examples of methods used in development research and planning. Yet, most of the tools available focus on the household and community level. As proponents of sustainable development have come to realize that solutions to many of the deeply rooted problems must also involve planning and changes at a larger level (regional planning, national policies, and so on), the tools used in social – and particularly gender – analysis have not kept pace. Thus, there should be greater emphasis on developing analytical tools that can be applied at the large community, regional, national and even international levels.

In recent years, many valid objections have been raised to the existing social, economic and environmental indicators used to measure conditions and set future policies – the tools which are currently used at the macro-policy level. The challenge to achieve true transformation would be to reorient indicators to measure what is important for biodiversity. A reorientation would encompass such things as accounting for the value of women's unpaid labour in GNP; calculating the loss/depreciation of capital from natural resource degradation; and re-evaluating indicators of agricultural productivity; a transformation goes beyond just tinkering with economic measures. There are important values which contribute to human well-being that must be reflected in the orientation and evaluation of development. These values include inter- and intra-generational equity, family and community stability, social networks, cultural heritage, self-sufficiency and a clean and safe environment. Indeed, how to reorient indicators to reflect rather than dictate values is the challenge.

Conclusion

The documentation of the social, economic and ecological value of women's knowledge is important if we are to increase our understanding of sustainable biodiversity management and to gain support and recognition for women. In addition to learning what people do, and why they do it, we also need to understand the social and political context in which they operate and the strategies they employ to overcome obstacles. However, it is also critical to support women and biodiversity for their own sake, irrespective of their potential utility to others. We should not lose sight, nor should we allow others to lose sight, of the fact that this is also an issue of social justice and human rights.

References

Abramovitz, Janet N. and Roberta Nichols (1993) 'Women and Biodiversity: The Critical Link in Conservation and Development', in Lea M. Borkenhagen and Janet N. Abramovitz (eds) *Proceedings of the International Conference on Women and Biodiversity*. Committee on Women and Biodiversity and World Resources Institute, Washington, DC.

—— (1992) 'Women and Biodiversity: Ancient Reality, Modern Imperative', in *Development* 1992: 2, pp 85-90.

Addo, Florence A. and Emmanuel O.A. Asibey, Kate B. Quist, Mary B. Dyson (1992) 'The Economic Contribution of Women and Protected Areas: Ghana and the Bushmeat Trade.' Paper prepared for the IV World Congress on Parks and Protected Areas, Caracas, Venezuela, 10-21 February.

Agarwal, Bina (1992) 'The Gender and Environment Debate: Lessons from India', in *Feminist Studies* 18(1), pp. 119-58.

Asibey, E.O.A. (1974) 'Wildlife as a Source of Protein in Africa South of the Sahara', in *Biol. Conservation* 6, pp. 32-9.

Badri, Amna (1993) 'Women and Biodiversity in The Sudan'. Paper presented at the Society for International Development/WUMEN Roundtable on Women, the Environment, and Alternative Development, The Hague, 25-28 May.

Borkenhagen, Lea M. and Janet N. Abramovitz (eds) (1993) *Proceedings of the International Conference on Women and Biodiversity*. Committee on Women and Biodiversity and World Resources Institute, Washington, DC.

Chambers, Robert, Arnold Pacey and Lori Ann Thrupp (eds) (1989) *Farmer First: Farmer Innovation and Agricultural Research*. Intermediate Technology, Croton-on-Hudson, NY.

Charkiewicz-Pluta, Eva and Sabine Häusler (1991) *Remaking the World Together: Women, the Environment and Sustainable Development*. Report for INSTRAW. Institute for Social Studies, The Hague.

Collins, Jane L. (1991) 'Women and Environment: Social Reproduction and Sustainable Development', in Rita S. Gallia and Anne Ferguson (eds) *The Women and International Development Annual*, vol. 2. Westview Press, Boulder and London.

Dalrymple, Dana G. (1986) *Development and Spread of High-Yielding Wheat Varieties in Developing Countries*. US Agency for International Development, Washington, DC.

Falconer, J. and J.E.M. Arnold (1991) *Household Food Security and Forestry: An Analysis of Socio-economic Issues*. Food and Agriculture Organization of the United Nations, Rome.

Farnsworth, Norman R. (1988) 'Screening Plants for New Medicines', in E.O. Wilson and Francis M. Peters (eds) *Biodiversity*, pp. 83-97. National Academy Press, Washington, DC.

Food and Agriculture Organization of the United Nations (FAO) (1989) *Forestry and Food Security*, FAO Forestry Paper 90. FAO, Rome.

FAO and Swedish Development Authority (1987) *Restoring the Balance: Women and Forest Resources*. Community Forestry Note 1. FAO, Rome.

Fortmann, Louise and Dianne Rocheleau (1985) 'Women and Agroforestry: Four Myths and Three Case Studies', in *Agroforestry Systems* 2, pp. 253-72.

Fowler, Cary and Pat Mooney (1990) *Shattering: Food, Politics, and the Loss of Genetic Diversity*. University of Arizona Press, Tucson.

Government of Indonesia, Ministry of Population and Environment (KLH) (1989) *National Strategy for the Management of Biodiversity*. KLH, Jakarta.

Griffith, Victoria (1991) 'Diseases Put Brazil's Oranges at Risk', in *Financial Times*, 14 June, p. 34, London.

Haisla Nation and Ecotrust (1991) *A Cultural and Scientific Reconnaissance of the Greater Kitlope Ecosystem*. Ecotrust and Conservation International Canada, Portland, Oregon.

Hecht, Susanna (1993) 'Sustainable Extraction in Amazonia', in Lea M. Borkenhagen and Janet N. Abramovitz (eds) *Proceedings of the International Conference on Women and Biodiversity*. Committee on Women and Biodiversity and World Resources Institute, Washington, DC.

Ireson, Carol (1991) 'Women's Forest Work in Laos', in *Society and Natural Resources* 4, pp. 23-36.

Jiggins, Janice (1986) 'Women and Seasonality: Coping with Crisis and Calamity', in *IDS Bulletin* 17(3), pp. 9-18.

Jodha, N.S. (1986) 'Common Property Resources and Rural Poor in Dry Regions of India', in *Economic and Political Weekly* 21(27), 1, pp. 169-81.

Kainer, Karen A. and Mary L. Duryea (1992) 'Tapping Women's Knowledge: Plant Resource Use in Extractive Reserves in Acre, Brazil', in *Economic Botany* 46(4), pp. 408-25.

Kaur, Ravinder (1990) 'Women in Forestry in India', in *World Bank Review Paper*, World Bank, Washington, DC.

Lindstrom, Jan and Rose Kingamkono (1991) *Foods from Forests, Fields and Fallows: Nutritional and Food Security Roles of Gathered Food and Livestock Keeping in Two Villages in Babati District, Northern Tanzania.* Working Paper 184. Swedish University of Agricultural Sciences, International Rural Development Centre, Uppsala, Sweden.

Molnar, Augusta (1991) 'Women and International Forestry Development', in *Society and Natural Resources*, 4, pp. 81-90.

Norem, Rosalie Huisinga, Rhonda Yoder and Yolanda Martin (1989) 'Indigenous Agricultural Knowledge and Gender Issues in Third World Agricultural Development', in D. Michael Warren, L. Jan Slikkerveer and S. Oguntunji Titilola (eds) *Indigenous Knowledge Systems: Implications for Agriculture and International Development.* Iowa State University, Ames.

Plucknett, D.L., N.J.H. Smith, J.T. Williams and N.M. Anishetty (1987) *Gene Banks and the World's Food.* Princeton University Press, Princeton.

Prescott-Allen, Robert and Christine Prescott-Allen (1990) 'How Many Plants Feed the World?', in *Conservation Biology*, 4(4), pp. 365-74.

Pretty, Jules and Robert Chambers (1992) 'Turning the New Leaf: New Professionalism, Institutions and Policies for Agriculture'. Overview paper for IIED/IDS Beyond Farmer First, Rural People's Knowledge, Agricultural Research and Extension Practice Workshop, 27-29 October, University of Sussex, UK.

Reid, Walter V., Sarah A. Laird, Carrie A. Meyer, Rodrigo Gamez, Ana Sittenfeld, Daniel H. Janzen, Michael A. Gollin and Calestous Juma (1993) *Biodiversity Prospecting: Using Genetic Resources for Sustainable Development.* World Resources Institute, Instituto Nacional de Biodiversidad, Rainforest Alliance, African Center for Technology Studies, World Resources Institute, Washington, DC.

Rocheleau, Dianne E. (1991) 'Gender, Ecology, and the Science of Survival: Stories and Lessons from Kenya', in *Agriculture and Human Values*, Winter/Spring, pp. 156-65.

Sachs, Carolyn (1992) 'Reconsidering Diversity in Agriculture and Food Systems: An Ecofeminist Approach', in *Agriculture and Human Values*, Summer, pp. 4-10.

Schoonmaker Freudenberger, Karen (1992) 'Challenges in the Collection and Use of Information on Local Livelihood Strategies and Natural Resource Management'. Paper prepared for IIED/IDS Beyond Farmer First: Rural People's Knowledge, Agricultural Research and Extension Practice Workshop, 27-29 October, University of Sussex, UK.

Shiva, Vandana, Patrick Anderson, Heffa Schucking, Andrew Gray, Larry Lohmann and David Cooper (1991) *Biodiversity: Social and Ecological Perspectives.* World Rainforest Movement, Penang, Malaysia.

Thrupp, Lori Ann (1989) 'Legitimizing Local Knowledge: From Displacement to Empowerment for Third World People', in *Agriculture and Human Values*, Summer, pp. 13-24.

Timothy, David H., Paul H. Harvey and Christopher R. Dowswell, (1989) *Devel-*

opment and Spread of Improved Maize Varieties in Developing Countries. US Agency for International Development, Washington, DC.

Wachiira, Komoji K. (1987) 'Women's Use of Off-farm and Boundary Lands: Agroforestry Potentials'. Final report to the Ford Foundation, Nairobi, Kenya.

Waters-Bayer, Ann (1992) 'Beyond the Farm: Women's Knowledge and Skills in Marketing Farm Products'. Paper prepared for IIED/IDS Beyond Farmer First: Rural People's Knowledge, Agricultural Research and Extension Practice Workshop, 27-29 October, University of Sussex, UK.

Weigand, J.F. (1991) 'Coastal Temperate Rain Forests: Definition and Global Distribution (a working manuscript)'. Ecotrust and Conservation International Canada, Portland, Oregon.

Williams, Paula J. (1992a) *Women, Trees and Forests in Africa: A Resource Guide.* Environment Liaison Centre International, Nairobi, Kenya.

—— (1992b) *Women, Trees and Forests in Africa: Project Summary and Policy Recommendations.* Environment Liaison Centre International, Nairobi, Kenya.

World Resources Institute/World Conservation Union(IUCN)/United Nations Environment Programme (1992) *Global Biodiversity Strategy.* World Resources Institute, Washington, DC.

PART FOUR

Population: Linking Women, Environment and Development

15

Women, Poverty and Population: Issues for the Concerned Environmentalist

Gita Sen[1]

Introduction

Differences in perceptions regarding the linkages between population and environment became particularly acute during the preparatory build-up to the UN Conference on Environment and Development, variously known as the Earth Summit and Rio 92. Disagreement between Southern and Northern countries on the extent of attention to be given to population received considerable publicity. At the non-governmental level too, the issue of population has been, of late, a subject of considerable debate among environmentalists (especially those from the North), feminists and population lobbyists.

The basis of these differences often appears baffling; the apparent lack of willingness to compromise, or to acknowledge the obvious merits of opposing views seem to indicate a lack of analytical rigour. The debate appears, to some at least, to be based on passionately held but ultimately ephemeral differences. I wish to argue that, although the positions taken in the policy debate have been exaggerated at times, some of the oppositions have deeper roots. They arise from conceptual and possibly paradigmatic differences rather than from disagreements regarding the 'truth-value' of particular scientific propositions. These shape the protagonists' perceptions of problems, the analytical methods used, and the weights assigned to different linkages and relationships. In particular, varying views regarding development strategies, the linkages between poverty and population growth, and the role of gender relations in shaping those links colour the positions taken in the debate.

This chapter is an attempt to examine the different perspectives on these issues held by environmental scientists and environmental activists[2] on the one hand, and women's health researchers and feminist activists on the other. Its motivation is twofold: first, to identify the positions taken by these two broad groupings within the larger discourses on development and on population; secondly to propose a possible basis for greater mutual understanding.[3]

Gender in the population field

In the history of population policy, women have been viewed typically in one of three ways. The narrowest of these is the view of women as the principal 'targets' of family planning programmes; of women's bodies as the site of reproduction, and therefore as the necessary locus of contraceptive technology, and reproductive manipulation. The early history of population programmes is replete with examples of such views; but even more recently, the 'objectification' of women's bodies as fit objects for reproductive re-engineering, independent of a recognition of women as social subjects, continues apace. (Hubbard, 1990)

A second view of women which gained currency after the Bucharest Population Conference in 1983 was women as potential decision-makers whose capabilities in managing childcare, children's health in particular, could be enhanced through greater education. Women began to be viewed as social subjects in this case, but the attention given to women's education has not spun off (in the population policy literature) into a fuller consideration of the conditions under which the education of girls takes hold in a society, and therefore the extent to which education is embedded within larger social processes and structures. While this view represented a step away from objectification, women were still perceived as a means to a demographic end, with their own health and reproductive needs becoming thereby incidental to the process.

A third view which grew in the 1980s focused on maternal mortality as an important health justification for family planning. This view, which was at the core of the Safe Motherhood Initiative, attempted to claim a health justification for family planning on the basis of rates of maternal mortality. In practice, the initiative has received relatively little funding or support.

Conceptual approaches

Economic theories of fertility are closely associated with the 'new' household economics. Premised on the belief that children are a source of both costs and benefits to their parents, such theories argue that parents determine their 'optimum' number of children based on a balancing of costs and benefits at the margin. As a description of differences between societies where children are viewed as a source of both present and future streams of income vs. those where children are essentially a cost to parents (balanced by a measure of psychological satisfaction but not by a significant flow of money income), the theory has an appealing simplicity. It purports to explain why the former societies may be more pro-natalist than the latter. It also suggests that shifting children away from child labour (a source of parental income) towards schooling (a parental cost) might work to reduce fertility.

Such theories have been criticized on a number of grounds. (Folbre, 1988) The main criticism centres on the assumption that actual fertility is the result of choices made by a homogeneous household unit innocent of power and authority relations based on gender and age. Once such relations are acknowledged, and there is enough anthropological and historical evidence of their existence, the basis of decision-making within households has to be rethought in terms of differential short-term gains and losses for different members, as well as strategic choices by dominant members which will protect and ensure their continued dominance. For example, if the costs of child-raising increase, *ceteris paribus*, there may be little impact on fertility if the increased costs are largely borne by subordinate members of the household (such as younger women) who do not have much say in household decision-making.

Traditionally, in many societies the costs of high fertility in terms of women's health and work-burdens are rarely acknowledged as such, as long as the benefits in terms of access to a larger pool of subordinate children's labour or the social prestige inherent in being the father of many sons continue to accrue to men. Such authority relations are further cemented by ideologies which link woman's own personal status within the authoritarian household to her fertility. Newer game-theoretic models of household behaviour (Sen, 1987) provide more interesting and complex theories that take better account of the differential distribution of types of assets as well as gains and losses within the household. These have not thus far, however, generated adequate explanations of fertility outcomes.[4]

Against the stream: gender relations and reproductive rights

Many of the influential approaches to theory and policy within the population field have been less than able or equipped to deal with the complexity and pervasiveness of gender relations in households and the economies and societies within which they function. Both feminist researchers and activists within women's health movements have been attempting to change the terms of the debate and to expand its scope. An important part of this challenge is the critique of population policy and of family-planning programmes as being biased (in gender, class and race terms) in their basic objectives and in the methods that they predominantly use.

The definition of a social objective of population limitation[5] which does not recognize that there may be costs to limiting family size that are differential across social classes and income groups, has long been criticized.[6] In particular, such costs are likely to be less than transparent in non-democratic polities or even within democratic states where the costs are disproportionately visited on groups that are marginal on ethnic racial bases and therefore do not have sufficient voice.[7]

Population policy has also been criticized by some as being a substitute for rather than complementary to economic development strategies that are broad-based in their allocation of both benefits and costs. For example, if impoverished peasants were persuaded or coerced to limit family size on the premise that their poverty is a result of high fertility, independent of the possible causal impact of skewed land-holding patterns, commercialization processes, or unequal access to development resources, then it is questionable whether smaller families would make them more or less poor.

The critique becomes more complicated once the gender dimension is introduced. Critics of population policy on class grounds have sometimes been as gender blind as the policy itself. Having many children may be an economic imperative for a poor family in certain circumstances, but the costs of bearing and rearing children are still borne disproportionately by the women of the household. Gender concerns cannot be subsumed under a notion of homogeneous national or global concerns. For feminist critics of population policy, development strategies that otherwise ignore or exploit poor women, while making them the main target of population programmes, are highly questionable. But they do not believe that the interests of poor women in the area of reproduction are identical to those of poor men.

In general terms, the feminist critique agrees with many other critics that population control cannot be made a surrogate for directly addressing the crisis of economic survival that many poor women face. Reducing population growth is not a sufficient condition for raising livelihoods or meeting basic needs.[8] In particular, the critique qualifies the argument that reducing fertility reduces the health risks of poor women and therefore meets an important basic need. This would be true provided the means used to reduce fertility did not themselves increase the health hazards that women face, or were considerably and knowably less than the risks of childbearing. If family-planning programmes are to do this, critics argue, they will have to function differently in the future than they have in the past.

The most trenchant criticism questions the objectives (population control rather than, and often at the expense of, women's health and dignity), the strategies (family planning gaining dominance over primary and preventive health care in the budgets and priorities of ministries and departments), the methods (use of individual incentives and disincentives for both 'target' populations and programme personnel, targets and quotas for field personnel, overt coercion, the prevalence of 'camps' and absence of medical care either beforehand or afterwards, inadequate monitoring of side-effects), and the birth-control methods (a narrow range of birth prevention methods, technology that has not been adequately tested for safety, or which has not passed regulatory controls in Northern countries) advocated and supplied through population programmes. A now extensive debate around the 'quality of care' has focused particularly on the implications of alternative programme methods and birth-control techniques for the quality of family programme services. (Bruce, 1989) More broad-ranging evaluations of population policy objectives and strategies have found them guilty of biases of class, race/ethnicity and gender. (Hartmann, 1987)

Viewed as a development strategy, the critics see population policies as usually falling within a class of strategies that are 'top-down' in orientation, and largely unconcerned with (and often violating) the basic human rights needs of target populations. Even the developmentalist concern with improving child health and women's education has received little real support from population programmes despite the extensive research and policy debate it has generated.

The critical perspective argues that ignoring co-requisites, such as economic and social justice and women's reproductive health and rights, also makes the overt target of population policies (a change in birth rates) difficult to achieve. Where birth rates do fall (or rise as the case may be) despite this, the achievement is often predicated on highly coercive methods, and is antithetical to women's health and human dignity. The women's health advocates argue for a different approach to population policy – one that makes women's health and other basic needs more central to policy and programme focus, and by doing so increases human welfare, transforms oppressive gender relations, and reduces population growth rates. (Germain and Ordway, 1989)

Around the world there is a growing emergence of positive statements about what human rights in the area of reproduction might encompass. (Petchesky and Weiner, 1990) Many of these statements are culturally and contextually specific, but they usually share a common critique of existing population programmes, and a common understanding of alternative principles. Many of them prioritize the perspective of poor women, although they recognize that the reproductive rights of all women in most societies are less than satisfactory. Their attempt to recast population policies and programmes is also, therefore, a struggle to redefine development itself to be more responsive to the needs of the majority.

Enter the environmentalists

Environmentalist concern with population growth pre-dates the public debate sparked by the UN Conference on Environment and Development (UNCED). Probably some of the most influential early documents were the Club of Rome's *Limits to Growth* and Ehrlich and Ehrlich's *The Population Bomb*. (Ehrlich, 1969) The interest in global and local carrying capacity, vis-à-vis growing human population sizes and densities, stimulated the production of considerable literature, both scientific and popular. Unfortunately, the popular and activist literature has tended to ignore some of the important anthropological debates about carrying capacity, as well as to disregard the inconclusiveness of empirical evidence linking environmental change to population growth.[9] It tends, furthermore, to treat the population-environment linkages as simple mathematical ones, linking numbers of people to their environments through technology.

But the argument of both developmentalists in the population field and women's health and rights advocates has been precisely that population is not just an issue of numbers, but of complex social relationships which govern birth, death and migration. People's interactions with their environments can be only partially captured by simple mathematical relationships which fail to take the distribution of resources, incomes and consumption into account; such mathematical relationships by themselves may therefore be inadequate as predictors of outcomes or as guides to policy.[10]

Furthermore, from a policy point of view, more precise modelling of population-environment interactions has not, thus far, provided much better guidance about appropriate population policy programmes. Ignoring the wide disparities in the growth rates of consumption between rich and poor within developing countries and hence their relative environmental impacts, as well as the critiques of women's health advocates outlined in the previous sections, leads to single-minded policy prescriptions directed once more simply to increasing family-planning funding and effort. The leap from over-aggregated population-environmental relations to policy prescriptions favouring increased family planning becomes an implicit choice of politics, of a particular approach to population policy, to environmental policy, and to development. Because it glosses over so many fundamental issues of power, gender and class relations, and of distribution, and because it ignores the historical experience of population programmes, it has come to be viewed by many as a retrograde step in the population-development discourse.

Population actors

The preceding discussion suggests that important actors in the population field are as follows.

First come those population specialists who traditionally have focused on the size and growth of populations, on age structures, migration and population composition. In general, they enter the development discourse primarily through their concern with what impact population growth might have on rates of economic growth. In addition, population projections are mapped onto planning needs in areas such as food production, energy, and other infrastructures, as well as health, education, and so on. These mappings can be said to belong to a class of simple mathematical planning models which usually ignore problems of distribution (based as they tend to be on per capita needs and availabilities), as well as the social and institutional aspects of making a plan actually work.

The second group are the developmentalists who focus less on the impact of demographic change, and more on the prerequisites of sustained decline in mortality and fertility rates. In particular they stress the importance of improving health and women's education. They thus represent a major revision of traditional population approaches, but all too often stop short of addressing the problem of sustainability or of livelihoods.

A third group, the fundamentalists, has become increasingly important in the population field during the 1980s, gaining political legitimacy through their links to mainstream political organizations. Their primary interest is not the size or growth of populations, but rather control over reproduction and a conservative concern to preserve traditional family structures and gender roles. The moral overtones of the US abortion debate notwithstanding, their interest in procreation appears to derive largely from an opposition to changing gender relations in society.

The fourth group are the Northern environmentalists. At the risk of oversimplification, one might argue that many of these individuals and groups focus mainly on the links between economic growth and ecological sustainability on the one hand, and the size and growth of population on the other.

The fifth important group of actors are the women's health groups which have evolved either out of the feminist movement or out of other social movements or population organizations. Their understanding of the population problem is distinctive in that they define it as primarily a question of reproductive rights and reproductive health, in the context of livelihoods, basic needs and political participation. They often acknowledge that economic growth and ecological sustainability are concerns, but believe these ought to be viewed in the context of reproductive rights and health. In particular, many of them give priority to the needs and priorities of poor women in defining issues, problems and strategies.

Each of these sets of population actors has a view of the population question that is consistent with a particular view of development; as such they tend to overlap with particular sets of development actors, and find a niche within a particular set of development ideas. For example, population specialists are attracted to problems of economic growth, developmentalists to basic needs issues, and women's health activists to the problems of livelihoods, basic needs and political empowerment. Many Northern environmentalists, on the other hand, tend to view population solely through the lens of ecological sustainability, and this accounts for a considerable amount of the dissonance between their views and those of grassroots groups in the South.

Towards more synergy between environmentalists and feminists

Despite the dissonance provoked by the population-environment debate, there is much in common between feminists and environmentalists in their visions of society and in the methods they use. Both groups (or at least their more progressive wings) have a healthy critical stance towards ecologically profligate and inequitable patterns of economic growth, and have been attempting to change mainstream perceptions in this regard. Both use methods that rely on grassroots mobilization and participation, and are therefore sensitive to the importance of political openness and involvement. As such, both believe in the power of widespread knowledge and in the rights of people to be informed and to participate in decisions affecting their lives and those of nations and the planet. Indeed, there are many feminists within environmental movements (North and South) and environmentalists within feminist movements.

Greater mutual understanding on the population question can result from a greater recognition that the core problem is that of development within which population is inextricably meshed. Privileging the perspective of poor women can help ground this recognition in the realities of the lives and livelihoods of many within the South.

Economic growth and ecological sustainability must be such as to secure livelihoods, basic needs, political participation and women's reproductive rights, not work against them. Thus, environmental sustainability must be conceptualized so as to support and sustain livelihoods and basic needs, and not in ways that automatically counterpose 'nature' against the survival needs of the most vulnerable. Where trade-offs among these different goals exist or are inevitable, the costs and burdens must not fall on the poorest and most vulnerable, and all people must have a voice in negotiating resolutions through open and genuinely participatory political processes. Furthermore, environmental strategies that enhance livelihoods and fulfil needs can probably help lay the basis for reduced rates of mortality and fertility.

Population and family-planning programmes should be framed in the context of health and livelihood agendas, should give serious consideration to women's health advocates, and be supportive of women's reproductive health and rights. This has to be more than lip-service; it requires reorienting international assistance and national policy, reshaping programmes and rethinking research questions and methodologies. Using the language of welfare, gender equity or health, while continuing advocacy for family planning as it is at present practised will not meet the need.

Reproductive health strategies are likely to succeed in improving women's health and making it possible for them to make socially viable fertility decisions if they are set in the context of an overall supportive health and development agenda. Where general health and social development are poorly funded or given low priority, as has happened in the development agendas of many major development agencies and countries during the last decade, reproductive rights and health are unlikely to get the funding or attention they need. Reproductive health programmes are also likely to be more efficacious when general health and development are served. A poor female agricultural wage-labourer, ill-nourished and anaemic, is likely to respond better to reproductive health care if her nutritional status and overall health improve at the same time.

The mainstream Northern environmental movement needs to focus more sharply on gender relations and women's needs in framing its own strategies, as well as on the issues raised by minority groups. These issues (such as those raised by native peoples and African Americans in the US) tend to link environmental issues with livelihoods and basic needs concerns in much the same way as do the people's organizations in the South.[11] Greater sensitivity to the one, therefore, might bring greater awareness of the other.

Wide discussion and acknowledgement of these principles could help to bridge some of the current gaps between feminists and environmentalists, and make it possible to build coalitions that can move both agendas forward.

Notes

1. This chapter is based on a longer article written for a collaborative project of the International Social Sciences Association, the Social Science Research Council, and Development Alternatives with Women for A New Era (DAWN) on 'Rethinking Population and the Environment'. I am grateful for comments on an earlier draft by Carmen Barroso, David Bell, Lincoln Chen, Adrienne Germain and Jael Silliman. The usual disclaimers apply.

2. The dissonance addressed in this chapter is between mainstream environmentalists from the North and women's health researchers and activists from both North and South.

3. My own position is that of someone who has come to these debates from a background of working on issues of gender and development, and this chapter will perforce tilt heavily towards spelling out the positions taken from within the women's movements. I do not claim to be able to explicate how the mainstream of the environmental movement (especially in the North) has come to the particular definitions it has of 'the population problem'.

4. A different theoretical approach that takes better account of the shifts in

patterns of inter-generational transfers, and therefore of age-based hierarchies, is contained in the work of Caldwell and Caldwell (1987).

5. Or, in the case of many parts of Europe, of population expansion through increased fertility.

6. For an influential early critique see Mamdani (1974).

7. See Scott (n.d.) for a look at Norplant use in the contemporary United States.

8. Even rapid fertility decline may sometimes be indicative of a strategy of desperation on the part of the poor who can no longer access the complementary resources needed to put children's labour to use.

9. Examples of the former are Little (1992), Blaikie (1985); of the latter, Shaw (1989) and UN (1992). The latter argues, for example, that 'The failure to take fully into account the possible effects of other factors that might contribute to environmental degradation characterizes many analyses of population-environmental interrelationships at the national and global levels and thus limits their value in assessing the impact of demographic variables'.

10. An example is the well known Ehrlich-Holden identity, I = PAT, linking environmental impact (I) with population growth (P), growth in affluence/consumption per capita (A), and technological efficiency (T).

11. Personal discussion with V. Miller, co-founder of West Harlem Environmental Action in New York City.

References

Bruce, J. (1989) 'Fundamental Elements of the Quality of Care: A Simple Framework'. The Population Council, Programmes Division Working Papers No. 1, May, New York.

Caldwell, J. and P. Caldwell (1987) 'The Cultural Context of High Fertility in Sub-Saharan Africa', in *Population and Development Review*, 13:3, September, pp 409-38.

Ehrlich, P. (1969) *The Population Bomb*. Ballantine Books, New York.

Folbre, N. (1988) 'The Black Four of Hearts: Towards a New Paradigm of Household Economics', in J. Bruce and D. Dwyer (eds) *A Home Divided: Women and Income in the Third World*. Stanford University Press, Stanford.

Germain, A. and J. Ordway (1989) *Population Control and Women's Health: Balancing the Scales*. International Women's Health Coalition, New York.

Hartmann, B. (1987) *Reproductive Rights and Wrongs: The Global Politics of Population Control and Contraceptive Choice*. Harper and Row, New York.

Hubbard, R. (1990) *The Politics of Women's Biology*. Rutgers University Press, New Brunswick.

Little, P. (1992) The Social Causes of Land Degradation in Dry Regions (manuscript). Institute of Development Anthropology, Binghamton.

Mamdani, M. (1974) *The Myth of Population Control*. Monthly Review Press, New York.

Petchesky, R. and J. Weiner (1990) *Global Feminist Perspectives on Reproductive Rights and Reproductive Health*. Report on the Special Sessions at the Fourth International Interdisciplinary Congress on Women, Hunter College, New York City.

Scott, J. (n.d.) 'Norplant: Its Impact on Poor Women and Women of Color'.

National Black Women's Health Project Public Policy/Education Office, Washington, DC.

Sen, A.K. (1987) 'Gender and Cooperative Conflicts'. Discussion Paper No. 1342. Harvard Institute of Economic Research, Cambridge.

Shaw, R.P. (1989) 'Population Growth: Is It Ruining the Environment?', in *Populi*, 16:2, pp. 21-9.

16

Finiteness, Infinity and Responsibility: the Population-Environment Debate

Franck Amalric

Introduction

Mitchell (1989) describes the opposition between the modern order of the colonizers, notably that of their army, and the (hidden) order of the medina, engrained in the balance between the space reserved to women and the one reserved to men. What appeared to the external modern observer as the freedom of men opposed to the oppression of women was in fact a subtle combination of two different visions of the world, one turned towards the exterior and portraying the world as open, the other turned towards the interior and portraying it as closed. And the heart of life takes place at the meeting of these two worlds. Ivan Illitch (1982) goes so far as to argue that it is this balance which characterizes the humanness of human societies.

But the argument need not lie in the gender division of labour in society. Banuri speaks of the tension between 'impersonal' and 'personal' maps as a characteristic of any culture, and infers what he calls the 'impersonality postulate of modernity', that is, 'that impersonal relations are inherently superior to personal relations'. (Banuri, 1990: 79) Personal relationships suggest the idea of a limited sphere in which they take place: another way to consider Banuri's tension between the 'personal' and the 'impersonal' is to look at the balance between what Appudarai (1990) called 'centripetal' and 'centrifugal' organizations of society. Again, the exterior is in balance with the interior. From there, it is only a small step to speak about finite and infinite visions of the world, a discourse which will sound familiar to scholars interested in environmental and demographic issues.

The concept of sustainable development brings into play the two ideas of finiteness and infinity. Development in the sense of modernization is a process of opening up. What was not possible at the traditional community level becomes possible at higher levels of aggregation. New opportunities arise and the boundaries to human freedom recede. The ideology of modernization is built around this idea of infinity. The French philosopher Pierre Lecourt (1990) suggests that modernity started with the taste for adventure. For Baudelaire, modernity was the ephemeral, the new always replacing the new. Economic theory is also built around this idea. If scarcity is felt at the individual level, in the aggregate there is no limit to the expansion of human activity. Indeed, economists tend to see the world as infinite.

By contrast, the concept of sustainability is closely linked to that of limits, the limits that the biosphere put on the expansion of human activity. Following the seminal work of Malthus, these limits were associated with land, and then with other natural resources. But other limits have been identified more recently, which have to do with the capacity of the biosphere to recycle the waste of human activities, whatever form these activities take. The use of energy is for instance not only limited by the supply, but also by the level of pollution the process of consumption entails.

Sustainable development therefore aims to reconcile the drive for infinity, which characterizes modernity, with the finiteness of our biosphere. A conventional approach, in the wake of the Brundtland Report (*Our Common Future*, 1987) is to try to reorient this drive towards yet other spheres which still appear infinite. Hence the call for 'better' growth, supported by 'better' technology, and modulated by economic incentives such as taxes. The drive remains unrestrained; only its direction is changed.

It is within this context that the more specific debate on the interlinkages between population growth and environmental degradation takes place. The ambiguity of the process of population growth is that it inscribes itself within modernity by being another form of human expansion, while at the same time it is a state of being of those at the fringes of modernity, the poor in Southern countries. This explains why the process appears less responsive to the above-mentioned reorienting devices, and why the topic has become such a controversial and emotional one.

This chapter is an attempt to outline the broad framework for the study of the interlinkages between population growth and environmental degradation by proposing a different analysis of the concept of sustainability, and focusing on how to encourage people to take responsibility for environmental protection. Although it does not take a feminist perspective *per se*, it shares with it the idea that sustainability requires the challenging of modernity, both as a certain contruction of reality (knowledge/power systems) and as a mode of investigation of reality (Western science, for example). The analysis developed in this chapter should thus be considered as complementary to those developed in the other chapters, with the common goal of constructing an alternative world view in which sustainability could have a place. Sustainability, in fact, requires the coexistence of different ways of perceiving the world, of different cultures. The feminist perspective focuses on gender issues, and notably stresses the importance of restoring a balance between 'masculine' and 'feminist' ways of being. Connected to this is the need to reconcile infinity and finiteness. The primary argument is that this reconciliation cannot be realized outside society, but must be embedded within all its institutions. This is the condition of responsibility.

The background

The link between population growth and environmental degradation is without doubt controversial. For some, population is the central cause of environmental degradation; for others, it plays a marginal role. They instead blame wasteful consumption or inadequate technology. (Commoner, 1988) Others point to the politico-economic environment which prevails in many developing countries and which pushes the poor to degrade their environment in order to survive.

As Paul Harrison (1992) recognized, 'all [these] schools of thought are partly right. There is good evidence to support all good contenders. That is why the controversy has kept going for so long.' (Harrison, 1992: 236) Thus there is no universal law, no universal policy. But just as we have to accept and recognize this diversity, we have to move towards a synthesis which alone can provide the ground for adequate and legitimate policies.

The form this synthesis has often taken is to elaborate a larger model which incorporates population, technology and consumption, and derive from it the respective shares of each factor in the different environmental degradations. The equation which synthesizes the model ($I = PTC$, where I = impact; P, population; T, technology; and C, consumption) has been presented as the theoretical synthesis of the issue (Ehrlich and Ehrlich, 1990; Harrison, 1992), and has been applied empirically to measure the contribution of population growth to global warming (Bongaarts, 1992), deforestation (Harrison, 1992), and increase in the use of pesticides, nitrogenous fertilizers and motor vehicles (Commoner, 1988). Except for Commoner's, all the other studies have concluded that population is the most improtant factor.

Thus, despite the differences of opinion, there seems to be at least a consensus that if population is not the major cause of environmental degradation, then consumption or technology must be. The finiteness of the biosphere is represented by an upper limit to the impact on the environment (I), while the other factors are supposed to evolve in a world supposedly infinite. Thus C would tend towards infinity because people always like to consume more; T is constant in the short run, but in the long run it can supposedly tend towards zero as better and more efficient forms of technology are invented.

It is thus the population factor which becomes particularly suspect, for the simple reason that a constantly growing population does not fit well with the figure expected from modernization. After all, demographic transition theory predicted that fertility rates would fall as development took place. Thus, whereas consumption and technology have a 'right' to infinity, population does not.

There are however a number of problems with this framework which render it quite dubious, and which lead us to the implicit assumption that the different variables (consumption, technology and population) are independent, as well as to the absence of reference to the institutional and cultural context. Hence, a common hypothesis is to treat population growth as exogenous to the model, that is, independent of the interaction between environment, level of consumption, technology and the size of the population. If this hypothesis is in accordance with the central tenet of demographic transition theory – that population growth is mainly due to the decline in mortality rates brought about by the introduction of modern medicine – it does not accord with more recent development of theories of fertility which have stressed the voluntary aspect of having large families, as well as the link between the institutional structure of society and fertility. (McNicoll, 1980; Greenhalgh, 1990) As Laesteghe remarked, 'mechanisms of social control of fertility and of population growth in general to some degree reflect basic institutional arrangements that pertain to the functioning of society as a whole'. (Laesteghe, 1980: 527)

Moreover, the model claims validity at all levels of aggregation, whereas the independence of consumption, technology and population can only be broadly supported at the global level because of the absence of noticeable feedback effects at that level, which is not the case at the local or even national levels. Boserup (1965), for instance, defended the thesis that technology was directly responsive to growth in population. At the local level, it must also be explained why environmental degradation has no feedback effect on fertility.

Furthermore, the model fails to incorporate the historical dimension, notably that development has led to a more extensive and more intensive integration of hitherto broadly independent communities within a larger economic and political realm. This integration has notably relieved people's dependence on their immediate natural environment – urbanization is the extreme example – although without necessarily expanding people's possibilities for survival. The relation between population growth and environmental changes at the local level (notably in rural areas of Southern countries) should thus be considered within this process of integration, notably by focusing on the institutional changes to which it leads.

Towards a different approach: on modes of sustainability

An alternative approach to the study of the interlinkages between population growth and environmental degradation starts by considering the process of development (in the sense of integration) as the main engine of change in developing countries, and particularly in rural areas. It notably brings about changes in the institutional structure of society through which the effects and causes of population growth are mediated. In this framework, population growth is thus no more the first cause of change, but rather a consequence of broader societal transformations, just as is environmental degradation, in part.

The second consideration is to define sustainability within a framework of integrated levels of aggregation. The Brazilian rainforest provides a good example. At the local level, it has been the environment in which Indian societies have lived sustainably over a long period of time. But it is also the natural environment which new settlers try to conquer in order to impose a different form of livelihood, thereby leading to important environmental changes, as well as to the destruction of native cultures. As noted by the WCED, 'it is a terrible irony that as formal development reaches more deeply into rainforests, deserts, and other isolated environments, it tends to destroy the only cultures that have been able to thrive in these environments'. (WCED, 1987: 115) But the irony is a false one: for sustainability can no longer be considered at the local level in the case of the new settlers. Their goal is not to live in the forest, but to use the forest or the land to live in Brazil, that is in a modern society. The issue of sustainability must thus be considered at the national level, which in no way implies that large-scale deforestation is indeed the path towards sustainable development. Finally, at the global level, the importance of the Brazilian rainforest as a reserve of biodiversity or as a regulator of climates, for instance, needs to be considered. And requirements of sustainability at the global level might well conflict with possible paths of sustainable development at the national level.

This example shows that we cannot simply speak about sustainability at the local level, and then at the national level, and finally at the global level, but we need to take a more integrated perspective: sustainability at the local level will have meaning only within a model of sustainability at the national level, itself defined within a model of sustainability at the global level.

Moreover, the division of sustainability constraints between the different levels of aggregation is only partially determined by the nature of the resources considered. If the depletion of the ozone layer, or climatic changes linked to the emission of greenhouse gases, are issues that are intrinsically global, others can be addressed at different levels, as in the case of the forest. Food systems are another case in point. Even if the Earth's carrying capacity (of humans) could indeed be assessed, it would only set the biological limit to world population size. But for other considerations, other levels of sustainability may be preferred: the national level for strategic considerations, or the local level to protect particular livelihoods and cultures, for instance.

There is, therefore, a plurality of (biologically) sustainable organizations of society – what could be called modes of sustainability. And if these different modes are determined by biological factors, the technology available and possibilities of substitution, the choice between different modes is basically a political one. Unsustainability can thus be interpreted as the political failure to implement a particular choice of mode of sustainability, inasmuch as such a mode is available given the physical constraints.

To a mode of sustainability thus corresponds a form of governance (that is, the set of institutions that regulates the functioning of society). At each level of aggregation as defined by the mode of sustainability, there must exist an institution that can address the question of sustainability, by taking and implementing decisions, and by monitoring this implementation. A framework of governance must thus cohere with the requirements of an integrated mode of sustainability. This is simply a generalized version of the simple model of a village 'republic' taking care of sustainability at the village level.

A first implication to note is that a shift in the mode of sustainability will entail environmental changes. In general, development (as integration) will lead to a shift towards higher levels of aggregation. By replacing local constraints with national ones, it will logically lead to some environmental degradation. A number of case studies in rural communities of Pakistan have notably revealed that most of the male villagers considered that neither population growth nor environmental degradation were major issues – despite important population growth and what we, as external observers, interpreted as environmental problems – whereas they were considered major issues at the national level. (Amalric and Banuri, 1992) In fact, due to the integration of local communities within the larger political and economic realm, there is no longer a direct relationship between population growth and environmental degradation at the local level.

We could thus speak of an environmental transition, by analogy with the demographic transition, which implies that it is not environmental degradation as such that needs to be analysed, but the aspect of degradation which exceeds what could have been logically expected from the process of development. To this excess corresponds a failure of the transition between forms of governance: the checks at the national level, which were to modulate the environmental transition, failed to operate. In the case of Pakistan, if, heuristically speaking, the adverse link between population growth and the environment does exist at the national level, there are no institutions at that level that can influence behaviours to respond to this problem.

We thus need to examine how sustainability can be regulated at different levels of aggregation, how these different levels interact one with another, and how these interactions evolve under formal development.

Different levels of aggregation

Sustainability can first be defined at the level of the family as an adequate set of incentives that yield a sustainable number of children. Confronted with the problem of having many children, a number of Pakistani women replied that their husbands say that it is not a women's problem, since it is men's responsibility to provide for the entire family. In fact, it is now a widely held view that the empowerment of women is of crucial importance for managing sustainably the local environment as well as for lowering fertility rates. For instance, in a comparative study of North and South India, Dyson and Moore (1983) linked the difference in demographic performance to the degree of autonomy enjoyed by women in the different cultural settings.

Conversely, we could wonder to what extent population growth is not itself a consequence of a disempowerment of women within the household. The process of development has touched unevenly the different spheres to which men and women were traditionally attached. Indeed, it is in those societies in which the prescribed role of women is attached to the household – as in Islamic societies – that the demographic transition seems the more delayed. (Sathar *et al.*, 1988) Typically, modernization tends to raise the status of those who are directly in contact with it (men in this case) to the detriment of those who remain more attached to the traditional order. This unbalanced form of development would lead here to a crisis within the household, of which population growth is but one consequence.

The analysis can be extended to the village level: excessive reliance on external resources undermines traditional forms of management of local resources, thereby leading to environmental degradation. The 'tragedy of the commons', as rendered famous by Hardin (1968), is a misinterpretation of what the commons were in many non-modern societies. The resources were not openly accessible, but were managed by the community, in some instances precisely to preserve sustainability. The 'real' tragedy of the commons is the breakdown of these community-level forms of organization, often due to the aggressive intervention of the state and of market forces. (Repetto and Holmes, 1983) But the responsibility of local populations should not be overlooked. In some instances, it is the villagers themselves who push for the marketization of local products, notably wood. To single out one actor as generally responsible for environmental degradation is too simple.

Rather, as in the case of the family, it is more enlightening to look at changes in the villagers' bargaining power brought about by the processes of modernization and globalization – more precisely, to discover to what extent villagers are pushed or constrained to act cohesively. The direction of change is clear: there are fewer incentives for the group to act together. In certain cases, those who can control the relations of the village with the external world can gain a dominant status and thereby reduce communal initiatives to protect the environment. In other cases, the introduction of new technologies and the growing dependence on external resources bring about profound change in the social relations within the community. It is in this context that Appudarai (1990) spoke of 'centripetal' versus 'centrifugal' organizations of society, looking at the consequences of technological change in an Indian village; in the first case, social relations are a major goal pusued for itself, in the second, they become a burden. The consequence is that solutions for problems arising at the village level will increasingly be sought at the national level. In the case studies from Pakistan referred to above, a striking feature was the alienation of the populace from public matters, and the way they saw the government as responsible for solving almost any problem, from the collection of waste in the streets to the amelioration of irrigation canals, from the purveyance of social services to the protection of the forest. Even population growth was seen as the government's problem, rather than that of the village, the region or the country as a whole. Thus, local institutions, which in the past could respond in a balanced manner to internal changes, have been destabilized by the growing intervention and appeal of the external world, so much so that unsustainable forms of behaviour have arisen.

If it is true that the consequences of population growth are less felt at the village level because of the possibilities of adaptation through integration within the national entity, this is not the case at the national level. A growing number of governments around the world tend to see in population growth a major impediment to the achievement of national priorities such as modernization and human development. In this perspective, we can thus speak of national population growth problems. The failure of governments to address efficiently this public issue and gather the support of the population is a failure of governance. Some countries, such as China, the Republic of Korea, Thailand or Sri Lanka, have been able to bring down rates of fertility in a relatively short span of time, whereas others, like India, Pakistan or Bangladesh, have failed to do so in spite of a relatively long tradition of family-planning policies.

Lessons should be drawn from these failures when we view the problem at the global level. First, it should be recognized that population growth is not the historical cause of global environmental problems such as the depletion of the ozone layer or of possible climatic changes due to the over-emission of greenhouse gases. To put it differently, even with a rapid stabilization of world population, the problems would remain because they are inherently linked to wasteful forms of consumption in Northern countries. Secondly, even if world population growth posed some form of problem at the global level, it could not be addressed in a global perspective. Again, as at the other levels, the issue should be considered in terms of governance. The failure of some centralized Southern states to cope with these issues makes the success of an even larger institutional framework (like some world institutions) more than doubtful.

The concept of responsibility

We have identified a number of issues related to population growth and environmental degradation at different levels of aggregation. The crux of the argument is that these issues are not independent, but rather interdependent. For instance, the failure of governments to address population problems is but the other side of the coin of the incapacity of local communities to take and implement collective decisions. What constitutes the thread between them is the lack of responsibility.

Inasmuch as in the past local communities did feel responsible for questions of sustainability at the local level, we can say they have been de-responsibilized as local institutions have broken down and national institutions have not been able to gather popular support. Development as de-responsibilization is therefore central to an understanding of both environmental degradation and population growth.

This process has two aspects. One is the growing intervention in local communities of the state and the market, which have taken over the control of natural resources and denied customary rights of usage of former commons. This has been documented most extensively in the case of forests where (presumably because of difficulties of regulation) local populations were abruptly forbidden to exercise their customary rights to graze their animals and collect fuel wood and fodder as well as edible roots. Thus, almost overnight the guardians of the forests were transformed into poachers and destroyers.

The second is the state's incapacity to deliver the goods it had promised. The intervention of external forces has not been followed by a significant improvement in conditions of life, or by an empowerment of the populace, or by an alleviation of needs or uncertainties. Thus it is the external forces that have tended to reshape the world, with little consideration for local aspirations and needs. In a recent book on modernity, the French sociologist Alain Touraine concluded:

> *Concluons: pas de modernité sans rationalisation; mais pas d'avantage sans formation d'un sujet-dans-le-monde qui se sente responsable vis-à-vis de lui-même et de la société. Ne confondons pas la modernité avec le mode purement capitaliste de modernisation.*

(To conclude: no modernity without rationalization; nor without the emergence of a subject-in-the-world who feels responsible for herself/himself and for society. Let us not mistake modernity for the purely capitalist mode of modernization.) (Touraine, 1992: 238)

It is precisely the emergence of this subject-in-the-world that has failed. But it cannot be commanded. It arises from a long process of participation, of democratization; from a just balance between internal and external dynamics.

Conclusion

It is a cruel irony to interpret environmental degradation as a consequence of population growth, for it leads to closing the world by restraining the behaviour of those who already face limits in all directions: limited access to resources, limited power, limited education, limited health and limited voice.

By contrast, we define sustainability as a balance with which internal components and external constraints determine the functioning of a given institution (family, local bodies and government). In this definition, sustainability is not opposed to development (as in sustainable development); rather it defines a form of society. This balance could also be defined as the condition of responsibility: the responsibility to define limits inseparable from the responsibility to respect them. In this perspective, the issues of population growth and environmental degradation call for adequate forms of governance which would give greater voice to the local populations. Participation and democratization are therefore prerequisites to move society towards a sustainable path, which can take place only within wider changes of the political and economic systems.

This is quite distinct from more conventional analyses that focus upon the need for education, particularly of women, and the importance of literacy as an indirect way to reduce fertility.

The difference lies in the interpretation of the phenomena observed. To focus on the education of women without considering the relationship within the family or the household is tantamount to saying that women have hitherto been acting somewhat irrationally, and that, once educated, they will be more aware of the implications of their actions. A similar ambiguity with respect to the concept of rationality had already been denounced by Caldwell (1976) in the case of demographic transition theory: development as modernization and as urbanization was to bring down fertility rates. Yet proponents of the theory were also speaking about resistances to change, to lags in making fertility adjustments to new conditions of life. The same logic applies here: the framework is the same, and only the content of development is changed, education and literacy replacing modernization and urbanization.

By contrast, the interpretation proposed here focuses on the bargaining power between different actors and different forms of knowledge. It is not the level of education of women *per se* which matters, but the relative status of women within the household. (Sathar, 1988)

The same holds true at the village level. Here again, behind the interpretation of environmental degradation along the lines of the tragedy of the commons is hidden the assumption that local populations cannot act collectively. Local participation thus becomes the catchword of new development schemes, thereby disregarding many anthropological studies that have documented how different traditional societies have been able to adapt to resilient environments. But local participation is intrinsically impeded by the aggressive intervention of external forces within local communities. To make the local communities stronger is but a dream: external forces have shown their unrestrained ability to grow always faster and stronger.

Is this not also the way to interpret the ongoing confrontation of the impact of population growth on the environment at the global level? Theroretically, the direct effect of curbing population growth would be to slacken the environmental constraint on levels of consumption, on the principle that 'the fewer people there are, the more they can consume'. Yet the historical capacity of Northern countries to take over surpluses suggests that if some sort of environmental surplus is released it will be taken over by them. In other words, Southern countries would not collect the global benefits of a reduction in world population growth, whereas they would incur the cost of adjustment.

References

Amalric, Franck and Tariq Banuri (1992) 'Population, Environment and De-Responsibilisation'. Working Paper WP/POP/1992/1, SDPI, Islamabad.

Appudarai, Arjun (1990) 'Technology and the Reproduction of Values in Rural Western India', in F. Apffel-Marglin and S. Marglin (eds) *Dominating Knowledge*. Clarendon Press, Oxford.

Banuri, T. (1990) 'Modernization and its Discontents: A Cultural Perspective on the Theories of Development', in F. Apffel-Marglin and S. Marglin (eds) *Dominating Knowledge*. Clarendon Press, Oxford.

Bongaarts, John (1992) *Population Growth and Global Warming*. The Population Council, New York.

Boserup E. (1965) *The Conditions of Agricultural Growth*. Allen and Unwin, London.

Bulatao, Rodolfo A. and Ronald D. Lee, (eds) (1983) *Determinants of Fertility in Developing Countries* (2 vols). Academic Press, New York.

Caldwell, John C. (1976) 'Towards a Restatement of Demographic Transition Theory', in *Population and Development Review*, 2.

Commoner, B. (1988) 'Rapid Population Growth and Environmental Stress'. Paper presented to the United Nations Expert Group on Consequences of Rapid Population Growth, 24-26 August, (mimeographed). United Nations, New York.

Dyson, Tim and Mick Moore (1983) 'On Kinship Structure, Female Autonomy, and Demographic Behavior in India', in *Population and Development Review*, 9, 1.

Ehrlich, P. and A. Ehrlich (1990) *The Population Explosion*. Touchstone, New York.

Greenhalgh, Susan (1990) 'Toward a Political Economy of Fertility: Anthropological Contributions', in *Population and Development Review*, 16.

Hardin, Garrett (1968) 'The Tragedy of the Commons', in *Science*, 1162, 1.

Harrison, Paul (1992) *The Third Revolution: Environment, Population and a Sustainable World*. I.B. Tauris, London and St Martin's Press, New York.

Illitch, Ivan (1982) *Gender*. Pantheon Books, New York.

Lecourt, Pierre (1990) *Contre la Peur*. Seuil, Paris.

Laesthaege (1980) 'On the Social Control of Human Reproduction', in *Population and Development Review*, 6.

McNicoll, Geoffrey (1980) 'Institutional Determinants of Fertility Change', in *Population and Development Review*, 6, 3.

Mitchell, Timothy (1989) *Colonizing Egypt*. Cambridge University Press, Cambridge.

Repetto, Robert and Thomas Holmes (1983) 'The Role of Population in Resource Depletion in Developing Countries', in *Population and Development Review*, 9.

Sathar, Zeba *et al.* (1988) 'Women's Status and Fertility Change in Pakistan', in *Population and Development Review*, 14, 3.

Sen, Amartya (1989) 'Co-operation, Inequality, and the Family', in McNicoll and Cain (eds) *Rural Development and Population: Institutions and Policy. Population and Development Review*, 15 (suppl.).

Touraine, Alain (1992) *Critique de la Modernité*. Fayard, Paris.

United Nations (1990) *Results of the Sixth Population Inquiry Among Governments*. United Nations, New York.

UNDP, *Human Development Report 1992*. Oxford University Press, New York.

WCED (1987) *Our Common Future*. Oxford University Press, Oxford.

17

Consumption and Fertility

Helga Moss[1]

Consumption and fertility are not commonly linked in Western feminist discourse. Maria Mies' books are an important exception. She has pointed out clear North-South differences, wherein women of the North are encouraged to breed and buy, while women of the South should not breed, but sell their labour power cheaply within the context of the world market – becoming 'integrated into development'.[2] Consumption and fertility, however, have become politically linked in the course of the UNCED negotiations. Countering the North's preoccupation with population growth in the South, many Southern voices – and some Northern ones too – have rightly pointed to the non-sustainability of the Western development model that creates poverty at one end and wealth at the other. In this chapter, I shall try to map some conditions for the North to change its ways.

Solidarity from diversity

Northerners experience a complex and fragmented reality, together with an enormous excess of information. We find it difficult to produce theoretical analyses that can act as concrete guidelines for individuals, groups and organizations. Our theories, often all too abstract, aim to explain complex relations which seem far removed from the everyday life where we actually act. Moving too quickly to a generalized level of picturing reality has the effect of silencing other perspectives and other realities. The feminists of the North have been doing this too much.

Accordingly, I must point out that my thoughts, reflections and knowledge are those of a white, urban, intellectual Norwegian mother in her thirties. It is quite impossible for me to reflect – fully or significantly – the diverse realities of all women living in the North. These are women of different class and ethnic backgrounds, different occupations, young and old.

Creating an analysis for action in the area of consumption, therefore, must be a collective effort among and between diverse groups of women. It will have to be an ongoing process of sharing and critique. I believe that the most important challenge facing Western women today is how to act in order to reduce Western consumption, yet secure the well-being of all in our societies.

Consumption patterns

Norway's Minster of Development Cooperation, Grete Faremo, has stated that, in both the areas of over-consumption and over-population, the most dangerous thing is 'inaction'. This is questionable. It is possible to argue that the most dangerous thing now is action based on an analysis showing that population growth causes poverty and constitutes a major threat to the environment.

Inspired by DAWN and other feminist approaches[3] in addressing the consumption patterns of the North, I will try to move from the level of everyday life. In a Southern context, this analytical starting point leads to an understanding of how decisions made in the inner chambers of the World Bank have a profound and adverse impact on women in their everyday life as well as on their environment.

But if I start with the one kilo of paper that landed on my doorstep over the last ten days, where will it lead me? These advertisements for hundreds of commodities, distributed to every household in Oslo, where I live, most people usually throw away.

I do not grow any food, or weave or sew clothes; I have not built my house or made the furniture in it. Everything I use has been made by other people. It is like a global household. But of course, normally you do not reflect on that. If you have the money, you buy things in stores. When they are no longer useful, they become waste and will be disposed of by a public service. If I look around my flat I see hundreds of items whose history I know nothing about; in this respect, I am a 'normal' Western urban individual.

Buying and knowing

I have to buy all the things I need, sometimes ten items a day; and usually I am in a hurry to get home to my children. Each item has a price tag and a label describing the contents, and sometimes a label saying 'environmentally friendly product', words which cannot be trusted, as 'green' capitalists try to make money out of our environmental concerns. Every commodity I buy involves a choice. There are many things to be considered. The price factor often wins, and, if it is food, whether it is produced in Norway. I avoid the products singled out by campaigns; otherwise, my choices are not very informed. I feel guilty about this. I should do more, know more. I buy so many things! And I am always in a hurry. The task of becoming a conscious, informed consumer seems so vast. And I suspect that there would be reasons to boycott most of the items I buy, were they critically scrutinized for their social and environmental costs.

Investigating a radio

I have tried to make a model of my consumption practices, to clarify to myself what I need to know in order to make really informed choices in compliance with the demands of 'sustainability'. My point of departure is that I need to know the history of the commodity from its beginnings to the point at which it reaches me. (In this investigation, I have disregarded the problems of waste.) Let us say that I want to buy a radio. What would I need to know in order to evaluate the sustainability of this purchase? Figure 1 shows in a very simplified manner the different categories of steps the radio-in-the-making takes as it moves from raw material to my house as a complete radio apparatus. These steps include the retailer (R), the

Figure 1

ONE COMMODITY, FROM CRADLE TO ME:

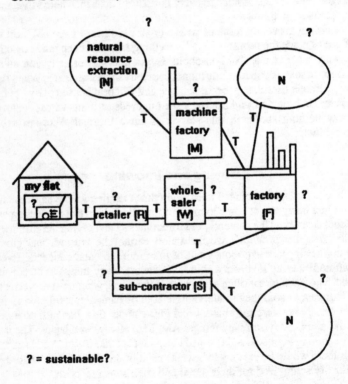

wholesaler (W), the factory (F) that produced the radio, the sub-contractors (S) who contributed the accessories, the machine factories (M) that contributed to F and S (and M), and, finally, the extraction of the raw materials necessary (N) to supply the factory and an unknown number of S's and M's. All these steps would have to be investigated for the radio's impact on sustainability. The evaluation of sustainability includes both the environmental impact assessment of the various production processes, and assessment of the intermediate transport arrangements (T).

There should also be an evaluation of the human aspect of its production (Figure 2), because we are also interested in the social sustainability of commodities. We must then take into account the workers: first, their working conditions, possible health hazards, and so on; secondly, their part in a web of consumption and production relations.

In order to arrive at an environmental and social impact assessment of this particular radio in terms of concrete reality, we have to combine both models (Figures 1 & 2) in order to arrive at a realistic model of investigation.

Already, the model is becoming too complex; the realistic model is not very clear. I have, however, learned several things:

(1) An understanding of my profound ignorance regarding my/our relationship to nature in any concrete sense. I am – to use Maria Mies's expression – delinked from nature and people as producers of the things I use to live.

(2) A vivid impression of my fundamental dependence on a very complex structure, a web of seemingly infinite concrete relations to the varying ecosystems and working people of the world. This is a hard blow to the liberal theses of the independent actor on the market, the 'self-made man'. The fact is that within the market economy, the people and ecosystems that contribute to the making of my radio are invisible.

(3) I am caught in a serious ethical dilemma. If I want to live in harmony with nature, its plants and living beings, including women and children, and men, all over the planet, I and my children would have to starve, freeze and become outcasts in our own society and community. My subsistence work – my household – is totally dependent upon consuming from this global household even if I reduce our consumption to the things most essential for survival. This is the final blow to the liberal thesis of free choice. As a consumer, I am forced to violate the very value system that I try to teach my children: care, sharing, solidarity and responsible action.

(4) The liberal split between politics and economics does not apply. Considering the possible, indeed probable, link between my consumption-based life-sustaining work at home and the life-destroying production at the other side of the market place opens my eyes to the fact that buying is

Figure 2

ONE COMMODITY, MORE CONCRETELY:

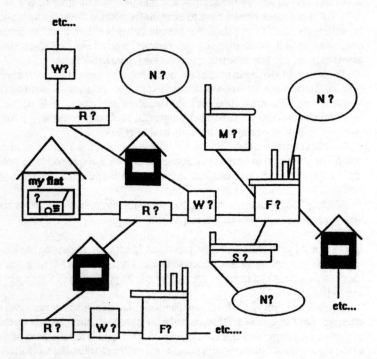

THEIR
  – CONSUMPTION?
  – WORKING CONDITIONS?
  – ENVIRONMENTAL AND SOCIAL SURROUNDINGS?

a political act.[4] It is an act in which my money carries the power and my moral judgement has to be suspended.

A divided household

In looking at this global household, one can discern the North-South division, which is also a class, race and gender division. Increasingly, peoples of the Third World, particularly women, have become the industrial workers of the world. They contribute to my household with their labour power and their natural resources; and to such an extent that their environment is being destroyed (through such activities as cash cropping, for example). For these efforts, however, they receive precious little in return. The goods a woman in the South produces for the world market I can buy very cheaply, which in turn increases the quantity of items I am able to buy. Living in the North, I can buy cheaply because the Southern woman is paid very little for her work; her wage is so small that it cannot sustain her or her children. Hence, her children have to work in order to contribute to the family income. More children, then, means increased chances of survival.

But in view of the fact that underconsumption in the South is directly linked to overconsumption by the North, who are we to say that there are too many people in the South?

The population rhetoric

The rhetoric of the population discourse is so dangerously seductive because thinking in numbers closes our eyes to these links and divisions in the global household, including the power relations embedded in it.

At her opening statement at UNCED, the Norwegian Prime Minister, Gro Harlem Brundtland, stated that 'we must reconcile human activities and human numbers with the laws of nature'. The problem with this reasoning is that it tends to reduce reality to the question of numbers. Numbers are easy to deal with: we can add, subtract, multiply and divide. Numbers speak simple truths and provide us with simple answers that cannot be questioned.

For instance, it is often claimed that it is the high and increasing number of people which creates environmental destruction in Bangladesh. But there are countries in Europe, such as Belgium, with a higher population density than Bangladesh. In Belgium, we find no World Bank conditionalities on reducing population. Belgium's ecosystem, however, could hardly sustain such a heavy density of people were it not for their integration into the world market. The fact that we – as part of this global household, are affecting the ecosystems of Bangladesh and all other nations integrated in the world market, is not considered. In this demographic, 'population explosion' line of thinking, it will always be the poor who are too many, no matter (or because of) how little they consume.

As long as we live and subsist within this global household, there is no way of justly assessing the balance of national environmental carrying capacity against the number of people within the nation. It is not the number of people that is significant, rather it is how different people relate to the ecosystems. To put it rhetorically: what is the earth's carrying capacity for agro-businesses, for world market, profit-oriented industrialists, for the military, or presidents? How can 'the number and activities' of these people be 'reconciled with the laws of nature'?

Fertility in the North

'Why do you women in the North have so few children?' asked medical doctor Jurema Werneck when she met Norwegian women at a conference in Oslo in 1991. Jurema works in the *favelas* (slums) of Rio, and is campaigning against the excessive number of sterilizations of black Brazilian women.

Many of the answers from the women included the words I used when speaking of myself as a consumer: choice, lack of time, energy and money. Many women say, if:

> I received more help from the father;
> I had my family (mother) close by;
> there were nurseries;
> our rent was not so high;
> we could afford to live on one wage only;
> the local environment was not so unfriendly;
> my job was less absorbing;
> I did not feel so exhausted after my first . . .

then I would have had more children.[5]

In societies where people are less dependent upon the market economy and the global household, they depend upon social networks of kinship and friendship to manage material survival; they have an 'extended' household. Or rather, we should say that our household 'shrinks' when integrated into the global one. These social networks are built through exchange on a person-to-person basis, which means that they also provide emotional bonds between people. They are a source of mutual support, fun, exchange of knowledge, as well as goods (gifts) and services.[6]

If you are totally dependent upon the market economy – working long hours, buying all the things you need – you have neither the motivation nor the surplus energy to put into extensive social networking at a community level. Bonding between people demands frequent interpersonal interaction in a variety of different situations. Lack of social bonding, with all it entails, is a major problem in the North, because our communities are torn apart by the way production and reproduction are organized. Thus, women's reproductive choices are made within a framework of social poverty.

For example, in Norway it is quite normal for a woman who has had her first-born to be left alone, most of the day, for months. When the baby cries night and day, she does not know why, and there is nobody to ask.

Even if her mother is there, her advice is not trusted, because professional child-rearing theories have taken away her authority. We are taught that a child's mother means everything to its well-being, and whatever goes wrong eventually, as mothers we blame ourselves. Motherhood is loneliness. Adding to the problems of merely being a mother are the frustrating gender relations. Divorce rates are high (especially since the mid-1970s), and it is usually the woman who leave the man. She feels lack of support, or experiences outright physical abuse.

Women in the North are, of course, linked to the economy not only as consumers, but also as producers. Correlating to the statistics of decreasing fertility and increasing divorce rate, is the number of mothers with one or two children entering (or staying within) the labour market, increasingly on a full-time basis. Many women in this category develop some sort of health problems sooner or later.

Conclusion

I have painted this rather gloomy picture of social poverty and suffering in the North because it is important to counter the image being constructed in international discourse of all problems being in the South, whereas the solutions are in the North. It should not be forgotten, however, that many traits of the consumption-based livelihood I have described here would also apply to middle- and upper-class segments of Southern societies.

Many people, mostly women, organize in many ways, in their local community as well as at a national level. There is a strong and growing understanding that current development with its emphasis on economic growth is tearing apart the very foundations of our societies, the way we live our everyday lives and develop as human beings. People who in various ways sustain life: women, workers, farmers, indigenous and fisher people and many others, subscribe to values in the reproductive/household sphere which assume that the economy should be adapted to sustain people. On the other side, there are those who claim that people must adapt to promote the modern market economy.[7] These latter are predominantly men; the urban, powerful, rich, who speak as if they have the solution to all problems; although, deep down, I am sure they know otherwise.

My own conclusion after this futile search for my relationship to nature is that:

- We must search for ways not only to reduce our consumption, but to reduce our dependence as an exploitative and energy-consuming global household.
- In the attempt to achieve these changes, the women's movement has the opportunity to restructure our societies according to its own values. Our children do not need all these commodities. As Freud noted:

'The reason why money never makes the adult satisfied is that the child never desired money.'

Notes

1. Based on a paper presented to the Planeta Femea '92 Global Form, UNCED, Rio de Janeiro, 6 June 1992.

2. Maria Mies, *Patriarchy and Accumulation on a World Scale*, Zed Books, London and New Jersey, 1986.

3. For instance, Dorothy Smith, *The Everyday World as Problematic: A Feminist Sociology*, Northeastern University Press, Boston, 1987.

4. In fact, the Norwegian language does not distinguish between the two; both words ('buy' and 'act') are translated as 'handle'.

5. Cf. Tone Schau Wetlesen, *Fertility Choices and Constraints: A Qualitative Study of Norwegian Families*, Solum Forlag, Oslo, 1991.

6. Although blind to the gender aspect of exchange, Marcel Mauss has opened our eyes to a different conception of economy, describing 'traditional' exchange systems as sources, or vehicles, of communality and spirituality. (Marcel Mauss, *The Gift: The Form and Reason for Exchange in Archaic Societies*, Routledge, London, 1990) What kind of communality and spirituality is fostered by the world market system of exchange? Rather than meeting us as a Stranger on the market, the Other is erased and sometimes expelled.

7. The underlying assumption is that money, or capital, is the true creator and sustainer of life. As I have shown in my example, this corresponds to ordinary people's dependence on market consumption. Hence the system is not challenged.

Index